Seriously Good
Chili Cookbook

177 of the Best Recipes in the World

by *New York Times* Best-Selling Author
Brian Baumgartner

Foreword by Oscar Nuñez

FOX CHAPEL
PUBLISHING

© 2022 by Brian Baumgartner and Fox Chapel
Publishing Company, Inc., 903 Square Street,
Mount Joy, PA 17552.

Seriously Good Chili Cookbook is an original work,
first published in 2022 by Fox Chapel Publishing
Company, Inc.

ISBN 978-1-4971-0201-9

Library of Congress Control Number:
2022937580

To learn more about the other great books from
Fox Chapel Publishing, or to find a retailer near
you, call toll-free 800-457-9112 or visit us at
www.FoxChapelPublishing.com.

We are always looking for talented authors.
To submit an idea, please send a brief inquiry to
acquisitions@foxchapelpublishing.com.

Printed in China
First printing

Dedication

This book is dedicated to folks who love to gather together with friends and family and enjoy a pot of chili.

Acknowledgments

I want to acknowledge all of the hardworking people who worked tirelessly to make this cookbook a reality:

- David Miller, Gretchen Bacon, Elizabeth Martins, David Fisk, Diana Kern, Wendy Reynolds, Aubrey Vonada, and all of the folks at Fox Chapel.

- Ted Gekis, Megan Smith, Ryan Zachary, Daniel Ribera, and Megan Dunn from my team.

- Paul Castrataro and Dylan Chant for their help.

To the chefs and fans and World Champions who contributed recipes: THANK YOU.

And finally— a huge thank you to my friends and family who have tasted more chili over the last year than anyone thought possible. This could not have happened without YOU!

—Brian

Foreword

When Brian first told me he was writing a chili cookbook, I thought, "Really? Is Brian a chef?" I know he can cook, but I wasn't sold. Sure enough, the following day, I received a manila envelope with photographs of Brian wearing a chef's hat and apron while holding cooking utensils. In addition to the photos, there was a notarized document confirming that he is indeed a chef!

That is just a glimpse into the light-hearted, and often comical, communication we enjoy as friends.

During the filming of *The Office*, Brian was always committed to his character and his craft, so I wasn't the least bit surprised when I found out he was filming the chili scene. Sprawling across a pile of fresh chili was nothing short of doable for him. On top of that, it was his idea to use the folders to try scooping the fumbled chili back into the pot, which was pure

chili /'CHil⁻e/ 1 a : a hearty stew that is also used as a topping on other dishes and has varied recipes and ingredients, with or without meat, ultimately derived from the Mexican-style chili con carne

comedic genius. It's extremely impressive he did it in one take. However, I wasn't expecting him to show up to our "Accountants Dinner" afterward reeking of chili. But as Brian, Angela, and I fought to enjoy our meals, we had zero inkling as to how Brian's chili fall was the catalyst for Kevin's most famous moment.

I know Brian to be hardworking and meticulous in everything he does. Not only is he a talented actor and celebrity—and now chef—he is also a devoted husband and father. He enjoys golfing, cooking, watching professional sports, and, of course, chili.

Brian is extremely dedicated to seeing how chili brings people together—something that started out as part of his character but has grown into making and sharing his own chili and supporting others as they share their recipes and cooking skills. His chili cookbook is just one example of that dedication.

Brian's cookbook is a compilation of 150 of the best chili recipes made by celebrities, chefs, cooks, and friends from across the nation. There is something for everyone, whether you enjoy your chili on a hot dog, in a cup or bowl, vegetarian, meaty, spicy, or mild. Honestly, there's no wrong way to enjoy chili. You be you! On top of that, Brian has combined the recipes with his own fun tips and chili facts. To me, that sounds like a great book to add to or to start a cookbook collection.

It is with a profound sense of joy that I close this foreword I promised Brian I'd do. So join me, won't you? Lift your chili bowls on high, and gulp down delicious mouthfuls of Brian's favorite chilis. Taste the deliciousness. Now, bow your head solemnly, and do what the ol' beloved nursery rhyme commanded . . .

**"Chili, chili everywhere
so eat it up
and make some more"**

Enjoy,

Oscar Nuñez

Oscar Nuñez is best known for his role as Oscar Martinez in NBC's Emmy-winning TV series, *The Office*. Additionally, Oscar has appeared in several movies and TV shows, including *Malcom in the Middle, Reno 911!, It's Always Sunny in Philadelphia, New Girl, Shameless, The Goldbergs*, and countless others. He's also appeared on *Worst Cooks in America: Celebrity Edition* on Food Network, therefore qualifying him as the perfect candidate for writing the foreword of a cookbook.

Contents

SERIOUS ABOUT CHILI

Introduction

On April 30, 2009, at roughly 9:02pm, my life changed forever. I became known as "the chili guy."

For those of you who don't know, I played Kevin Malone on NBC's comedy television show *The Office*. By 2009, we were into our fifth season, and it was humming—with an audience regularly over 10 million viewers when we aired on Thursday nights, and sometimes more! In fact—in February of that year—we aired after the Super Bowl, where over 26 million people watched Dwight organize a fake fire drill and Kevin raid the vending machine. We were a hit. A classic "watercooler show." But more than that, it was a job I *loved*, with people I *loved*. I considered myself the luckiest guy on the face of the earth. What could possibly go wrong?

Well, in March of that year—just a few weeks after the Super Bowl, in fact— I was given a script for the episode "Casual Friday," written by

> "I started to realize something—it's not just that Kevin spilled *something*; he spilled his *famous chili*. And folks take chili very seriously."

Anthony Q. Ferrell and directed by Brent Forrester. In the opening of that episode, Kevin prepares and brings in to work a pot of his "Famous Chili" . . . and promptly spills it all over the floor. "Funny," I thought, "but this may be difficult to shoot."

It was the last scene we filmed that week, at the end of the day on Friday. My character was the only one in the scene, so all the other actors had left for the day. Angela Kinsey, Oscar Nuñez, and I had dinner plans that night. The three of us would periodically plan "Accountants Dinners" and all get gussied up and go to a fancy steakhouse for good food and better drinks. That night was one of my favorite destinations—Maestros in Beverly Hills. As they left for the day to go home and change, I told them I would come straight from *The Office* and meet them there.

We rehearsed this scene a lot. I mean . . . *a lot.* Because the reality of having to reset and refilm this scene would be a *monumental* task. After all, no carpet could survive this explosion, so new carpet had been cut. No props would be salvageable, so all props had duplicates. My wardrobe and hair and makeup would certainly not survive, so new clothes and a shower were standing by. The pressure was high—"we only have three pieces of carpet!" I was told more than once.

But I did it. I spilled the chili. And I needed only one take.

I'm not going to bore you with a detailed scene description or actor tricks I employed to try to convincingly "accidentally" spill the chili. But as I stood by the monitor watching the scene playback, chili dripping from my clothes as our key wardrobe dresser was trying to peel my chili-soaked sport coat off me, I found myself deeply moved. Yeah, ok, the scene is funny—*but it is so much more!* Here is a guy who does *one* great thing in this world: he makes great chili. And like all great makers of chili, all he wants is to share it with folks. But he fails.

With the help of more people than one would think necessary, I got cleaned up and showered as best I could, and then left to meet Angela and Oscar. Dinner was a disaster. My hands were stained a distinctive reddish-brown color. I attempted to enjoy my steak—and the others at the table did as well—*but all we could smell was CHILI!* I think it was seeping from my pores. I suppose I shouldn't have been surprised. I had, after all, practically taken a bath in it.

From the moment the episode aired, I started hearing from folks:

"It was so sad!?!?"
"I felt so bad for Kevin."
"Chili!!!!!!"
"I wish he could have shared it with everyone."
"Don't forget to undercook the onions."
"It's probably the thing he does best . . ."

To make Kevin's Famous Chili, *see* page 244.

The episode "Casual Friday" first aired April 30, 2009, and quickly became a sensation.

Brian partnered with Bush's Beans in 2020 to share a chili recipe that they co-authored.

I started to realize something—it's not just that Kevin spilled *something*; he spilled his *famous chili*. And folks take chili very seriously. And because, in a way, I *am* Kevin, people started associating *me* with chili as well. On the street, at the airport, in a restaurant, or in a bar, everyone wanted to talk to me about . . . chili.

My favorite chili story happened at a hotel bar in Pittsburgh, Pennsylvania. I was there traveling for work, alone, sitting at the bar eating dinner. I had just finished my meal, and my food had been cleared, when the bartender set some food down in front of me. Without looking at the food, I looked up at him and said, "No, sorry, this isn't mine. I just finished." The bartender got a wry smile on his face and like a character out of a movie from the 1950s, he cocked his head to the side and softly said, "This is from the woman at the end of the bar." I looked down, and of course, it was a bowl of chili.

> "I love the *people* I have been fortunate to meet through my experiences with chili. And let me tell you, I have traveled far and wide searching for the "perfect pot of chili."

So, I decided I better learn to make some seriously good chili myself. My recipe has slowly developed over time. Prior to April of 2009, I can honestly say I had never made chili in my life. But now . . . I make it all the time. And I'm perfecting different types as well, from turkey chili to chili con carne. And from Cincinnati chili—where my father was born—to Texas chili—where I spent many years in my youth. I love the nuance and variety. The cultural and regional differences. But most of all now, I love the *people* I have been fortunate to meet through my experiences with chili. And let me tell you, I have traveled far and wide searching for the "perfect pot of chili."

In 2021, I traveled to Myrtle Beach, South Carolina, to attend the World Championship Chili Cook-Off, hosted by the International Chili Society (ICS). I was blown away by how many chefs were there. And these were just the ones who had made

Nationals! Their passion for chili knew no bounds. I judged one category and enjoyed many more. It was so much fun, and all the chilis were *so good* I decided right then and there that I needed to assemble the very best chili recipes from across the country to create the greatest collection of chili recipes the world has ever seen!

Seriously Good Chili Cookbook includes recipes from past national champions, world-renowned chefs, and people who just make awesome chili. I hope you will try a few varieties, get outside your comfort zone, and experience them with people you love. Because chili is meant to be shared . . . not spilled.

Yes, my life changed forever on April 30, 2009. Forever for the *better*. I embrace being "the chili guy" and hope you and yours enjoy this cookbook as much as I enjoyed eating my way through the recipes.

Cheers,

Brian Baumgartner

Brian judging at the 2021 World Championship Chili Cook-Off, hosted by the International Chili Society (ICS).

A Brief History of Chili and Fun Facts

I like history. Do you like history? Before diving into the recipes, I want to touch on chili's (or chilli's) rich history and share a few stories. Can these accounts be proven? Not by me. But its complex past is sure to stir up the imagination as you prepare to make that food we call chili.

Chili's history is anything but settled

Chili's history is incredibly rich, and, as it turns out, even a bit . . . *heated*. The details of exactly how chili con carne—which translates to "chili with meat"—originated are blurry, but whether fact or fiction, they are fascinating either way.

By many accounts, it is a red-blooded American dish; it did not originate in Mexico. In fact, Mexico denies any association with chili, and only a handful of spots serve it. Parts of Mexico that do serve chili only do so to please tourists.

Some think it originated in the 1800s

A lot of historians claim the earliest versions of chili were made in the 1800s by the poorest class of people to stretch what little meat they could afford at market and stew it with as many peppers as there were pieces of meat.

Sister Mary's traveling spirit

A Southwestern Native American legend claims the first chili con carne recipe was written in the 17th century by a mysterious nun, Sister Mary of Agreda of Spain, who was known as *La Dama de Azul* ("the lady in blue"). While she never *physically* left her convent, she claimed to have out-of-body experiences, when her spirit traveled to preach in faraway countries. After "returning" from one such trip, Sister Mary wrote down a recipe that called for venison or antelope meat cooked with onions, tomatoes, and chile peppers.

CHILI TIMELINE ❯ ❯ ❯ ❯ ❯ ❯ ❯ ❯

Soup of the Devil

Another (and more realistic) theory is that in 1731, a group of 16 families (about 56 people) emigrated to Texas, to what is now San Antonio, from the Canary Islands by order of King Philip V of Spain. His intention was to colonize and cement Spanish claims to the region. Historians say the women in those families would make a "spicy Spanish stew."

However, these steamy new stews brought surprising controversy. A few Spanish priests assumed that chile peppers were aphrodisiacs and began to condemn their consumption. The priests' warnings about the "Soup of the Devil" only fed people's hunger more, and the popularity of chili spread like wildfire.

A cowboy's staple

Everette DeGolyer was a rootin'-tootin' Dallas millionaire who loved a zesty bowl of the good stuff. He found records of the first chili mix that dated to 1850. Written by Texan cowboys, it revealed their reliance on chili as a staple during their long travels. It noted that they pounded dried beef, fat, pepper, salt, and chile peppers together into rectangles, or "chili bricks," that could be rehydrated with boiling water.

Jailbird stew

Chili was apparently common in the prisons of Texas, where the cheapest available ingredients were bread, water, and spiced beef. Turns out, the Texas prison system made such good bowls of chili that inmates would rate each jail based on that provision alone! Freed inmates would even write back to their favorite chili-serving prisons to ask for the recipe, while expressing it was what they missed the most from their time doing time.

Pre-1700
Legend says Sister Mary writes a recipe with chile peppers from a dream

1731
Families in Texas make "spicy Spanish stew"

1850
Texas cowboys eat chili during long travels

San Antonio "Chili Queens"

Now we get to some *serious* chili ladies who were *so* serious about their dishes, they were dubbed chili royalty. In the 1880s, a group of women in San Antonio called the "Chili Queens" would feed people a stew they called chili at the Military Plaza, their first of many market locations. The women would make their renowned chili at their homes, load it onto their vibrant wagons donned with colored lanterns, and transport it to the market where they'd build mesquite fires to keep the food warm. From chili con carne to tamales and enchiladas, no matter who you were or where you were from, a day at the market wasn't complete unless you paid the chili queens a visit!

Unfortunately, they were forced to close their business in 1937 once the town implemented sanitary standards. Their only two violations were flies and "poorly washed dishes," and just like that, a 50-year tradition was gone. (Curse those 20th-century health inspectors.)

To commemorate the iconic Chili Queens, San Antonio held the first annual "Return of the Chili Queens Festival" in the 1980s in Market Square during its Memorial Day celebrations. For over a decade now, there is also an official Chili Queens Cook-Off event, along with the larger-than-life Tackiest Queen fashion contest.

Chili at the Chicago World's Fair

Eventually, Texas-made chili received national attention (finally!) when a San Antonio chili stand was set up during a little event called the World's Columbian Exposition, also known as the Chicago World's Fair, in 1893.

A special blend of spices

Another Texan chili icon was DeWitt Clinton Pendery who owned a grocery store. Unfortunately, said store burned down. Fortunately, DeWitt discovered something great! He started to make and sell a special spice blend under the name Mexican Chili Supply Company. Today, Pendery's spices and seasonings are still sold through members of his family.

1880
San Antonio "Chili Queens" fed the Spanish army

1893
Chili appears at the Chicago World's Fair

1895
Lyman T. Davis makes the first branded chili

CHILI TIMELINE ❯ ❯ ❯ ❯ ❯ ❯ ❯ ❯

Wolf Brand Chili was born

The first "branded" chili came to fruition in 1895 with a man named Lyman T. Davis. After making chili he'd sell from the back of his wagon for 5 cents a bowl, he opened a meat market and began to sell his chili in brick form under the brand name "Lyman's Famous Homemade Chili." By 1921, he was ready to can, and he named his new brand after his pet wolf. (Yes, you read that correctly—A pet *wolf*.) And thus, Wolf Brand Chili® was born!

The inventor of chili powder

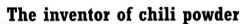

William Gebhardt, owner of the Phoenix Café (now the Phoenix Saloon), is credited for inventing the all-powerful chili powder. He dedicated a lot of his time to perfecting the spices he used in his chili. In order to serve his dish year-round (at the time, chili was a seasonal food), Gebhardt would import Mexican ancho chiles from 500 miles away in large quantities so he could stock up his supply. He only had to figure out a way to store it all.

He started running the peppers through a home meat grinder. Eventually, he made a powder with ground chile peppers, cumin seed, oregano, and black pepper. He packaged the product in tiny bottles, then loaded them into a box for trade. He called it "Tampico Dust" at first, then later Gebhardt's Eagle Brand Chili Powder in 1896. The factory he opened in San Antonio produced five cases of chili powder a week. From there, his business exploded and is known today as the popular brand, Gebhardt Mexican Foods Company.

The chili craze spreads

Around 1900, chili joints began popping up not only all over Texas, but also nationwide. Usually no more than a shed or a room with a hung blanket to separate the kitchen—that's how you know it's going to be really, *really* good—almost every town had somewhere to go to enjoy a bowl of steaming chili.

By the time the Great Depression hit, chili was the difference between starvation and surviving. It was cheap and crackers were free. There was even a saying that chili saved more lives than the Red Cross!

1896
Gebhardt's Eagle Brand Chili Powder was born

1921
Wolf Brand Chili was born

1922
Cincinatti chili was born

Chili vs. Chilli

You know things are getting heated when an entire city insists on spelling chili their own way. There are two theories as to why and how Springfield, Illinois, spells it "chilli." The first points to a man named Dew Brockman in 1909—owner and founder of the Dew Chilli Parlor—who argued with the man who was painting his parlor's sign. After insisting that the dictionary spells it both ways, Dew "won," and "chilli" was born. The other theory is the spelling was simply made to match the first four letters in "Illinois."

In 1993, Illinois' state government passed legislation that declared Illinois as the "Chilli Capital of the Civilized World" and, yes, recognized its spelling *their* way.

Cincinnati chili is born

When you think of chili, you probably think of Texas first. But Cincinnati, Ohio, can arguably be thought of as a close second. Cincinnati chili differs from Texan chili in a few ways: the way the meat is cooked, its thinner consistency, and its unusual blend of spices that consists of cinnamon, cocoa, allspice, and Worcestershire. It's also served on top of spaghetti.

This unique dish was born in 1922, created by a man named Tom Kiradjieff. An immigrant from Macedonia, Tom and his brother John opened a hot dog stand with a Greek-inspired spin. The only problem was no one cared about Greek food, so their business was failing. To stir up some attention, they then started to cook chili using Middle Eastern spices that could be served in different ways and called it "spaghetti chili." "The works," or Five-Way Chili, consisted of a pile of spaghetti topped with chili, onions, red kidney beans, and shredded cheese with a side of oyster crackers and hot dogs topped with more cheese.

Chili goes Hollywood

The most famous chili, however, brings us to Chasen's Restaurant in Hollywood in 1936, where owner Dave Chasen kept his legendary recipe under lock and key. Everyone from actors to film crews to chauffeurs would come to the back door of Chasen's to buy his chili. These chili-craving icons included Jack Benny, J. Edgar Hoover, Eleanor Roosevelt, and others. It's even said it was Clark Gable's last meal and that Elizabeth Taylor had 10 quarts sent to her while she was filming *Cleopatra* in Rome, Italy.

CHILI TIMELINE > > > > > > > >

The first chili cook-off

While most say the first official World's Chili Championship was held in 1967, *technically*, the very first cook-off was held on October 5, 1952, at the Texas State Fair Chili Championship in Dallas, Texas. The winner was Mrs. F. G. Ventura. Her recipe was declared the "Official State Fair of Texas Chili Recipe," and she was named the first "World Champion Chili Cook." She went on to hold her title as champion for the next 15 years.

A man named Joe E. Cooper was the event's planner, and while chili cook-offs went on to explode in popularity across the nation, he died in December of 1952 and would never live to see any other than the very first one he himself orchestrated. A true chili tragedy.

A tale of chili and racecars

There were two things the famous racecar driver Carroll Shelby loved: racecars (of course) and chili—what a true American. Known for being a professional racing driver, automotive designer, and entrepreneur, one of his non-Ford related projects included organizing the iconic 1967 chili cook-off at Terlingua. It started as a party for chili fanatics, but evolved into an annual, world-famous championship. Shelby and his fellow judge, C.V. Wood, then founded the International Chili Society and its World Champion Chili Cook-Offs that still exist today!

During those yearly events, Shelby would go around handing out his own chili seasonings in brown paper bags he designed himself. His mix grew so popular that by the 6th ICS cook-off event, "Carroll Shelby's Original Texas Chili Kit" was available on the market and, of course, still is.

Chili today

With such a joyride of a history, it's no wonder why there are countless chili organizations, including the International Chili Society (my people!) and the Chili Appreciation Society International, which has about 50 subgroups across the United States and Canada. This one organization alone sanctions over 400 chili cook-offs each year that draw thousands of participants. And they're all, you guessed it, *serious* about chili. And seriously good at making it!

Clearly, chili has become an iconic American dish that means so much more than just a bowl of beef and peppers. It represents a culture of food fanatics who love to share their recipes for generations to come, and that's the goal of this book: to share with you a collection of seriously good recipes—whether they are passed down from days of old or new and original takes. But, no matter what, it's yours to make, serve, and share.

1936
Chasen's Chili serves Hollywood

1952
First cook-off held at the Texas State Fair Chili Championship in Dallas

1967
First World Champion Chili Cook-Off is held

The Recipes—My Search for the Perfect Pot of Chili

There I was in Myrtle Beach, South Carolina, surrounded by pots and pots of chili. A judge at the World Championship Chili Cook-Off, hosted by the International Chili Society. You know, the famous competition that Carroll Shelby helped organize. I looked around at the chili competitors—*my people*—rosy from the work of perfecting their dishes, anxiously awaiting the announcement of the winners, happy to gather in celebration of chili. "How did I get here?" I pondered.

It all began that fateful night of April 30, 2009. I spilled the chili and became "the chili guy." Little did I know that I'd discover a new passion in my life—chili! I've been blown away by the chili community and their dedicated passion. So many people of different cultural backgrounds and differing tastes brought together by one dish! Vegans and carnivores, bean advocates and bean avoiders, Texans, South Africans, and others from around the globe—all here in search of the winning chili!

Inspired by their passion, I knew I just *had* to assemble a cookbook that features the best-of-the-best

chili recipes for anyone to recreate some seriously top-tier dishes! I needed to find a chili for every unique flavor and secret ingredient.

But how? Where would I start?

And then it hit me—I knew exactly what I had to do. My *only* option to discover the world's best chili recipes was to go on an epic voyage. To purely indulge myself, I'd refer to it as *The Quest to Find the Best*. I packed my bags, kissed my wife and children goodbye, and set out to find my destiny!

Determined and hungry, I trekked through deserts, swam across oceans, scaled mountainsides, battled wind and sky, rain and snow, searched high and low across the globe on a hunt for the most downright delicious bowls of chili I could find. Eventually, word of my epic chili expedition got out. I remember I was deep in the Amazon when I heard rustling leaves and breaking branches from right behind me. Quickly, I snapped around to find someone panting and thirsty, holding out a crumbled-up piece of paper. Puzzled, I traded her the paper for my canteen as she wiped her brow.

A Note About the Chili Categories

In my *Quest to Find the Best*, I uncovered so many different chili recipes, I needed to find a way to keep them all straight! I decided to group them into 10 different categories. I chose a category for each recipe based on the ingredients used, the inspiration behind the dish, and the description given by the contributor. Many of these categories are not "Official Competition" categories, and rarely are they agreed-upon or clearly defined, so I've included the generally accepted definitions for each at the beginning of their sections.

Chili Categories
- Chili con Carne
- Chili Verde
- White Chicken Chili
- Texas Chili
- Cincinnati Chili
- Turkey Chili
- Vegetarian Chili
- Black Bean Chili
- Homestyle Chili
- Chili Takes: Chili Dogs, Nachos, Cornbread, and More

"I've been trying to catch up with you since you crossed the Andes!" she puffed out. She gestured a tired hand to the paper. "That's my great-great-grandmother's chili con carne. It's been passed down for generations. Maybe you'll like it enough for your cookbook I heard you're writing?"

I was flabbergasted. And inspired! One by one, more and more people were popping up everywhere along my trek. Carrier pigeons were swooping from the sky, smoke signals were sent, boats were docking along coastlines, and soon I had more chili recipes than I could carry! I hitchhiked my way back home where I found a swarm of people waiting for me on my front lawn, waving their beloved chili recipes in the air. A single tear glistened in my eye; it was the most beautiful sight I had ever seen. I literally had millions of chili recipes!

With so many recipes to review came the daunting task of narrowing it down. I spent the next eight months cooking, eating, and choosing. I was up day and night like a mad scientist wreaking total kitchen havoc. Some nights I manically laughed with glee, and other nights I cried like I was mourning a beloved friend. Every cut recipe hurt like a sucker punch to my heart. It was arguably one of the hardest things I've ever done in my life, but eventually, I had done it. I had a whopping 177 of the best chili recipes the world would ever know. And now, for the first time ever in chili history, they're yours, too.

The recipes that follow were carefully (one might even say *seriously*) vetted and selected based on taste (of course) as well as originality. I scoured regional styles, from Texas to Cincinnati, and I also wanted to accommodate all taste buds, so you'll find plant-based vegan and vegetarian recipes, white chicken chili, and the inclusion of unique ingredients, from mango and pumpkin to beer, coffee, wine, and more—even alligator for the adventurous eater! I can assure you that you'll taste flavors that will absolutely blow your mind.

By making these recipes yourself, you're taking part in the once-in-a-lifetime journey I went on myself to find them. What surrounds chili is a culture of sharing. It's not only my honor that so many amazing people have shared their recipes with me, but it's also my honor to share them with you. Compiling these recipes was an absolute joy, and after I eventually recovered from intense frostbite, I was completely floored by how talented and creative chili lovers are with their recipes. Trust me, there are ingredients you wouldn't even *think* to put in chili but may not leave out ever again.

Not to sound boastful, but I'd be hard pressed to find a more eclectic and impressive collection of chili recipes anywhere else. I encourage you to challenge your chili skills and cook as many new styles as your chili pots can muster. The goal of creating this cookbook was to build the ultimate chili resource with the biggest assortment of recipes ever on the planet, all in one place—and I think we've gone and done it.

Enjoy, friends and chiliheads! And thank you for joining me on this chili journey.

Watch for the QR Codes

But wait, there's more! I wanted to take things a step further to really bring this best-of-chili book to life, so I've included exclusive cooking videos. When you come across a QR code, simply open the camera on your phone or device, scan the code, and a link will appear for you to click and watch!

Brian's Seriously Good Chili Recipe

This is it, folks. My own personal go-to chili recipe. Has it been passed down for generations? No. But it serves as my own best chili recipe that I cook all the time. Don't be afraid to play! Like it spicier? Add red pepper flakes or Spicy Bush's® Chili Beans. Like it thicker? Feel free to cook this over the stove all day. (Just add water as needed for best consistency.) I felt it was important to add my personal favorite recipe to this book, but know that it is always changing. I love exploring new flavors and employing new techniques every time I make it—so *you* should feel free to make any adjustments you love and send them along to me! Enjoy.

COOK TIME
1 hr.
Makes 6–8 servings

WATCH HOW TO MAKE THIS RECIPE

INGREDIENTS

- 1 tablespoon grapeseed oil (or cooking oil)
- 1 large yellow onion (or 1 cup shallots), chopped
- 1 green bell pepper, chopped
- 2 cloves garlic, diced
- 2 pounds lean ground turkey (or lean ground beef), undrained
- One 6-ounce can tomato paste
- One 24-ounce can diced tomatoes
- One 16-ounce can tomato sauce
- ½ cup water (optional)
- ½ teaspoon black pepper
- 2 teaspoons salt
- 4 teaspoons chili powder
- 2 teaspoons ancho chile powder
- 4 teaspoons oregano
- 1 teaspoon sugar

- One 16-ounce can Bush's® Pinto Beans in a Mild Chili Sauce, undrained
- One 16-ounce can Bush's® Kidney Beans in a Mild Chili Sauce, undrained
- Garnish: shredded cheddar cheese

Good-to-Know Info

Have fun with your garnishes! Sour cream and shredded cheese are classic options, but you can change it up with pickled jalapeños, avocado mash, or crumbled tortilla chips. Just make sure what you choose complements your chili.

DIRECTIONS

1. In a large pot, sauté the chopped onion, green bell pepper, and garlic in oil over medium-high heat. I like to use grapeseed oil because it's a little less oily.

2. Add in the ground turkey or beef. Before the meat has completely cooked, add the tomato paste. Finish browning the meat completely.

3. Stir in the remaining ingredients, except the beans and the cheese. Bring to a boil. Reduce heat. Cover and simmer on low heat for 30 minutes (or longer until the desired consistency is reached), stirring occasionally.

4. Then, 20 minutes before serving, add the beans. You can't add the beans in right away or they get mushy.

5. Finish with sharp cheddar cheese. Any leftovers are easy to freeze!

Sauté the onion, green bell pepper, and garlic over medium-high heat.

Add in the ground turkey or beef. Before the meat has completely cooked, add the tomato paste. Finish browning the meat completely.

Stir in remaining ingredients, except the beans and the cheese. Bring to a boil. Reduce heat. Cover and simmer on low heat, stirring occasionally.

4

Add the beans 20 minutes before serving.

5

Finish with sharp cheddar cheese.

Good-to-Know Info

Freezer tip! Pour individual portions of your chili into a gently greased muffin tin, then put the muffin-sized portions in their own freezer bags so you can individually reheat them as needed.

Recipe Conversions

Many recipes in this book use volume-based ingredients and can be converted to their metric volume equivalent (given below). If you would rather convert to mass (grams), you should research the correct conversion for the exact ingredient being measured, since different ingredients have different masses.

⅛ teaspoon = 0.6 mL	1 tablespoon = 15 mL	1 cup = 240 mL
¼ teaspoon = 1.2 mL	⅛ cup = 30 mL	1 fluid ounce = 30 mL
½ teaspoon = 2.5 mL	¼ cup = 60 mL	1 ounce = 28 grams
1 teaspoon = 5 mL	½ cup = 120 mL	1 fluid pound = 500 mL
½ tablespoon = 7.5 mL	¾ cup = 175 mL	1 pound = 453 grams

Hot Pepper Heat Scale

Scoville Heat Unit (SHU) heat ranges given are approximate. Because some chilies come in such a wide range of heats, not all chilies necessarily fit perfectly within the listed ranges.

Heat Level 1:
SHU 0–750

 Antohi Romanian

 Boldog

 Choricero

 Pepperoncini

 Pimiento

 Santa Fe Grande

 Shishito

Heat Level 2:
SHU 500–1,200

 Ají Dulce

 NuMex Big Jim

 Peppadew

Heat Level 3:
SHU 1,000–2,500

 Ancho

 Cascabel

 Chilhuacle Rojo

 Costeño Amarillo

 Georgia Flame

 Goat's Horn

 Guindilla

 Kashmiri Degi Mirch

 New Mexico Sandia

 Pasilla

 Poblano

 Poinsettia

 Prairie Fire

 Sebes

Szentesi Semi-Hot

Heat Level 4:
SHU 1,000–5,000

 Ammazzo

 Anaheim

 Casabella

 Chilhuacle Negro

 Cyklon

 Garden Salsa F1

 Hungarian Yellow Wax Hot

 Inferno F1

 Mirasol (Miracielo)

 Mulato

 New Mexico No. 9

 Pasado

 Pimiento de Padron

Heat Level 5:
SHU 2,000–8,000

 Capónes

 Cherry Bomb F1

 Chilhuacle Amarillo

 Chimayó

 Chipotle

 Fresno

 Jalapeño

Heat Level 6:
SHU 8,000–20,000

 Christmas Bell

 Joe's Long

 Serrano

Heat Level 7:
SHU 15,000–35,000

 Bangalore Torpedo

 Brazilian Starfish

 Bulgarian Carrot

 Criolla Sella

 De Árbol

 Fish

 Japóne

 Jwala

 Orozco

 Peter Pepper

 Takanotsume

Tears of Fire

Tokyo Hot F1

Heat Level 8:
SHU 20,000–50,000

 Ají Amarillo

 Bacio di Satana

 Cayenne

 Dagger Pod

 Facing-Heaven

 Filius Blue

 Firecracker

 Jaloro

 Manzano

 NuMex Twilight

 Piquin

 Super Chili F1

 Tabasco

 Tepin

Heat Level 9:
SHU 40,000–200,000

 Ají Cereza

 Ají Limo

 Ají Limón

Ají Pinguita de Mono

Apache F1

Bird's-eye

Charleston Hot

Chi-Chen

Ornamental Firecracker

Jamaican Hot Chocolate

Piros F1

Riot

Thai Dragon F1

Heat Level 10:
SHU 100,000–2,200,000

 Carolina Reaper

 Datil

 Fataali

 Habanero

 Habanero Red Savina

 Naga/Bhut Jolokia (Ghost Pepper)

 Paper Lantern Habanero

 Scotch Bonnet

Surinam Red

Chili con Carne

In this traditional chili dish, beef, peppers, and spice are essentials. Tomatoes, onions, and beans are commonly included, but meat is a must!

The Recipes

JB's Deep Heat Sweet Feat Chili

Electric Pressure Cooker Chili

Asian-Spiced Pork Chili with Butternut Squash

Braised Short Rib and Chorizo Chili

JK's Go-To Chili

For me, chili is comfort food. Although I usually get a hankering for this dish as autumn approaches, sometimes I want this comfort on a hot summer day. Remember, chili is always better warmed up the second day! Enjoy!

COOK TIME
1 hr. 30 mins.
Makes 6–8 servings

INGREDIENTS

- 2–3 tablespoons bacon drippings, duck fat, or butter
- ½ cup onion, diced
- ¼ cup bell pepper, diced
- 1 clove garlic, minced
- 2 pounds ground beef, lamb, or turkey
- 1¼ cups canned plum tomatoes, crushed with your hand
- 4 cups cooked kidney or black beans, drained
- ½ cup canned corn, drained (optional; I only use corn with turkey)
- 1 bay leaf
- 2 teaspoons to 2 tablespoons chili powder, depending on your taste and the powder's strength
- Salt and pepper, to taste
- Serve with: cornbread, tortillas, or buttermilk biscuits

Directions

1. Melt the bacon drippings, duck fat, or butter in a pan. I use bacon drippings with beef or lamb, duck fat for turkey, and butter when I have neither.

2. Sauté the onion, bell pepper, and garlic in the fat over medium heat for 1–2 minutes.

3. Add the meat. Stir and sauté until well done.

4. Add the remaining ingredients (tomatoes, beans, corn, bay leaf, chili powder, salt, and pepper). Cover and cook slowly for 1 hour to 1 hour 30 minutes.

5. Serve with your choice of either cornbread, tortillas, or buttermilk biscuits.

CHEF JEFFREY VADEN,
White Plains, New York

New York chef Jeffrey K. Vaden was the owner of the former JK Restaurant & Bar, and currently owns Soul Luxe Caterers, bringing elevated and innovative soul food utilizing classic techniques to Westchester, NY. A contestant on Food Network's *Next Food Network Star*, Jeffrey expanded his brand to both coasts. He also began teaching in 2015, is an adjunct professor of culinary arts, and has been a spokesperson and lecturer for HealthFirst Insurance Co., A.D.A., and The Cooking Studio at Zwilling's U.S. Instagram: @soulluxe101

COOK TIME
2 hrs. 30 mins.
Makes 4–6 servings

Peruvian Chile Con Carne

The use of Peruvian Chile pastes really takes this chile con carne to a new flavor destination. The spice of the amarillo and earthy nature of the panca are a refreshing twist on this Tex-Mex classic.

INGREDIENTS

- 4 pounds chuck steak, chunked
- 1 pound cured pork jowl, diced
- ½ cup Peruvian ají panca chile paste
- ½ cup Peruvian ají amarillo chile paste
- ¼ cup espresso chile rub (I use Spiceology® Cowboy Crust)
- ⅛ cup cumin, roasted
- ⅛ cup coriander
- 2 tablespoons dried oregano
- 1 tablespoon salt
- ½ cup garlic, minced
- 2 cups onion, diced
- ¼ cup tomato paste
- One 14-ounce can fire-roasted tomatoes
- 8 cups beef stock
- 1 cup flour
- 1 teaspoon salt
- 4 tablespoons canola oil
- Garnish and serve with: tortillas, pickled jalapeños, green onions

Directions

1. Dice the chuck steak and dust with salt and flour. Reduce pork jowl in a large stockpot. Add the steak to the pot and slowly brown the beef on all sides in small batches, making sure not to crowd the bottom of the pot. Remove from the pot and drain.

2. Heat the canola oil in a pan. Sauté onions and garlic for 3 minutes. Add beef back to the pot with onions and garlic.

3. Add the espresso chile rub and all other spices. Incorporate the ají pastes, tomato paste, and tomatoes. Add beef stock and bring to a boil. Once thickened, reduce heat and simmer for 2 hours, stirring often to keep from sticking.

4. Serve with tortillas, pickled jalapeños, and green onions.

CHEF CHRISTIAN GILL,
Cincinnati, Ohio

Chef Christian Gill is the chef-owner of Boomtown Biscuits and Whiskey. Along with the many awards won by the restaurant and team, Chef Gill has made a multitude of appearances on the Food Network. Coming out a champion from multiple shows, Chef Gill's recipe for chili con carne is sure to win at your next chili cook-off.
Twitter: @bodybybiscuit
Instagram: @foodbrushninja
TikTok: @only_yams

Papa Youngblood's Chili

I love chili, so I experimented until I found my own perfect chili. It's not a quick-to-make recipe, but it is easy. I toned down the heat, but it does have a bite. My motto is, if it ain't hot, it's just soup!

COOK TIME

4 hrs.

Makes 7+ servings

INGREDIENTS

- 2 pounds rib eye steak
- Salt, to taste
- 1 teaspoon pepper
- 2 tomatillos
- 2 sprouts green onion
- 2 jalapeños
- 2 serranos
- 2 yellow chiles
- 1 pound ground beef (steak)
- 1 tube beef chorizo
- 1 tablespoon butter
- 1 onion, diced

- 1 bunch cilantro, chopped
- 5 tomatoes, diced
- One 15-ounce can kidney beans
- 1 tablespoon red wine vinegar
- 4 slices American cheese (I use Kraft®)
- ½ cup breadcrumbs
- 1 shot tequila (I use Don Julio 1942®)
- 1 tablespoon New Mexico chile powder (or to your taste)
- 2 serranos
- Juice of 1 lemon

Directions

1. Season the steaks with salt and pepper. Barbecue on a grill until brown on the outside. Charred is better, but make sure they're rare on the inside. Remove from the heat and set aside.

2. Grill the whole tomatillos, green onions, and all the chiles until charred. Then remove them from the heat and allow them to cool.

3. In a large pot on high heat, combine the ground steak and chorizo with 1 tablespoon of butter. Cook until the ground steak is brown. Remove some excess fat, making sure to leave at least some in.

4. Cut the grilled steak into small cubes and add it to the chorizo and ground beef mixture. Stir and turn the heat to low.

5. Dice the grilled tomatillos, green onion, and chiles. Combine these with the diced onion, cilantro, and tomatoes in a food processer. Give it a few bursts to chop everything more finely to make a sauce. Add this to the meat in the pot.

6. Add the kidney beans, red wine vinegar, and lemon juice. Stir well.

7. Add the cheese and stir well.

8. Add the breadcrumbs and stir well. Bring the whole mixture to a boil, stirring often. Add chile powder and stir well.

9. Turn the heat to low and simmer for 2 hours. Stir occasionally to make sure the bottom does not burn. Salt to taste.

10. Add the shot of tequila and stir. Continue to simmer for another hour. Let sit for 30 minutes. Then eat!

STEVE YOUNGBLOOD,
Thousand Oaks, California

Steve is a small business owner, husband, father of 5 and grandfather (or Papa) of 9. He loves to cook, loves to fish, and has been playing classic rock music since before it was classic. There is nothing better than playing in the band and having his grandchildren front and center. At a family or friend's gathering, you will find him at the grill or with a guitar in his hands.

Mom's Chili

Simplicity meets excellence in this handed-down masterpiece that screams warmth and comfort. Nothing fancy going on here, just the classic combination of good ol' ground beef (or turkey!), hearty beans, and warm spices that is best simmered low and slow. From my family to yours, enjoy. Grandma would be proud.

COOK TIME

1 hr.

Makes 6 servings

INGREDIENTS

- 1 pound ground meat of choice
- 1 small sweet onion, chopped
- One 16-ounce can tomato sauce
- One 16-ounce can red kidney beans
- ¼ teaspoon garlic
- 1 teaspoon salt
- 3 teaspoons chili powder
- 1 tablespoon vinegar

Directions

1. Brown the ground meat with the onion.
2. After the meat has cooked, drain off the grease.
3. Add the remaining ingredients and simmer for 45 minutes.

BRIANA FEDORKO,
Salisbury, Maryland

Briana is a Doctor of Physical Therapy in Maryland, and she really loves chili. She frequently requested chili for her "birthday dinner" as a child, and now makes this recipe herself. Briana's husband does the majority of the cooking in their household, but chili night is her time to shine.

COOK TIME

1 hr.

Makes 7+ servings

Double Meat Five-Alarm Habanero Chili

Chili, to me, is something that should be spicy! I love a good kick in the mouth with a hearty chili. I'm a chef and a lover of all things extreme—when I'm not in the kitchen grinding away, I'm out BMXing, skateboarding, or doing parkour—and my chili reflects that. This recipe can be executed very quickly and produces a chili that will make your guests feel like you've been cooking for days. Come have a taste of my world!

INGREDIENTS

- 2 pounds pork shoulder, cut into ½-inch cubes
- 1 tablespoon olive oil
- 1 large red onion, diced
- 2 jalapeños, diced
- 4 cloves garlic, minced
- 2 pounds 80% lean ground beef
- 3 habaneros
- ¼ cup paprika
- ¼ cup chili powder (Anaheim chile if possible)
- 2 tablespoons onion powder
- 2 tablespoons garlic powder
- 2 tablespoons salt
- 1 tablespoon coriander
- 1 teaspoon cumin
- 1 teaspoon mustard powder
- 1 teaspoon black pepper
- 1 bay leaf
- Two 28-ounce cans crushed tomatoes

Directions

1. Sear the pork shoulder in batches and remove from the pot.
2. Add the oil, onions, and jalapeños to the pot and cook for 2–3 minutes.
3. Add the garlic and cook for 30 seconds.
4. Add the ground beef and cook for 3–4 minutes or until brown.
5. Put slices in habanero. Leave the stem intact to easily remove the pepper later. Add to the chili.
6. Add the seared pork, all the spices, and the crushed tomatoes. Stir.
7. Bring the chili to a simmer and cook, partly covered, for 30–40 minutes or until the pork is tender.
8. Alternatively, add all the ingredients to slow cooker and cook on low.

ARA ZADA,
Chatsworth, California

Born and raised in Los Angeles, Ara spent his younger years skateboarding and snowboarding, but always had his heart in the kitchen. He attended culinary school at Le Cordon Bleu and built a career as an Executive Chef specializing in recipe development and food styling. He has worked with Jamie Oliver's Food Revolution, Food Network, ABC, CBS, NBC, Breville, Gelson's, and a range of others. He has had multiple TV appearances and written a cookbook *Lavash* with coauthors Kate Leahy and John Lee. He trains in parkour, is a triathlete, and an avid bowhunter. Facebook, Twitter, Instagram: @arazada YouTube: Ara Zada TikTok: @chefarazada

JB's Deep Heat Sweet Feat Chili

My chili is a labor of love with tremendous reward. I learned how to perfect building depths of flavor over years of trial and error. This recipe is something I poured myself into, a chili I can truly call my own. It does carry some sneaky heat, a heat you do not realize is there until you are a few bites in. My mantel has several "people's choice" awards that attest to the quality of this recipe—so I hope you enjoy it!

COOK TIME

1 hr. 45 mins.

Makes 7+ servings

INGREDIENTS

- ½ pound bacon
- 1 pound ground beef or your preferred meat; venison works wonderfully
- 1 pound ground pork
- 1 green bell pepper, diced
- 1 yellow onion, diced
- 1 cup pickled jalapeños
- 1 habanero, seeds removed
- 3 cloves garlic, minced
- 1 tablespoon cumin
- ½ tablespoon crushed red pepper

- 3 tablespoons chili powder
- 2 tablespoons beef bouillon
- One 28-ounce can crushed tomatoes
- Two 16-ounce cans whole peeled tomatoes, drained
- 1 can beer (light lager preferred)
- 3 ounces tomato paste
- 2 cups water
- Tabasco® sauce, to taste
- 1 ounce chili paste
- Salt and pepper, to taste

Directions

1. Cook the bacon in a pan until crispy. Chop it into bite-size pieces and set aside.
2. Brown the ground beef and pork in a large pot until no longer pink.
3. When the meat is browned, stir in the bell pepper, onion, jalapeño, habanero, garlic, all spices (including bouillon), all tomatoes, beer, tomato paste, and water.
4. Reduce the heat to low and simmer, uncovered, for 45–60 minutes in order to build the heat and flavors. As a wise man once said, "Everybody is going to get to know each other in the pot."
5. Add the bacon and simmer for an additional 15 minutes. Add the remaining ingredients to taste.
6. Enjoy with friends.

JACK BELLAMY,
Sparta, Michigan

A self-proclaimed chef from the Mitten state, raised on a midwestern palate, Jack Bellamy grew up in a household that thrived on a mac & cheese and a cereal diet. Jack started to explore the kitchen with great mentors at a young age. A chef was born (several burns and cuts later) out of a newfound love for cooking. The greatest thing that cooking has taught him, simply put… "No matter who you are or where you came from, there is one universal truth: food is the shortest distance between two people." Facebook: @jack.bellamy.10 Instagram: @jb_ington

Chili Recipe Awards

- 2015 "People's Choice" Award, Local Competition
- 2016 People's Choice Trophy (local award)
- 2017 "People's Choice" Award, Local Competition
- 2018 Moose Lodge "Best-of-the-Best" category
- 2019 Teacher's Union "People's Choice," Local Competition
- 2019 Best of the Midwest (West Michigan Award)
- 2020 Winter Fest "People's Choice" Trophy
- 2020 Sparta Moose Lodge "New Member Category: Best of the Best"
- 2020 "Best of the Midwest," Local Competition, Chili con Carne Category
- 2020 "Moose Lodge Winner," Best submission, all categories, over 50 competitors
- 2021 Best in "Hot/Spicy" Category (local award)
- 2021 "Overall Winner," Grand Rapids Charity Competition
- 2021 "I am so proud of you" award from my grandma

Chef Keriann's Drunken Chili

This is a chili recipe I have been perfecting for a few years now. I love the balance of heat and sweet that the use of the different chiles will give you. Also, the tiny hint of cinnamon really sets it all off. But the real secret is the buildup of flavor through the whole cooking process. I have won a few chili competitions with this one, so I hope you enjoy it!

COOK TIME
6 hrs.
Makes 7+ servings

INGREDIENTS

- ¼ cup bacon grease
- 3 pounds tri-tip, cut into ½-inch cubes
- 1 pound ground pork
- 1 pound ground beef
- 1 large onion, chopped
- 4 jalapeños, chopped
- 5 cloves garlic, chopped
- 3 dried Anaheim chiles, boiled and puréed
- 3 dried New Mexico chiles, boiled and puréed
- One 4-ounce can diced green chiles
- 8 tablespoons chili powder

- 2 tablespoons ground cumin
- 3 teaspoons oregano
- 1 teaspoon cinnamon
- 2 teaspoons brown sugar
- 2 teaspoons salt
- 1½ teaspoons pepper
- One 10-ounce can diced tomatoes
- One 14-ounce can kidney beans
- 2 bottles amber beer
- 2 ounces bourbon
- One 8-ounce can tomato sauce
- 5 cups beef stock

Directions

1. In a large pot, heat the bacon grease over high heat. Add the tri-tip and sear, then remove it and set it aside.

2. Add the pork and beef to the pot and cook until brown, then remove and set aside.

3. Lower the heat to medium. Add the onions, jalapeños, garlic, chiles, and chili powder. Cook, stirring constantly, until the onions are tender, about 5 minutes.

4. Add the cumin, oregano, cinnamon, brown sugar, salt, pepper, and tomatoes. Add the beer and bourbon and cook to deglaze the pan.

5. Add the tomato sauce, kidney beans, and beef stock. Return all the meat back into the pot and simmer for 5 hours.

6. When you're ready to serve, adjust the seasoning as desired, and enjoy!

KERIANN VON RAESFELD-HARRIGAN,
San Jose, California

Chef Keriann is a world-renowned chef with many international awards under her belt. She currently owns her own private catering company in San Jose, CA, focusing on high-end farm-to-table experiences. She was also a contestant on Bravo's *Top Chef*. Website: www.chef keriann.com

Chili Recipe Awards

- California Chili Cook-Off (2015)
- San Jose Chili Cook-Off (2016)
- Willow Glen Chili Cook-Off (2018)

Electric Pressure Cooker Chili

This chili recipe is made in an electric pressure cooker, making it a quick option for days when you don't have hours to let the chili cook. Even though you're saving time, this chili still turns out hearty and flavorful with the addition of jalapeños, southwestern seasoning, and dark cocoa powder.

COOK TIME
1 hr. 15 mins.
Makes 6 servings

INGREDIENTS

- 1 cup dry (uncooked) black beans
- 1 cup dry (uncooked) kidney beans
- 1 cup dry (uncooked) pinto beans
- 1 tablespoon cooking oil
- 1 onion, diced
- 2 jalapeños, diced, seeded if desired

- 4 cloves garlic, smashed and sliced
- 1 pound ground beef
- 2–3 tablespoons southwestern seasoning
- 1 tablespoon dark cocoa powder
- 3–4 cups beef broth
- One 32-ounce can tomatoes

Directions

1. Rinse the beans and combine in the inner pot of your electric pressure cooker (I use an Instant Pot®). Cover with water and secure the lid. Set the cooker to "beans/chili" and cook for 25 minutes. Natural release.

2. Drain and rinse the beans and clean out the inner pot.

3. Set the cooker to "sauté" and add the cooking oil. Once the oil is hot, add the onion and diced jalapeños. Cook for 3 minutes.

4. Add the garlic and continue cooking for 1 minute, stirring occasionally.

5. Add the ground beef, seasoning, and cocoa powder. Stir well and cook until the ground beef is well browned.

6. Turn off the cooker and add the cooked beans, broth, and tomatoes into it.

7. Secure the lid and set the cooker to "beans/chili" for 20 minutes. Natural release.

JENNIFER TAMMY,
London, Ontario, Canada

Jennifer Tammy is the blogger behind www.SugarSpiceAndGlitter.com where she shares delicious recipes, fun kids' activities, and travel tips to make family life easier and add a bit of magic to your day. Her recipes have been enjoyed by millions of people all over the world and have been featured in cookbooks and magazines, from *Southern Living* to the BBC.
Website: www.sugarspice andglitter.com
Facebook, Instagram: @sugarspiceandglitter
Pinterest: @jennifertammy
Twitter: @sugarspiceglitr

Dump Chili

I call this "dump chili" because you dump all the ingredients into a large slow cooker and let it go—overnight is best. What could be simpler than that?

INGREDIENTS

- 1½ pounds coarsely ground beef
- 1 large yellow onion, coarsely chopped
- 3–4 cloves garlic, peeled, crushed, and smashed
- ½ cup chili powder (I use McCormick®)
- One 24-ounce can tomato purée
- One 24-ounce can stewed tomatoes
- One 24-ounce can water
- ½ teaspoon each salt and pepper
- 1 tablespoon sugar

Directions

1. Turn the slow cooker on high. Dump the meat, onions, garlic, and chili powder into the cooker. Stir until mixed well.
2. Add the tomato purée, stewed tomatoes, water, salt, pepper, and sugar to the mix and stir well.
3. Cover the pot and walk away.

Good-to-Know Info

One teaspoon of red chili powder meets the recommended daily intake for Vitamin A.

ROBERT SHAND,
Port Lavaca, Texas

Robert is a 73-year-old man, originally from Maine and now living in Texas. He has been married for 52 years and has one child. Robert has always loved to cook and create in the kitchen.

COOK TIME
30 mins.
Makes 7+ servings

Asian-Spiced Pork Chili with Butternut Squash

This easy chili recipe is on the table in just 30 minutes! The addition of the Chinese five spice, cumin, coriander, and sambal oelek puts this comforting chili over the top with flavor. It is vibrant with butternut squash, multi-colored bell peppers, onions, and garlic, plus three kinds of beans. You'll be bookmarking this one for years to come!

INGREDIENTS

- 1 pound ground pork
- 1 tablespoon canola oil
- 3 cloves garlic, minced
- 1 large onion, chopped
- 1 yellow bell pepper, seeded and chopped
- 1 red bell pepper, seeded and chopped
- 1 small butternut squash, peeled, seeded, and cubed
- One 14.5-ounce can black beans, rinsed and drained
- One 14.5-ounce can white cannellini beans, rinsed and drained
- One 14.5-ounce can garbanzo beans, rinsed and drained
- Two 14.5-ounce cans petite diced tomatoes
- 1 teaspoon ground cumin
- 1 teaspoon coriander
- 1 tablespoon Chinese five spice
- ½ teaspoon salt
- ½ teaspoon pepper
- 1 tablespoon sambal oelek
- ¼ cup fresh cilantro
- 1 avocado, sliced
- Sour cream, to taste

Directions

1. Sauté the pork on medium-high heat until just browned. Let it sit on paper towels to drain.
2. Add the oil to the pot over medium-high heat. Sauté the garlic and onions until translucent, about 2 minutes.
3. Add in the bell peppers and butternut squash. Sauté for another 5 minutes until just softened.
4. Stir in all the beans and tomatoes and cook for 2 minutes.
5. Stir in all the spices and the sambal oelek. Cover and simmer for 10 minutes.
6. Add the pork back into the chili and stir to combine well. Let simmer for another 5 minutes.
7. Garnish with the cilantro, avocado, and sour cream.

LESLI SCHWARTZ,
Atlanta, Georgia

Lesli Schwartz is a self-taught cook specializing in crazy-delicious Asian-fusion recipes. After traveling the world several years ago, Lesli fell in love with Asian cuisine and wanted to share that love through her food blog, AsianCaucasian.com. She realized that many people are intimidated by cooking Asian food at home, which is why she brings simplicity to these recipes via her blog. No need for take-out when you make these creative dishes at home! Facebook, Instagram: @asiancaucasianblog Twitter: @asian caucasianB

The Dark Truth Stout Chili

I developed this recipe as an award-winning competitive home cook born with autism. It takes less than an hour to make this tasty chili. I took inspiration from my Red-Eye Cold Brew Chili, and it is unique because it uses Dark Truth Imperial Stout® from the Boulevard Brewing Company to bring coffee and hoppy notes to the flavor profile. I hope you enjoy it.

COOK TIME

1 hr. 15 mins.

Makes 6 servings

INGREDIENTS

- 2 pounds ground beef
- 1 onion, chopped
- 1 red bell pepper, diced
- 3 cloves garlic, minced
- 2 tablespoons chili powder
- 1 teaspoon ground cumin
- 1 teaspoon paprika
- 1 teaspoon onion powder

- One 15-ounce can chili beans, drained and slightly rinsed (I use Bush's®)
- One 15-ounce can fire-roasted tomatoes (I use Hunt's®)
- 1 bottle imperial stout beer (I use Dark Truth Imperial Stout® by Boulevard Brewing Company)
- Garnishes: cheddar, onions, sour cream, hot sauce

Directions

1. In a pot, brown the beef, onion, and bell peppers until the meat is rendered down. Drain the excess fat and return to the pot.
2. Add the garlic, spices, beans, tomatoes, and beer and stir.
3. Bring the mixture to a boil, then reduce the heat to medium and simmer for 30–35 minutes or until the chili has reduced down.
4. Divide the chili into bowls and top with cheddar, onions, sour cream, and hot sauce.

Chili Recipe Awards

- 2014 Honorable Mention South San Francisco Parks and Recreation Chili Cook-Off
- 2015 Honorable Mention South San Francisco Parks and Recreation Chili Cook-Off
- 2016 South San Francisco Parks and Recreation Chili Cook-Off

WATCH HOW I FINISH MY CHILI HERE.

AVA MARIE ROMERO,
South San Francisco, California

Chef Ava Marie is a food blogger and award-winning competition home cook born with autism. She was also a World Food Championship Dessert Finalist in 2018, a three-time chili cook-off competitor for South San Francisco Parks and Recreation Chili Cooks as a finalist, a 7 Mile House Ube BakeOff Champion in 2019, and a finalist in 2021. Chef Ava taught cooking classes at Williams-Sonoma and Grocery Outlet, and she has appeared on KQED. She creates recipes for content part-time, competes in competitions, and works at CDS at Costco as Product Demonstration Associate in the South San Francisco region. Ava currently lives with her parents, Carol Ann and Marty Romero, along with her sweet dog, Bellatrix.
Facebook:
@chefavamarie
Instagram:
@chefavamarie
Twitter: @chefavamarie

No-Fuss Chili

While chili is not really made here in South Africa, more and more local chefs and even supermarkets are coming out with their own version for consumers. While I don't often make chili in the traditional American sense, I do make my own special recipe that I use for everything from tacos and pizza to spaghetti Bolognese and sauces! It's also tasty eaten straight with some sour cream dolloped on top.

COOK TIME

1 hr. 45 mins.

Makes 6 servings

INGREDIENTS

- 3 tablespoons olive oil
- 2 medium red onions, sliced
- 1 teaspoon Korean chili flakes
- 1 teaspoon garam masala
- 1 teaspoon smoked paprika
- 1½ pounds ground beef
- 1 long red chili, chopped
- 3 cloves garlic, minced
- One 14-ounce can baby tomatoes
- One 14-ounce can borlotti beans (or use kidney or pinto beans)
- 1 tablespoon tomato paste
- 1 teaspoon sugar
- ¼ teaspoon flaky salt
- ¼ teaspoon pepper
- 1 tablespoon Worcestershire sauce
- Garnish: sour cream (optional)

Directions

1. Heat the oil in a large pot and fry the onions until soft.
2. Add the chili flakes, garam masala, and smoked paprika. Mix until combined. Add the ground beef and cook for 5 minutes.
3. Add everything else and cook for 20 minutes. Season to taste.
4. Serve straight with sour cream. Alternatively, use on pizza, in tacos with avocado, or serve over some cooked spaghetti in the Cincinnati style!

FATIMA SAIB,
Cape Town, South Africa

Fatima Saib is a cook, writer, and reader with a strong passion for food. She studied English Literature where she focused on food writing before working as a recipe developer, creating recipes for close to 20 major food brands in South Africa. Fatima is currently an editor of two food magazines in South Africa and has her own cooking and lifestyle blog on the side: www.fatimasaib.co.za and www.saibskitchen.com.
Twitter: @fatima_saib
Instagram: @fatimasaib
TikTok: @fatima_saib

COOK TIME

2 hrs.

Makes 4 servings

Sweet Paul's Easy Chili

This is an easy chili recipe, packed with lots of flavor. I always make it the day before as a night in the fridge makes the flavors really pop!

INGREDIENTS

- One 28-ounce can chopped tomatoes
- 1 cup ale
- 1 shot espresso or strong coffee
- 1 tablespoon honey
- 1 teaspoon cumin
- 1 teaspoon dried thyme
- 1 pinch (or more) red chili flakes
- 1 beef bouillon cube
- 1 large yellow onion, finely chopped
- 10 cloves garlic, minced
- ½ cup carrot, finely chopped
- ½ cup celery, finely chopped
- 1 tablespoon Worcestershire sauce
- Splash of soy sauce
- 1 tablespoon sriracha
- 1 pound lean ground beef
- One 10.5-ounce can white beans
- Garnishes: avocado, parsley, extra chili flakes

Directions

1. Place all the ingredients except for the beans in a slow cooker. Mix well and set heat to high. Let simmer for at least 2 hours.

2. After simmering, allow the chili to cool. Place it in the fridge for the next day.

3. When ready to serve, heat up the chili and add in the beans. Serve in large bowls with avocado, parsley, and extra chili flakes.

PAUL LOWE,
Palm Springs, California

Paul Lowe aka Sweet Paul was born in Oslo, Norway where he grew up crafting and cooking. Even as a young kid, he had his own knife, cutting board, and a favorite mixing spoon that no one else was allowed to touch. He first worked as a florist in Oslo, with the royal family as clients, before starting a career in food and prop styling. His work would take him all over Europe before settling in the US. He's worked with *Country Living, Vogue, ELLE, Cosmo, Real Simple*, and more. He started *Sweet Paul Magazine* in 2010 when it quickly grew into a printed publication that has sold all over the world. Instagram, Facebook: @sweetpaulmagazine Website: www.Sweet PaulMag.com

47

Carne Asada Chile with Cornbread Crumbles

This is my own chili recipe that I have served in several of my restaurants. I also won a chili cook-off in South Philly a few years back against twenty other competitors, including some hardcore BBQ guys who were bragging about how they were smoking their meats for twelve hours or more in the days before the competition. Then I walked in with my tried-and-true recipe and won!

COOK TIME

2 hrs.

Makes 7+ servings

INGREDIENTS

- 2 tablespoons canola oil
- 5 pounds carne asada–style small diced beef
- 1 large sweet onion, diced
- 10 cloves garlic, chopped
- 1 poblano
- Two 28-ounce cans crushed tomatoes
- One 28-ounce can diced tomatoes
- ½ cup dark chili powder
- 1 tablespoon chipotle powder
- 1 tablespoon ground cumin

- 2 tablespoons kosher salt, or to taste
- 1 tablespoon freshly ground black pepper
- Two 15-ounce cans small white beans
- Two 15-ounce cans small red beans
- Two 15-ounce cans small pink beans
- Garnishes: sour cream, shredded cheddar cheese, scallions, cornbread (crumbled and toasted in oven)

Directions

1. Heat a large Dutch oven or heavy-bottomed pot over high heat. Add oil and, once it is hot (appears slightly wavy), carefully add the beef. Brown the beef on all sides, doing it in batches if your pot is not large enough.

2. Roast the poblano over an open-flamed burner (or broil in oven) until skin is charred all over. Wrap in plastic wrap and allow to cool. Peel the charred skin off the pepper, remove the stem and seeds, then small dice the pepper.

3. Add the onions and garlic. Stir and sauté for a few minutes.

4. Add the tomatoes and lower the heat to medium. Add all the spices, stir, cover, and simmer for 1 hour.

5. Add the beans and simmer another 30 minutes or until the meat is tender.

6. Serve topped with cheese, sour cream, cornbread, and scallions.

GEORGEANN LEAMING,
Brigantine, New Jersey

Chef Georgeann is a Food Network *Chopped* Champion as well as a competitor on *Man Vs Master*. With a diverse background that spans over 20 years, her vast experience includes co-owning two popular Philadelphia eateries with a Best of Philly Award, as well as being the Executive Chef for two Gordon Ramsay restaurants. She is currently the Culinary Director for a new multi-concept virtual food hall based in Cherry Hill, NJ. This chili recipe is one that she won first place with at a chili cook-off in South Philly, beating out about twenty other competitors. Instagram: @georgeann_leaming

Chili Recipe Awards

- **Winner Chili Cook-Off in South Philly 2015**

Chili Dulce

Everyone who knows me knows that I never say no to a challenge. During the Covid-19 pandemic, a group of my friends decided to host a chili cook-off because our local Chili Fest was cancelled. I knew that this was a challenge that would surprise both my wife and friends. I developed this recipe based on my personal taste in chili. I wanted this to be something on the sweeter side and something I would enjoy eating if I was cooking for our family. To everyone's surprise, I took home first place in the mild division!

COOK TIME

45 mins.

Makes 6 servings

INGREDIENTS

- 2 pounds ground beef
- 1 large onion, diced
- 2 teaspoons garlic powder
- 2 teaspoons chili powder
- 1 teaspoon salt
- 1 teaspoon pepper
- 1 teaspoon oregano
- 1 teaspoon cumin
- Three 14.5-ounce cans tomato sauce
- 6 tablespoons brown sugar
- One 15.25-ounce can corn, drained
- 2 medium red sweet peppers, diced

Directions

1. Brown the ground beef, onion, and garlic powder in a pot. Once the beef is browned, drain the pot.

2. Mix in the chili powder, salt, pepper, oregano, and cumin. Then mix in the tomato sauce and brown sugar. Stir in the corn and diced sweet peppers.

3. Simmer for 15–20 minutes, stirring occasionally.

Chili Recipe Awards

- **First Place Mild Category, Zorns/Hash Chili Cook-Off Huntington, WV**

TREY JONES,
Huntington, West Virginia

Trey Jones is a small business owner from Huntington, WV. He is also a husband, father, and active social media woodworker. While he is not traditionally known for my cooking, he is not one to back down from a challenge. Trey decided to make this chili to enter a local chili competition, and to his surprise, he landed first place in the mild division.
Instagram:
@Handcrafted_by_Trey

COOK TIME

1 hr. 15 mins.

Makes 6 servings

Steak 'n Shake— Inspired Chili

Steak 'n Shake's chili is my all-time favorite restaurant chili. It's got a really specific, thick texture—almost like a sauce—that is unlike any other. After more than three tries, I finally was able to create my own version of chili inspired by theirs.

INGREDIENTS

- ½ pound ground beef
- 2 tablespoons oil
- ½ teaspoon salt
- One 10.5-ounce can French onion soup
- One 15.5-ounce can dark kidney beans
- 1 teaspoon chili powder
- 1 tablespoon cumin
- 1 teaspoon garlic powder
- 1 teaspoon paprika
- 2 teaspoons Worcestershire sauce
- ¼ teaspoon liquid smoke
- ½ cup tomato sauce
- ½ cup dark cola (such as Coke®, Pepsi®, etc.)
- Garnishes: diced onions, grated cheese, oyster crackers
- Serve with: spaghetti (optional)

Directions

1. Brown the ground beef and salt in oil in a Dutch oven–style pan (with high sides). Drain the beef and set aside.

2. Pour the French onion soup and half of the can of kidney beans (some liquid from the beans is fine—do not drain) into a mini blender. Blend for 1 minute, pulsing, until the mixture is completely puréed.

3. Add the soup and bean purée and all the remaining ingredients to the pot with the beef. Bring to a simmer, then turn the heat to the lowest setting and simmer for 1 hour.

4. Serve with diced onion, grated cheese and oyster crackers. You can also serve on top of spaghetti for a Steak 'n Shake three-way!

HEATHER JOHNSON,
Blanchester, Ohio

Heather Johnson is the hussy behind TheFoodHussy.com! She is a food and travel blogger that covers restaurants, recipes, and road trips. She is also a huge fan of *The Office* and is hopeful that you might see her on the Food Network (someday)!
Facebook: @TheFoodHussy
Instagram: @foodhussy
Pinterest: @foodhussy

Braised Short Rib and Chorizo Chili

This recipe is a classic take on chili con carne with an Arizona twist. Filled with tender chunks of steak and a subtle smokiness, the base is made with chorizo and ground beef to give it a spicy yet flavorful bite.

COOK TIME
2 hrs. 45 mins.

Makes 6 servings

INGREDIENTS

- 1 teaspoon garlic powder
- 1 teaspoon cumin
- 1 teaspoon red pepper flakes
- 1 tablespoon chili powder
- 1 teaspoon ground cinnamon
- 2 teaspoons salt
- 1 teaspoon black pepper
- 1 teaspoon paprika
- 1 teaspoon Mexican oregano
- 1 teaspoon white pepper
- 1 teaspoon cayenne pepper (optional)
- 1 pound boneless short rib, cut into 1-inch cubes

- 2 tablespoons olive oil
- 1 yellow onion, diced
- 2 jalapeños, diced
- 2 chipotles in adobo, diced
- 5 cloves garlic
- 1 pound chorizo sausage
- 1 cup tomatoes, diced
- 2 bay leaves
- 1 cup black beans, puréed
- 2 cups beef stock
- 2 tablespoons cornmeal
- Garnishes: diced red onions, sour cream, cheese, diced green onions

Directions

1. Preheat a Dutch oven or a large pot on the stovetop to medium-high heat. Combine all the spices (garlic powder, cumin, red pepper flakes, chili powder, ground cinnamon, salt, black pepper, paprika, Mexican oregano, white pepper, and cayenne pepper) in a separate bowl to create a homemade spice mixture.

2. Generously season the short rib cubes using half of the spice mixture. Pour the olive oil in the Dutch oven and sear the short rib cubes until brown on all sides. Remove the cubes from the Dutch oven and set aside.

3. Add the onion, jalapeños, chipotles, and garlic to the pot and cook until fragrant. Add the chorizo to the pot and mix with the vegetables. Cook until the chorizo is fully cooked, about 6–8 minutes.

4. Add the rest of the spice mixture, the diced tomatoes, the bay leaves, and the puréed black beans to the pot. Mix until all ingredients are well dispersed, then add the short rib cubes (including whatever juices have accumulated beneath them) and the beef stock to the pot. Stir the mixture and bring to a boil. One boiling, cover the pot and reduce the temperature to low. Let the chili simmer for 2 hours.

5. After 2 hours, remove the lid and stir the mixture. If the mixture is still soupy, sprinkle a small amount of cornmeal into the pot and stir. Continue to cook the chili for about 15 minutes with the lid off, stirring every few minutes.

6. Serve the chili topped with diced red onions, sour cream, cheese, and diced green onions.

Good-to-Know Info

The 4th Thursday in February is National Chili Day.

LEONARD HUDSON,
Mesa, Arizona

Leo Hudson runs a test kitchen and private chef business in Mesa, Arizona. He has had a passion to cook for years and recently left his 9 to 5 to pursue it professionally. He has written recipes for Country Bob's spices and sauces and has been a private chef for high profile clients, but he mostly enjoys cooking for friends and family! Instagram: @leohudsoncooks and @chefleotonight

Chili Without Borders

I created this recipe to balance out the many vegan chilis that inevitably show up at a San Diego neighborhood potluck. Influenced by day trips to Mexico, my recipe begins with bacon, uses hearty beef chuck rather than ground meat, and is finished with fresh jalapeño slices. This meaty chili recipe won Best of the Best at an annual church chili competition in 2008.

COOK TIME
4 hrs. 30 mins.
Makes 7+ servings

INGREDIENTS

- 3 tablespoons bacon, diced
- 2 pounds beef chuck
- 3 large onions, finely diced
- 5 cloves garlic, roughly minced
- ¼ cup chili powder
- 1 teaspoon ground coriander
- ¼ teaspoon dried oregano
- 1 teaspoon black pepper
- 14 ounces stewed tomatoes
- 3 cups beef broth or water
- 1 teaspoon Tabasco® sauce
- 4 tablespoons Worcestershire sauce
- One 16-ounce can pinto beans
- 2 jalapeños, sliced
- Garnishes: sour cream, chips, avocado

Directions

1. Brown the bacon and then the meat.
2. Add all the browned meat to a pot or slow cooker. Add in the rest of the ingredients, except for the jalapeños, in order, stirring each time you add something new.
3. Simmer for at least 4 hours.
4. Remove from the heat. Add the jalapeños. Taste and adjust the seasoning as desired.
5. Serve with sour cream, chips, avocado, and whatever else you like on your chili. Or put this on top of fry bread or a baked potato.

Chili Recipe Awards

- "Best" Award at the Annual Harvest Festival Chili Cook-Off 2008 (San Diego, CA)
- Local Church Chili Competition 2008 (San Diego, CA)

KARI RICH,
Vacaville, California

Chef Kari Rich began her career following in her brother's footsteps in professional kitchens. After culinary school, Chef Rich honed her skills in fine dining premier restaurants in San Diego, California. She continued in her career as a professional chef running kitchens for more than 20 years. After selling her successful food truck venture, Food Farm, Chef Kari has continued working as a restaurant consultant as well as food writing and research. Instagram: @Chef_K_Rich_

Coach's Not-So-Secret Chili

This is a fast, basic chili that I discovered during a local chili contest I was competing in. I was prepping my ingredients—chopped tomatoes, onions, and peppers—and I put them in a bowl for adding to the pot later while I was preparing the beef. I tasted the mixture and realized it was a pretty good salsa! Now, whenever someone asks me for a chili recipe, this is what I give them.

COOK TIME
30 mins.

Makes 4 servings

INGREDIENTS

- 1 pound 80% lean ground chuck
- One 16-ounce jar mild, medium, or hot salsa (use your favorite salsa)
- 2 tablespoons chili powder
- Salt, to taste

Directions

1. In a medium pan, brown the ground chuck and break it apart into crumbles. Drain off the fat if needed.
2. Add the salsa and chili powder. Stir and simmer for 30 minutes. Add salt as needed.
3. Eat it straight or use it as a topping on whatever you like!

TJ HEISER,
Madison, Wisconsin

From Madison, Wisconsin, TJ is 65 years old and has been cooking since she told her mother that she didn't like her chili. Her mom said, "Make your own!" So she did. Later, TJ entered a local contest and won! She was hooked and has been competing ever since. TJ enjoys experimenting with techniques and ingredients to gain valuable contest time management, meaning she has pared her recipe to the bare essentials. Whenever the inevitable question, "What's your recipe?" pops up, this is the recipe TJ gives.

COOK TIME
2 hrs.
Makes 5 servings

Wacipi-Inspired Chili

Years ago, a friend invited me to attend a local powwow or *Wacipi* (meaning "They Dance" in the language of the Dakota Sioux). It was a unique experience. I simply stood back and watched. One of my best memories of that event, though, was the chili that was served from large roasters into paper bowls with warm fry bread for dipping. It was a strong-flavored, ground beef chili with beans, and it was loaded with green bell peppers. Years have passed, and I am still struck by how wonderful that chili was.

INGREDIENTS

- One 15-ounce can chili beans
- One 15-ounce can crushed tomatoes
- One 8-ounce can tomato sauce
- Two 15-ounce cans chicken broth
- 2½ tablespoons dark chili powder
- 2½ tablespoons New Mexico chile powder
- 1 tablespoon ground cumin
- 2 teaspoons onion powder
- 2 teaspoons garlic powder, plus additional to taste
- ½ teaspoon sea salt, plus additional to taste
- 3 pounds ground round
- 1 medium yellow onion, chopped
- 2 green bell peppers, chopped
- ½ teaspoon dark brown pure cane sugar
- ½ teaspoon lime juice

Directions

1. Separate the beans from their liquid and set the beans aside for now. Combine the bean liquid, tomatoes, tomato sauce, broth, chili powders, cumin, onion powder, garlic powder, and salt. Mix well to remove any lumps.
2. Bring this mixture to a boil over medium heat. Then reduce the heat, cover, and simmer for 30 minutes, stirring occasionally.
3. Brown the beef and onion in a skillet. Drain, then add to the pot. Add the bell peppers. Simmer the mixture for 1 hour 30 minutes.
4. Add the brown sugar, lime, and beans. Return the pot to a boil, then remove it from the heat.
5. Add additional garlic powder and salt to taste 15 minutes prior to serving.

TIMOTHY STORLY,
Mitchell, South Dakota

In his hometown of Mitchell, South Dakota, Tim Storly is known for his delicious chili and as a judge at local cook-offs. He has competed at the International Chili Society World's Championships in 2008 and 2009 before leaving the circuit to pursue other family interests. His wife and children look forward to his upcoming 20-year retirement from active military service so the family can travel and spend more time together.

Chili Recipe Awards

- **Former ICS member with years of small awards**

Chili Verde

Chili verde includes marinated pork, green chiles, and tomatillos at its core. Sometimes white potatoes are used to thicken up this tasty green chili.

The Recipes

Stephanie's Chili Verde

BBQ Pulled Pork Chili

Darth Verde

Pork Green Chili—
Colorado Style

Off-the-Charts Good Chili Verde

COOK TIME

5 hrs.

Makes 6 servings

Ever since my husband and I were newlyweds, we have regularly dined at a favorite Mexican restaurant in San Diego called Marieta's. Later, our kids joined us in what became a family tradition; it's our special occasion spot. My husband always had the chili verde. When I published a cookbook and eventually started a food blog, I decided to recreate his favorite dish—especially since we made the move to Montana. This spicy chili is "off-the-charts good," at least according to him!

INGREDIENTS

- 1½ pounds tomatillos
- 3 poblanos
- 2 serranos
- 1 large yellow onion, coarsely chopped
- 1 head garlic, top sliced
- 3 tablespoons olive oil, divided
- 1 tablespoon salt
- 2 teaspoons black pepper
- 3 pounds pork, cubed
- ¼ cup cilantro, chopped
- 1 teaspoon cumin seeds or powder
- 1 tablespoon dried oregano
- 2 cups chicken broth

Directions

1. Peel the tomatillos and add them to a foil-lined sheet. Add the poblanos, serranos, onion, and garlic. Drizzle with 1 tablespoon of oil. Broil until charred.

2. Salt and pepper the cubed pork. Heat the remaining oil in a cast-iron skillet. Sear the meat in batches. Add the meat and juices to a slow cooker.

3. Peel the charred peppers and garlic. Add them to a blender with the other pan ingredients. Add the cilantro, cumin, oregano, and broth. Pulse.

4. Pour the mixture over the meat in the slow cooker. Cover and cook for 4–6 hours.

HILDA STERNER,
Trego, Montana

Hilda Sterner is a cookbook author and a food blogger at www.HildasKitchenBlog.com. She is involved in church ministry, is a Navy Veteran, and is a retired Deputy Sheriff. In 2008, Hilda published *Mom's Authentic Assyrian Recipes Cookbook*. Hilda is married to her best friend, Scott, and has two adult children, Nena and Scott.
Website: www.hildaskitchenblog.com
Facebook:
@HildasKitchenBlog
Instagram:
@hildaskitchenblog
TikTok:
@hildaskitchenblog

COOK TIME
4 hrs. 30 mins.
Makes 7 servings

Pork Green Chili—Colorado Style

In 2015, after judging many chili cook-offs and sampling many Colorado award-winning restaurant chili verdes, I created this recipe to combine the best of both worlds. International Chili Society cook-off winners use lots of meat, which is typically too expensive for restaurants. Restaurants often thicken their chili so it can double as either a sauce or a soup. So this chile verde is thick with plenty of pork and flavor—great in a bowl by itself or as a sauce for smothering a burrito or omelets.

INGREDIENTS

- 2 pounds pork roast
- Salt and pepper, to taste
- 4 tablespoons olive oil, divided
- 8 cups chicken broth (or 4 cans)
- 2 cups water
- 2 cups onion, chopped
- 8 cloves garlic, pressed
- ½ pound tomatillos (about 8 medium), chopped
- 1–2 serranos, minced
- 2 cups mild green chiles, diced
- One 14.5-ounce can diced tomatoes, with juice
- 1 cup hot green chiles, diced
- 1½ tablespoons ground cumin
- ½ teaspoon oregano
- ½ teaspoon cayenne pepper
- 1 cup flour

Directions

1. Cut the roast in half, salt and pepper it, and sear it in 2 tablespoons of oil on medium-high heat.
2. Put the roast in a slow cooker with the broth and water. Cook on high for 1 hour and then on low for 2–3 hours.
3. Sauté the onion, garlic, tomatillo, and serrano in 2 tablespoons of oil. Purée 1 cup of mild green chiles with ½ cup of liquid and set aside.
4. Remove the pork and 3 cups of the broth; set aside to cool for 15 minutes.
5. Add the onion mixture, tomatoes, all spices, and green chiles (including the puréed chiles).
6. Slowly add the broth to the flour, stirring. Blend this into the slow cooker.
7. Shred the pork with a fork and add to the slow cooker. Cook on low for 1 hour.

ANITA EDGE,
Conifer, Colorado

In 2006, Anita Edge combined her decade of web-design experience and her fascination for chiles and Southwestern cooking to create DenverGreenChili.com. The site has become a how-to resource for selecting, roasting, peeling, freezing, cooking, and even decorating with chiles. Anita has been featured in the *Denver Post*, the *Rocky Mountain News*, AAA's *EnCompass* magazine, and *Westword*. As a speaker at BlogHer and BlogHer Food, she has shared her insights on everything from must-have recipes to remedies for capsaicin overdose.
Website: www.Denver GreenChili.com
Facebook, Instagram: @DenverGreenChili
Twitter: @AnitaEdge
Pinterest: @denverchili

Chili Recipe Awards

- **537 shares on Yummly**

2Chefs Tomatillo Chicken Chili

This chili is like if pozole and chili verde made a hipster baby. It's light but hearty, it's spicy but tangy, and it's limey and refreshing but has a rich depth from warm spices. In the winter, we love spicy pozole, but with Austin's crazy-hot, humid summers, we needed something lighter. We created this recipe that retains the best of pozole, the rich broth, chewy hominy, and fresh herbs, but instead of needing a nap after you eat, you can don a swimsuit and float the river without feeling weighed down.

COOK TIME

1 hr. 45 mins.

Makes 4 servings

WATCH HOW TO MAKE THIS RECIPE

INGREDIENTS

- 2 tablespoons olive oil
- 1 onion, finely diced
- 2 green bell peppers, medium diced
- 2 cloves garlic, minced
- 2 teaspoons salt
- ½ teaspoon dried oregano
- 2 teaspoons cumin
- ⅛ teaspoon ground clove
- ¼ teaspoon cinnamon
- 4 cups chicken stock
- 1 pound tomatillos, oven roasted and puréed

- 1 poblano, broiled until charred, then peeled, seeded, and finely diced
- One 25-ounce can hominy, drained
- 4 bay leaves
- 1 lime, zested and one-half juiced
- 1 pound chicken breast, cooked and shredded
- 1 tablespoon fresh cilantro
- 1 tablespoon fresh oregano
- Garnish: Mexican crema or sour cream

Directions

1. Place a pot over medium-high heat. Add the olive oil and onion and sauté for 3 minutes.
2. Add the bell pepper, garlic, salt, dried oregano, cumin, clove, and cinnamon and sauté for an additional 3 minutes.
3. Add the chicken stock, tomatillo purée, roasted poblano, hominy, bay leaves, lime zest, and juice from half of the lime. Bring the chili back to a boil and then lower to a simmer. Let simmer for 40 minutes.
4. Add in the shredded chicken, cilantro, and fresh oregano and simmer for an additional 10 minutes.
5. When ready to serve, garnish with Mexican cream or sour cream.

CHEF MARA AND RYAN WOLLEN,
Austin, Texas

2Chefs are a husband-and-wife private chef team who prepare healthy weekly meals for their clients using quality seasonal ingredients. Additionally, they teach online cooking classes, for all levels of skill, from beginners seeking some cooking basics to seasoned home cooks who are looking for pro tips to up their game. Instagram, Facebook: 2chefs.food
YouTube: Cooking with 2chefs

Stephanie's Chili Verde

My wife is a lover of chili verde. She orders it whenever she can when we go out to eat. She is truly addicted to the porky goodness simmered in its mildly spicy green sauce. When we first started dating, I wanted to impress her by preparing one of her favorite dishes. I researched recipes and techniques and was not surprised to find all the different variations—like most dishes, recipes vary from region to region and grandmother to grandmother. I finally came up with this version. I love the bright flavors of the tomatillos as well as the richness created by roasting the chiles and tomatillos first before adding them to the pot. Feel free to increase the amount of jalapeño if you are looking for more heat.

COOK TIME

4 hrs.

Makes 8 servings

INGREDIENTS

- 4 pounds pork butt or shoulder, trimmed of fat and cut into 2-inch cubes
- Kosher salt
- Freshly ground black pepper
- Flour (for dredging)
- 2 tablespoons canola oil
- 1½ pounds tomatillos
- 2 jalapeños, halved and seeds removed
- 2 pasilla chiles, cored and halved
- 2 green bell peppers, cored and cut into halves
- 3 cloves garlic, left whole with skin on
- 2 teaspoons cumin seeds
- 2 tablespoons coriander seeds
- 2 yellow onions, diced
- 1 tablespoon dried Mexican oregano
- ½ cup cilantro leaves, cleaned and chopped, plus extra for garnish
- 3 cups chicken stock
- Garnish: sour cream
- Serve with: small flour tortillas

Directions

1. Preheat the oven to 375 degrees Fahrenheit. Season the pork generously with salt and pepper. Pour some flour into a medium-sized bowl to dredge the pork. Lightly flour the pork and place on a plate or tray.

2. Heat some of the oil in a heavy-bottomed pot over medium-high heat. Brown the pork in batches, paying attention to not crowd the pot. Brown until the pork has a nice crust on all sides. When you place the pork in the pot, leave it alone—don't stir it around. The pork may initially stick, but once the crust forms, the meat will release, letting you know it is time to turn it.

3. Move the browned pork onto another clean plate or tray and set aside. Remove the pot from the heat.

4. Place the tomatillos, jalapeños, pasilla chiles, bell peppers, and garlic in a large bowl. Coat with oil and season with salt and pepper. Spread the ingredients on a baking sheet. Roast in the oven for 25–30 minutes. Roast until the vegetables and garlic are soft.

5. Gently toast the cumin and coriander seeds in a small pan over medium heat. Once the oils start to release from the seeds and you can start to smell them, remove the pan from the heat so the seeds don't burn.

6. Allow the toasted seeds to cool, then transfer them to a spice grinder. Grind until the seeds are a powder.

7. Return the heavy-bottomed pot to the heat. Add the diced onions and sweat over medium heat for 5 minutes.

8. Add the ground spices and sauté for 1 minute.

9. Working in batches, transfer the roasted vegetables and garlic (removed from their skins) to a blender and blend until smooth.

10. Once the onions are softened, add the blended mixture to the pot. Add the oregano and cilantro. Return the meat and any juices that are on the plate to the pot. Cover with the chicken stock and stir to incorporate. Bring the mixture to a boil, then reduce and simmer for 2–3 hours uncovered or until the pork is fork tender.

11. Adjust the seasoning with salt and pepper.

12. Serve with flour tortillas and top with sour cream and cilantro.

JEFF SOLBERG,
Sacramento, California

Jeff Solberg is a self-taught social media chef. His love for cooking started at 5 years old when he would help his dad in the kitchen. That passion continued to flourish as he studied and worked to make restaurant-quality dishes in his own home. Jeff's only goal is to make meals for friends, loved ones, his beautiful wife, and occasional private dinner guests that evoke past food memories, and bring joy to them during their meal. Instagram, Facebook: @sactattooedfooddude

Mezcal Jalapeño and Tortilla Strips Chili Verde

Growing up, many of us have enjoyed a classic red chili. As the cofounder of *Athleisure Mag*, I also enjoy incorporating a number of ingredients that lean towards wellness with chili verde, turkey, sausage, and the use of mezcal with garnishes that include limes and avocado. It's still a hearty dish that can be enjoyed when the temperatures drop, for tailgating, etc. The mezcal creates a great smoky flavor that plays well with the spices and chiles that are used in this dish.

COOK TIME
4 hrs.

Makes 7+ servings

INGREDIENTS

- ¼ cup olive or avocado oil
- 2 pounds ground turkey
- 2 pounds sausage
- 1 tablespoon salt, divided
- 2 large onions, chopped
- 1 tablespoon ground cumin
- 1 tablespoon ground coriander
- 1 tablespoon oregano
- 4 cloves garlic, minced
- 2 serranos, chopped
- 2 Anaheim chiles, chopped
- 1–2 jalapeños, seeded and diced
- 1 pound tomatillos, peeled, cleaned, and chopped
- 2 bay leaves
- 1 large bunch cilantro, chopped
- 3 tablespoons masa (yellow/corn flour)
- 4 cups water or chicken stock
- 1⅔ cups mezcal
- Salt and pepper, to taste
- Garnishes: lime wedges, avocados, tortilla strips, Mexican lime crema (see recipe at right)

Directions

1. Heat the oil in a large pot over medium-high heat. Add the sausage, turkey, and 2 teaspoons of salt. Brown the sausage and turkey on all sides, stirring regularly. Remove the sausage and the turkey from the pot and pour out all the rendered fat, saving about 1 tablespoon.
2. Add the onions, remaining salt, cumin, coriander, and oregano to the pot. Sauté for 3–5 minutes.
3. Add the garlic and all of the chiles. Sauté for another 3–5 minutes.
4. Add the tomatillos, bay leaves, and cilantro. Toss the pork and turkey with the masa and add back into the pot. Stir well.
5. Add the water or chicken stock and the mezcal. Bring to a boil, then reduce the heat to low. Cover and simmer for 3 hours, stirring occasionally.
6. Add salt and pepper to taste.

KIMMIE SMITH,
New York City, New York

Kimmie is Co-Founder/Creative + Style Director of Athleisure Media, publisher of *Athleisure Mag*, and Host/Co-Producer of Athleisure Studio which includes the culinary podcast, Athleisure Kitchen. Kimmie has also been a food judge for Cochon555. She is a celebrity fashion stylist and TV personality and a contributor to *Vogue Italia*. Kimmie is an avid music, style, food, and sports fan.
Twitter: @ShesKimmie @AthleisureMag
Instagram: @Shes.Kimmie @AthleisureMag
Facebook: @ sheskimmie @ athleisuremag

Mexican Lime Crema

INGREDIENTS

For Mexican Crema:

- 1 cup heavy whipping cream
- 1 tablespoon plain yogurt
- 2 teaspoons lime juice
- ⅛ teaspoon kosher salt

For Mexican Lime Crema:

- 1¼ cup Mexican crema
- ¼ cup loosely packed cilantro
- 2 tablespoons lime juice, plus the zest of half of 1 lime (about ½ teaspoon)
- ¼ teaspoon garlic powder
- ¼ teaspoon sugar
- ¼ teaspoon kosher salt

Directions

For Mexican Crema:

1. In a sealable container, stir together the cream and the yogurt. Cover and let sit at room temperature for 36–48 hours, until it becomes very thick. (The mixture won't spoil on the counter, since the acid in the mix prevents bacteria associated with dairy products.)
2. Mix in the lime juice and salt. Taste and adjust the lime as necessary.
3. Mexican crema keeps in the refrigerator for up to 2 weeks; it will continue to thicken while refrigerated.

For Mexican Lime Crema:

1. By hand method: Finely mince the cilantro. Mix it together with the remaining ingredients.
2. Food processor method: Place all the ingredients in a food processor and whiz for a few seconds until combined.
3. Blender method: In a regular countertop blender or using an immersion blender, blend all ingredients, starting with three-quarters of the Mexican Crema, until combined. Stir in the remaining ½ cup of the crema (this prevents it from becoming too runny).
4. This crema will store up to 1 week in the refrigerator.

Darth Verde

When someone says "chili," most people think of traditional Texas chili (or Texas red chili). But after eating lots of different chilis at cook-offs, chili verde became a personal favorite of mine. However, cutting all the meat and dicing all the peppers is very labor intensive! So I created this quick-fix version based on many World Championship recipes. It gives the same great flavor in a lot less time!

COOK TIME

3 hrs. 30 mins.

Makes 6–8 servings

INGREDIENTS

- 2 tablespoons bacon grease or oil
- 2½ pounds pork tenderloin, cut into 1-inch cubes
- 4 jalapeños
- 1–4 serranos (seeded depending on your heat preference)
- 2 Anaheim chiles
- One 26-ounce can whole green chiles, cut into ½-inch squares, divided; save half to add at end
- 1 cup onion, diced
- 4 cloves garlic, crushed
- One 14-ounce can mild green enchilada sauce

- One 14-ounce can chicken broth
- One 7-ounce jar salsa verde (I use Herdez®)
- 2½ tablespoons cumin
- 1 tablespoon green chili powder (if you can find it; I order it online, but it's fine without it!)
- 1 teaspoon white vinegar
- 1 teaspoon celery salt
- Juice from 1 lime
- 2 teaspoons corn starch (optional for thickening)
- Salt, to taste (optional)
- Green Tabasco® sauce (optional for extra heat)

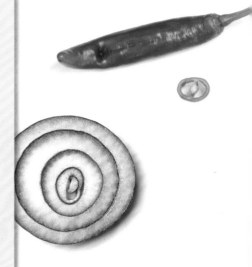

Directions

1. In a pot, heat the bacon grease, then brown the pork.
2. Cut all the whole chiles (jalapeños, serranos, and Anaheim chiles) in half. Using a spoon, scrape out and discard the seeds, then coarsely cut the chiles into smaller chunks.
3. You may need to do the following step in two batches, because everything may not all fit into a food processor. Into a food processor, add the chopped chiles, half of the can of whole green chiles, the diced onion, the garlic, and the green enchilada sauce. Pulse until the chiles and onion are finely diced. Pour the mixture into the pot with the browned pork.
4. Add the remaining ingredients to the pot: the chicken broth, salsa verde, cumin, green chili powder, vinegar, celery salt, and lime juice.
5. Bring to a boil, stirring often, then reduce the heat to low and simmer for 3 hours, stirring every 15 minutes to prevent sticking/burning. Add the rest of the chiles in the last 15 minutes of cooking.
6. Add a little cornstarch if the chili needs thickening. Add salt and/or green Tabasco® sauce as needed.

GREG HANCOCK,
Redondo Beach, California

From age seven, Greg grew up going to chili cook-offs with his mother Carol Hancock. She competed in chili cook-offs for years and always had him take a final taste before she submitted her chili to be judged. Greg's mom won the ICS World Championship in 1985 and went on to become the owner of the International Chili Society for 17 years. Let's just say, Greg's eaten a lot of chili, and he's judged a lot of World Championships!

Chili Recipe Awards

- This chili recipe is based on MANY World Championship Chili Verde recipes, and it has won a lot of local cook-offs . . . oftentimes beating out the traditional Texas red chili!

Northeast Connection Chili

From what I gathered from my first World Championship Chili Cook-Off, it's very rare to get there on your first try, but that is what we did! This recipe is very simple, but it is well rounded and extremely delicious. I took my years of culinary training and developed a recipe that everyone would enjoy. Living in New England, very few people have heard of chili verde, and I was happy to introduce something special. This chili is easy to prepare the night before and leave in the slow cooker all day if desired.

COOK TIME

3 hrs.

Makes 7+ servings

INGREDIENTS

- 1 pork butt, fat trimmed off and cut into ¼-inch chunks
- 2 Spanish onions, finely diced
- 1 bulb of garlic, peeled and minced
- 2 Anaheim chiles, seeded, charred, and peeled
- 2 poblanos, seeded, charred, and peeled
- 1½ pounds tomatillos, peeled and rinsed
- 1 bunch cilantro, rinsed and big stems chopped off
- 1 quart chicken stock
- 2 tablespoons cumin
- 1 tablespoon onion powder
- 1 tablespoon garlic powder
- Hatch chile powder, to taste
- Salt and pepper, to taste

Directions

1. In a pot, sear the pork butt chunks (a few at a time). Set aside when cooked.

2. Add the onions and garlic and sauté until soft.

3. Purée the roasted chiles, tomatillos, cilantro, and a little bit of the chicken stock. Add everything back into the pot along with the rest of the chicken stock. Add all the seasonings.

4. Bring to a boil, then drop down to a simmer. Simmer until the meat is nice and tender and the chili has thickened up slightly. Adjust the salt to your liking. This chili is great over rice!

Chili Recipe Awards

- **2019 ICS Meadowlands winner**

DANIEL FARM,
Shelton, Connecticut

After placing in many homestyle chili contests all over the Northeast U.S., Daniel was convinced by his brother Greg to compete in the International Chili Society Cook-Off. They researched and worked on their chili verde recipe and won their first-ever ICS cook-off. They were even invited to compete in the 2021 World Championships! It was extra special because the brothers were able to compete together. Instagram: @ comeonthefarm7812

COOK TIME
7+ hrs.

Makes 7+ servings

BBQ Pulled Pork Chili

In the Midwest, we love any version of pulled pork. When cooler weather hits, we also love chili! So, naturally, putting the two together seemed like a good fit. This chili is sweet and full of barbecue flavor.

CHILI VERDE

INGREDIENTS

- 2 pounds pork shoulder roast
- ¼ cup barbecue seasoning (I use John Henry's Pecan Rub®)
- 1 cup water
- 1 small onion, finely diced
- 2 strips bacon, chopped
- 32 ounces tomato juice
- 1 cup barbecue sauce
- One 15-ounce can chili beans (I use Mrs. Grimes® Original)
- One 15-ounce can petite diced tomatoes
- 1 tablespoon chili powder
- 1 tablespoon cumin
- ½ tablespoon garlic salt
- 1 pinch crushed red pepper flakes

Directions

1. Place the roast in a slow cooker and sprinkle on the barbecue seasoning. Add 1 cup of water.

2. Set the slow cooker to low and cook for 6–8 hours. Once the pork is done, remove and discard any fat. Shred the pork with tongs. Drain off and discard the extra juice from the roast.

3. In a skillet over medium heat, cook the diced onions and bacon until the onions are tender and the bacon is slightly crisp.

4. Set the slow cooker to warm. Add all remaining ingredients into the slow cooker with the pork. Mix everything together and let the chili heat for 1 hour.

ALLY BILLHORN,
Wilton, Iowa

A popular Midwest food blogger since 2009, Ally Billhorn highlights simple, family-friendly meals—ones that are homemade and easy, even for the non-cook! Ally has been featured in multiple Midwest newspapers, including *The Des Moines Register* and *dsm* magazine, as well various podcasts and local television shows. Her recipes have been featured by many national food brands and companies, including Blue Bunny®, Cuisinart®, ALDI®, Hy-Vee®, Iowa Beef Industry Council®, Cookies BBQ & Seasonings®, and more.
Facebook, Instagram, Twitter: @sweetsavoryeats
Pinterest: @allybillhorn

White Chicken Chili

Shredded chicken and white beans (such as cannellini) are the hallmarks of white chicken chili. This dish can be a great option for those who can't or don't eat beef or tomatoes. Peppers and spice can be added to give your dish some heat.

The Recipes

Great Northern Bean
White Chicken Chili

Slow Cooker White
Chicken Chili

Yummy Chicken Chili

Slow Cooker Cheesy
Chicken Chili

Slow Cooker White Chicken Chili

COOK TIME
2 hrs.

Makes 7 servings

This is a mouthwatering, mild Southwest chili that practically makes itself. This true toss-and-go recipe requires minimal prep and no precooking. In the morning, it will take you 5 minutes to add ingredients to the cooker, press one button, and then leave to go crush the busy day, knowing that a comforting chili dinner awaits you at the end of it. The texture is perfectly creamy, and each serving can be customized with endless toppings. It's a big winner in our home!

INGREDIENTS

- 1 pound boneless skinless chicken thighs
- Three 15-ounce cans white beans, rinsed and drained; reserve 1 cup for purée
- 2 cups chicken broth
- Two 4-ounce cans diced green chiles; do not drain
- Half of 1 large onion, diced
- 1 cup corn
- 3 cloves garlic, minced
- 1 tablespoon dried oregano
- 1 teaspoon ground cumin
- ¼ teaspoon chili powder
- ½ teaspoon kosher salt
- ¼ teaspoon black pepper
- 4 ounces cream cheese

Directions

1. Place the chicken thighs in the slow cooker. Add the white beans (reserving 1 cup), chicken broth, green chiles (with juice), onion, corn, garlic, oregano, cumin, chili powder, salt, and pepper.
2. Cover and set the cooker on high 2–4 hours or low 6–8 hours.
3. Transfer the cooked chicken thighs to a plate, shred them, and stir them back into the chili.
4. Mash the reserved beans into a paste and stir it into the chili to thicken.
5. Add the cream cheese, cover the pot, and allow to cook for 5 minutes to soften.
6. Serve warm.

TRACI ANTONOVICH,
Sonoma County, California

Traci owns and operates www.thekitchen girl.com, featuring hundreds of easy, delicious recipes for every occasion. As The Kitchen Girl, she prides herself in testing and developing every recipe to be approachable and successful for any cooking level. Her followers love her content for the use of wholesome, everyday ingredients and straightforward instructions. Traci invites you to find yourself among her countless readers saying, "This was so easy, and everyone loved it!" Facebook, Instagram, Pinterest: @thekitchengirl

COOK TIME

30 mins.

Makes 7+ servings

Patterson Family Hopeful Chili

Our white chicken chili has won the Annual Patterson Family Chili Cook-Off for 3 years running. It's a crowd-pleaser, and we love making it!

INGREDIENTS

- 2 pounds rotisserie chicken
- 1 large onion, chopped
- 2–3 cloves garlic, chopped or minced
- 8 tablespoons unsalted butter, divided
- ¼ cup all-purpose flour
- 2½ cups chicken broth
- 1 cup fat-free half-and-half
- 1 package white chicken chili seasoning (I use McCormick®)

- One 16-ounce can northern beans, mostly drained
- 2 cups frozen corn
- Two 4-ounce cans chopped mild green chiles
- 8 ounces shredded Monterey Jack cheese
- 1 cup light sour cream
- Salt and pepper, to taste

Directions

1. Shred the chicken.
2. Cook the onion and garlic with 2 tablespoons of butter until softened.
3. In a heavy pot, melt the remaining 6 tablespoons of butter over low heat. Whisk in the flour to make a roux. Cook the roux, stirring constantly for three minutes.
4. Stir in the cooked onion and garlic. Gradually add the broth and half-and-half, whisking the whole time.
5. Bring the mixture to boil, then simmer, stirring occasionally, for 5 minutes.
6. Stir in the white chicken chili seasoning, beans, corn, chiles, and chicken. Cook on low to medium heat for 20 minutes.
7. Add salt and pepper to taste. Add the sour cream and cheese when ready to serve.

JEN AND JOE PATTERSON,
Huntley, Illinois

The Patterson Family—Joe, Jen, Abby, Lorelai, and Cameron—live in the northwestern suburbs of Chicago. They have been making their chili since 2011 when they won 1st place in their family chili cook-off. The Pattersons would love for their chili to bring "hope" to all those who aspire to win their chili cook-offs with a non-traditional chili. Facebook: @jennifer.c.patterson.7 Instagram: @pea_nut79

Good-to-Know Info

Cooking with ground chicken runs the risk of turning rubbery, so try using bone-in chicken breasts. Brown it, poach it, then shred it!

Chili Recipe Awards

- **Annual Patterson Family Chili Cook-off winner: 2011, 2012, 2015**

Electric Pressure Cooker White Chicken Chili

This chili recipe was created due to my love for pressure cooking. I love how hands-off these kinds of recipes are—perfect for busy fall nights during back-to-school and sports season for my kids—and how the flavors meld together deliciously. This chili has just the right amount of kick, getting its spice from diced green chiles as opposed to chili powder, but it isn't so spicy that kids can't handle it. It's now a family favorite!

COOK TIME

1 hr.

Makes 6 servings

WATCH HOW TO MAKE THIS RECIPE

INGREDIENTS

- 2 teaspoons vegetable oil
- 1 medium onion, finely chopped
- 1½ cups chicken broth
- Two 15-ounce cans great northern beans, drained and rinsed
- One 15-ounce can corn, drained
- Two 4-ounce cans diced green chiles (with their juices)
- 1 teaspoon cumin
- 1 teaspoon salt
- ½ teaspoon ground black pepper
- ½ teaspoon garlic powder
- 1 pound boneless skinless chicken breasts, cut into thirds
- 2 tablespoons water
- 2 tablespoons cornstarch
- ½ cup sour cream
- Shredded Monterey Jack cheese, to taste

Directions

1. Select "sauté" on an electric pressure cooker (I use an Instant Pot®). Heat the oil in the cooker.

2. Add the onion and sauté for 3–4 minutes. Press "cancel."

3. Pour in the chicken broth and scrape the bottom of the pot with a spoon. Stir in the beans, corn, green chiles, cumin, salt, pepper, and garlic powder, then add the chicken.

4. Close the lid and cook on "high pressure" for 18 minutes. Natural release for 10 minutes, then quick release.

5. Whisk together the water and cornstarch. Open the lid, remove the chicken, and shred it with a fork.

6. Select "sauté." Stir in the sour cream, then the cornstarch slurry. Return the chicken to the pot and simmer for 3 minutes or until the sauce thickens. Press "cancel."

7. Serve topped with cheese.

RAMONA CRUZ-PETERS,
Round Rock, Texas

Ramona Cruz-Peters is a cookbook author and the founder and editor in chief of Fab Everyday®, a lifestyle website and social media presence that reaches over 10 million people per month. Ramona currently lives in Texas with her husband, two kids, and three dogs. Through Fab Everyday, Ramona inspires people to incorporate more fabulousness in their everyday life through quick recipes, easy home décor and entertaining ideas, and life hacks. Ramona's recipes and projects have been featured in *Allrecipes® Magazine*, *Good Housekeeping*, *Country Living*, BuzzFeed, *Reader's Digest*, and more.
Website: FabEveryday.com
Facebook, Instagram, Pinterest, Twitter, YouTube, TikTok: @fabeveryday

Kickin' Chickin' Chili

To develop this chili, I started with a basic white chicken chili recipe from my mother and added my own twist by including some new ingredients to make it special. I have frequently been told this is the best chicken chili recipe, and people ask for the recipe all the time. I have entered a few local fire department chili contests and have placed first for judges' choice and second for people's choice. I'm happy to share this chili with you now!

COOK TIME

1 hr.

Makes 7+ servings

INGREDIENTS

- 6 cups chicken, cooked and chunked
- 4 cans white navy beans, rinsed and drained
- One 4.3-ounce can mild green chiles
- 3 cans chicken broth, plus extra if needed
- 2 tablespoons chicken base
- 1½ cups heavy cream
- 2 packets white chicken chili seasoning (I use McCormick®)
- 4 slices white American cheese (I use Bongards®)
- 4 slices white hot pepper cheese (I use Bongards®)
- 1 cup sour cream dip (I use Top the Tator®)
- 2 onions, chopped
- 2 cloves garlic, minced
- 4 tablespoons butter
- 3 tablespoons sugar
- ⅓ cup flour

Directions

1. Put all the ingredients in a slow cooker except for the onions, garlic, butter, sugar, and flour.

2. Caramelize the onions and the minced garlic in the butter. Once they become transparent, add the sugar and cook for about 10 more minutes.

3. Add the flour to the mixture to make a roux and cook for about 3 minutes, stirring constantly so the mixture doesn't burn.

4. Add the mixture to the slow cooker. Cook on low heat for about 3 hours. The chili will thicken as it cooks. If it gets too thick, add a little more chicken broth and simmer for about 15 minutes with the lid off.

Good-to-Know Info

If using poultry like turkey or chicken, be careful that it doesn't dry out. Tip: add in a few strips of bacon to keep everything nice and juicy.

DAWN HANSEN,
Isanti, Minnesota

Dawn grew up in a small town in WI and moved to the Twin Cities when she got married. She has been married for almost 39 years and has 2 children and 4 grandchildren, and she loves spending time with them. Dawn enjoys cooking, sewing, crocheting, boating, and spending time at her cabin in Wisconsin. Facebook: Dawn Hansen

Chili Recipe Awards

- **First place Judges' Choice at North Sand Lake Chili Cook-Off**
- **Second place People's Choice at North Sand Lake Chili Cook-Off**

2Chefs White Chicken Chili

COOK TIME

1 hr. 30 mins.

Makes 4 servings

While working as cooks in Los Angeles restaurants, we had the opportunity to work alongside chefs from Mexico and Central America. They taught us how to get deep, smoky flavors from peppers by broiling them under high heat or over a flame. This technique softens the pepper, mellows out the spiciness, and leaves a well-rounded flavor. This chili is all about that smoky roasted pasilla chile. The depth of flavor makes you feel like you're sitting around a cooking campfire in the Old West days.

INGREDIENTS

- 1 pasilla chile
- 2 tablespoons olive oil
- 1 pound boneless skinless chicken thighs, medium diced
- 1 white onion, finely diced
- 2 cloves garlic, minced
- 1 green bell pepper, medium diced
- 3 cups chicken stock
- 3 bay leaves
- 1 lime, juice and zest
- Three 15.5-ounce cans cannellini beans
- 3 teaspoons salt
- 2 teaspoons cumin
- ½ teaspoon black pepper
- 2 tablespoons fresh oregano, chopped
- 2 tablespoons fresh cilantro, chopped

Directions

1. Under a broiler, completely char the pasilla chile. Remove the charred peel, stem, and seeds, then dice the chile finely.

2. Place a pot on medium-high heat. Add the oil and chicken and sauté for 5 minutes. Remove the chicken from the pot and set it aside.

3. Add the onion and sauté for 3 minutes.

4. Add the garlic, cumin, black pepper, and bell pepper and sauté for 3 minutes.

5. Add the chicken stock, bay leaves, pasilla chile, lime zest and juice, beans, and salt. Return the mixture to a boil, then lower it to a simmer and simmer for 45 minutes

6. Add back in the chicken. Add the fresh oregano and cilantro and simmer for 15 minutes.

CHEF MARA AND RYAN WOLLEN,
Austin, Texas

2Chefs are a husband-and-wife private chef team who prepare healthy weekly meals for their clients using quality seasonal ingredients. Additionally, they teach online cooking classes, for all levels of skill, from beginners seeking some cooking basics to seasoned home cooks who are looking for pro tips to up their game.
Instagram, Facebook: 2chefs.food
YouTube: Cooking with 2chefs

Great Northern Bean White Chicken Chili

This chili is full of white beans, chicken broth, and warm spices like cumin, oregano, and cayenne pepper. It is the perfect soup recipe when you are tired of normal chili.

COOK TIME
30 mins.

Makes 6 servings

INGREDIENTS

- 2 tablespoons olive oil
- 1 small onion, chopped
- 3 cloves garlic, chopped
- One 7-ounce can green chiles
- 2 teaspoons cumin
- 1 teaspoon oregano
- 1 teaspoon cayenne pepper

- Two 32-ounce boxes chicken broth, or you can use your own stock
- Two 14.5-ounce cans great northern beans
- 2 bone-in chicken breasts, boiled and shredded
- 2 cups shredded Monterey Jack cheese
- Salt and pepper, to taste
- Garnishes: sour cream, cilantro

Directions

1. Put the oil in the bottom of a soup pot. Add the onion and cook until tender.

2. Add the garlic and green chiles. Cook for 1 minute. Stir so you don't burn the garlic!

3. Add the cumin, oregano, and cayenne pepper. Cook for 1 minute. Stir so you don't burn the garlic.

4. Add the chicken broth and beans. Add the shredded chicken and 1 cup of the Monterey Jack cheese. Add salt and pepper to taste. Let simmer on the stove for about 30 minutes.

5. Enjoy garnished with fresh cilantro and sour cream, plus the remaining cup of the shredded cheese.

JENNIFER SIKORA,
Calvert City, Kentucky

Jennifer Sikora is a food and travel blogger living her best life in western Kentucky. She spends her days making delicious recipes to share with her friends and family. Her recipes are inspired by her Southern background, where she learned that a sprinkle of this and a pinch of that can make any dish sing. When Jennifer is not in the kitchen cooking, you can find her exploring and traveling with her family and her two Australian Shepherds.
Website: www.jenaround theworld.com
Instagram: @JenniferSikora
Facebook: @JenAroundTheWorld

COOK TIME
45 mins.

Makes 6 servings

Yummy Chicken Chili

This is a recipe that I learned right after I got married. It's simple to make and easy on the wallet—a match made in heaven.

INGREDIENTS

- 2 tablespoons oil
- Half of 1 medium onion, chopped
- 2 cloves garlic, minced
- 2 cups chicken broth
- 18 ounces tomatillos, drained and chopped
- One 16-ounce can diced tomatoes
- One 4-ounce can diced green chiles
- ½ teaspoon ground coriander seed
- ½ teaspoon pepper
- 1 pinch salt
- ¼ teaspoon cumin
- 2 cups chicken, cooked and shredded
- One 14.5-ounce can corn, drained
- One 15-ounce can white beans, drained

Directions

1. Heat the oil in a skillet. Add the onions and cook for 5 minutes, then add the garlic and cook for 2 more minutes.

2. In a stockpot over medium heat, add in the onions and garlic as well as all of the remaining ingredients except for the cooked chicken, corn, and beans.

3. Once the soup is boiling, lower the heat. Cover and simmer for 15 minutes.

4. Add the remaining ingredients and simmer for 10 more minutes.

5. Serve and enjoy!

SARA LUNDBERG,
Portland, Oregon

Sara Lundberg is a cookbook author and founder of the lifestyle blog BudgetSavvy Diva.com. She is a wife and a mother to five children, and she loves cooking and getting messy in the kitchen with her two oldest.

Facebook:
@thebudgetsavvydiva
Instagram:
@budgetsavvydiva
TikTok:
@budgetsavvydiva

Jalapeño Popper Chicken Chili

This chili has been a family favorite for years! It even won an online chili competition for food bloggers.

COOK TIME

45 mins.

Makes 7+ servings

INGREDIENTS

- 1 tablespoon olive oil
- 1 small onion, diced
- 1 red bell pepper, diced
- 4 jalapeños, diced and seeds removed
- 4 cloves garlic, minced
- 1 pound chicken breasts, cut into bite-sized pieces
- 1 teaspoon sea salt
- 1 teaspoon freshly ground mixed peppers (or black pepper)
- 2 teaspoons chili powder or other spice blend (I use Penzeys Arizona Dreaming® seasoning)

- 1 tablespoon ground cumin
- 1 teaspoon paprika
- One 15-ounce can diced tomatoes in juice
- 1½ cups chicken broth
- 2 cups cannellini beans
- 2 cups corn
- 8 ounces cream cheese
- 4 slices bacon, cooked and crumbled
- ¼ cup sharp cheddar cheese

Directions

1. In a large saucepan, heat the olive oil over medium heat. Add in the onion, red pepper, jalapeños, and garlic and sauté for 5–7 minutes or until soft.

2. Sprinkle the chicken with the salt and pepper. Add the chicken to the pan and lightly brown it on all sides.

3. Add in the spices (chili powder, cumin, and paprika). Stir to combine the spices with the chicken and vegetables. Stir in the diced tomatoes, chicken broth, cannellini beans, and corn. Simmer for 30 minutes. Add in the cream cheese and stir until melted.

4. Serve topped with crumbled bacon and cheddar cheese.

Chili Recipe Awards

- **Prevention RD Online Annual Chili Contest**

HEATHER KING,
Frostburg, Maryland

Heather King lives in Maryland with her husband and 4-year-old son. She is a full-time special education teacher and a food blogger who specializes in easy weeknight meals, as well as decadent desserts. Heather has been a food blogger for 11 years and spends numerous hours in the kitchen perfecting her recipes.
Twitter: @HezziD
Instagram: @hezzid
Facebook: @HezziDs
BooksandCooks
Food Blog: www.hezzi
-dsbooksandcooks.com
Pinterest: @26summer

COOK TIME
45 mins.
Makes 6 servings

Super Healthy White Chicken Chili

This chili is going to be a household favorite whether you're eating healthy or not. It's got big chunks of chicken, lots of veggies, and is just a touch creamy. It's now my favorite winter soup!

INGREDIENTS

- 3 chicken breasts
- 1 tablespoon garlic, minced
- 2 stalks celery, diced
- One-quarter of 1 red onion, diced
- One 15.8-ounce can great northern beans; do not drain
- One 14.75-ounce fire-roasted corn, drained
- 2 cups kale, coarsely chopped
- One 4-ounce can green chiles, diced
- 2 cups fat-free chicken broth
- 1 tablespoon cumin
- 2 tablespoons salt
- 10 ounces fat-free plain Greek yogurt
- Garnishes: cilantro, chives

Directions

1. Cook the chicken breasts. When the chicken is cooled a bit, shred it and set aside.
2. Spray a large soup pot or Dutch oven with non-stick cooking spray. Add the garlic, celery, and onion. Sauté for 3 minutes until the vegetables start to soften.
3. Add the shredded chicken and all remaining ingredients, except for the yogurt and garnishes, to your pot. Bring to a simmer and let cook for 15–20 minutes.
4. Once the mixture is cooked, remove from the heat and add the yogurt. Stir well.
5. Serve topped with cilantro or chives.

HEATHER JOHNSON,
Blanchester, Ohio

Heather Johnson is the hussy behind TheFoodHussy.com! She is a food and travel blogger that covers restaurants, recipes, and road trips. She is also a huge fan of *The Office* and is hopeful that you might see her on the Food Network (someday)!
Facebook: @TheFoodHussy
Instagram: @foodhussy
Pinterest: @foodhussy

Guajillo Chicken Chili

Whether it's a crisp fall day or a sunny summer eve, this Guajillo Chicken Chili is a surefire hit with spice lovers! The slow-building heat, savory beans, and simmered chiles make this a bowl of gold fit for chili royalty.

COOK TIME
1 hr. 45 mins.

Makes 6–8 servings

INGREDIENTS

- 10 dried guajillo chiles, destemmed
- 6 cups water
- 2 tablespoons canola oil
- ¼ cup garlic, minced
- 1½ pounds chicken breasts
- 3½ cups white onion, diced
- 2 serranos, thinly sliced
- 2 cups carrots, thinly sliced
- 1 cup green chiles, diced
- 6 cups chicken stock
- 2 tablespoons ground coriander
- 1 tablespoon cumin seed
- ⅛ cup parsley, chopped
- Two 16-ounce cans northern white beans
- Two 16-ounce cans cannellini beans
- 4 sprigs fresh thyme
- 2 teaspoons kosher salt
- 2 tablespoons corn starch (optional)
- 3 tablespoons cold water (optional)

Directions

1. In a medium saucepan, combine the guajillo chiles and 6 cups of water. Bring to a simmer to rehydrate the chiles, and turn off heat. Let sit, covered, while you continue to prep.

2. Dice the chicken into small, bite-sized chunks. In a Dutch oven over medium-high heat, add 2 tablespoons of canola oil. Once the oil begins to shimmer, add the garlic. Lightly sauté the garlic for one minute, then incorporate the chicken.

3. Once the chicken is lightly browned on all sides, add the white onion, carrots, serranos, and green chiles. Turn the heat down and let the ingredients soften for two minutes.

4. Using an immersion blender or countertop blender, purée the guajillo chiles in the lightly colored broth they have created. Add this chile purée to the Dutch oven and stir thoroughly.

5. Add the chicken stock, spices, chopped parsley, and beans to the Dutch oven. Bring to a light boil. Using the immersion blender, lightly pulse in one corner of the pot until approximately one-quarter of the chili has broken down. (If you don't have an immersion blender, pour one-quarter of the mixture into a countertop blender to blend it instead.)

6. Add the sprigs of thyme and the salt and bring back to a light boil. Cover and turn the heat down to low. Let simmer on low heat for 2 hours.

7. If desired, create a cornstarch slurry from the cornstarch and cold water, bring the chili back to a boil, and whisk in the slurry to thicken. Turn the heat off, let rest for 10 minutes, or wait until the next day.

CHEF CHRISTIAN GILL,
Cincinnati, Ohio

Chef Christian Gill is the chef-owner of Boomtown Biscuits and Whiskey. Along with the many awards won by the restaurant and team, Chef Gill has made a multitude of appearances on the Food Network. Coming out a champion from multiple shows, Chef Gill's recipe for Chicken Chili is sure to win at your next chili cook-off.
Twitter: @bodybybiscuit
Instagram: @foodbrushninja
TikTok: @only_yams

Smoked White Chicken Chili

This recipe is a favorite of everyone who eats it, whether that be coworkers or judges at chili competitions. It has won first place in the homestyle category at many International Chili Society cook-offs. It is also very popular when served to the public at competitions. Don't grab a bowl too big, or you will eat the entire pot!

COOK TIME

1 hr. 30 mins.

Makes 7 servings

INGREDIENTS

- 2 pounds boneless skinless chicken thighs
- 1 yellow onion, diced
- 3 jalapeños, diced
- 4 cloves garlic
- ¼ teaspoon cayenne pepper
- ¼ teaspoon Mexican oregano
- ⅛ teaspoon white pepper
- 1 tablespoon cumin

- 1 tablespoon granulated garlic
- 1 tablespoon granulated onion
- 2 cups chicken broth
- 8 ounces sour cream
- 12 ounces Monterey Jack or quesadilla melting cheese
- 1 cup frozen or fresh corn (optional)
- 1 can diced tomatoes and green chiles (I use Rotel®)

Directions

1. Lightly season and grill the chicken. Once it is cooked, cut it into small chunks.
2. Sauté the onion, jalapeños, and garlic in oil or bacon grease until tender.
3. Add the cayenne pepper, Mexican oregano, and white pepper into the vegetables. Also add the remaining spices (cumin, granulated garlic, and granulated onion); or, if desired, replace these three spices with 1 package of your favorite white chicken chili seasoning mixture. Let cook for one minute.
4. Add the chicken broth and bring to a simmer.
5. Add the chicken and let simmer for 20 minutes.
6. Add the sour cream and cheese and stir constantly. Simmer for 15 minutes.
7. Check the heat and salt levels. Add more cayenne or salt if needed.

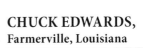

Recipe Awards

- 1st place homestyle chili at Tennessee State Championship
- 1st place homestyle chili at Tennessee Regional Championship
- Final table in homestyle category at the ICS Championship

CHUCK EDWARDS,
Farmerville, Louisiana

Chuck is a public health veterinarian who works in food safety. He and his wife Ashley enjoy traveling the country, cooking in chili and steak competitions as part of the High Steaks Cooking Team. In 2018, he was the National Points Champion in the Steak Cook-Off Association Championship.

When not traveling or cooking, Chuck enjoys playing golf, watching football, and taking care of his pets.
Facebook, Instagram:
@highsteakscookingteam

COOK TIME
6+ hrs.
Makes 7 servings

Cream Cheese White Chicken Chili

I've experimented with many chicken chili recipes, and this one takes the cake! My goal was a rich flavor that makes your eyes pop but which is super simple to make. It's just not possible to mess it up. Of course, you also won't find it on a low-calorie diet. It's perfect for a potluck, and it freezes well. If you stick to the basic seasoning combination (including bacon), you can vary the rest and still count on a fabulous chili every time!

INGREDIENTS

- 2 pounds boneless skinless chicken thighs
- 4 cups chicken broth
- 10 strips bacon, cooked and chopped
- One 1-ounce package ranch seasoning
- 1 tablespoon chili powder
- 1 teaspoon cumin
- 1 teaspoon onion powder
- One 8-ounce package cream cheese
- 1½ cups green chiles, diced
- One 11-ounce package frozen corn
- Two 16-ounce cans great northern beans in mild chili sauce (I use Bush's®)
- 1½ cups shredded white cheddar cheese (I use Tillamook®)

Directions

1. Put the chicken in a slow cooker. Add the chicken broth, bacon, ranch seasoning, all spices, cream cheese, and 1 cup of the diced green chiles.
2. Cook on low for 6 hours.
3. Remove the chicken and shred it using two forks. If the cream cheese is lumpy, use a whisk to blend it into the liquid. Return the chicken to the slow cooker.
4. Stir in the corn and beans, let cook for another 30 minutes, and then stir in 1 cup of shredded cheese.
5. Serve with the remaining shredded cheese and diced green chiles for garnish. This chili will gradually thicken more as it sits. Enjoy!

ANITA EDGE,
Conifer, Colorado

In 2006, Anita Edge combined her decade of web-design experience and her fascination for chiles and Southwestern cooking to create DenverGreenChili.com. Her mouthwatering insights have been guiding chile enthusiasts on where to buy the best green chiles in Denver ever since. The site has become a how-to resource for selecting, roasting, peeling, freezing, cooking, and even decorating with chiles. Anita has been featured in the *Denver Post*, the *Rocky Mountain News*, AAA's *EnCompass* magazine, and *Westword*. As a speaker at BlogHer and BlogHer Food, she has shared her journey and insights on everything from must-have recipes to remedies for capsaicin overdose.
Website: www.Denver GreenChili.com
Facebook, Instagram: @DenverGreenChili
Twitter: @AnitaEdge
Pinterest: @denverchili

Slow Cooker Cheesy Chicken Chili

This is no ordinary chicken chili! It is made in a slow cooker and is full of secret ingredients, but, most importantly, it is extremely cheesy. Everyone loves topping their chili with cheese, but putting the cheese into the actual chili is even more delicious and adds great texture and flavor.

COOK TIME
6+ hrs.

Makes 6 servings

INGREDIENTS

- 2 chicken breasts
- Two 25-ounce cans diced tomatoes and green chiles (I use Rotel®)
- Two 25-ounce cans black beans, drained and rinsed
- One 25-ounce can corn
- 32 ounces chicken broth
- 1 packet dry ranch seasoning
- 8 slices bacon, cooked and crumbled
- Salt and pepper, to taste
- 2 tablespoons chili powder
- 1 tablespoon cumin
- 1 tablespoon garlic powder
- 8 ounces cream cheese, at room temperature
- 1 cup shredded cheddar cheese
- Garnishes: extra cheese, Fritos® corn chips, hot sauce

Directions

1. Beginning with the chicken at the very bottom, add all the ingredients to the slow cooker except for the cream cheese, cheddar cheese, and toppings.

2. Set the temperature to low and cook for 6–8 hours or high for 4 hours. Halfway through the cook time, add the cream cheese.

3. When you're ready to eat, shred the chicken and add the cheddar cheese. Give the cheese a few minutes to melt, then serve with your desired toppings.

Good-to-Know Info

Using the right cookware is key! Pots that distribute heat evenly and prevent sticking are a must-have.

AMANDA DORICH,
Windber, Pennsylvania

Amanda Dorich is a wife, a high school Spanish teacher, a mom to two beautiful girls, and a food blogger. She blogs at Old House to New Home, where she shares easy, family-friendly recipes and home decor ideas from her 105-year-old historic home.
Amanda loves cooking because food truly is love!
Website: www.oldhouse tonewhome.net
Facebook, Instagram: @oldhousetonewhome

Texas Chili

Texas chili usually consists of chili pepper-marinated beef and some extra spices. Beans, tomatoes, and tomato-based ingredients traditionally aren't included.

The Recipes

Cin Chili

Terlingua
Championship Chili

Beef Mushroom
Quinoa Chili

Mike's Texas-Style Chili

George's Chili Gang Chili

This is my red chili recipe that I use in ICS Chili Competitions. I was able to cook it with Brian Baumgartner during a chili demo at the 2021 ISC World Championship Cook-Off. I had a great time with Brian.

COOK TIME

3 hrs.

Makes 7+ servings

INGREDIENTS

- 3 pounds tri-tip beef
- ½ pound mild pork sausage (I use Jimmy Dean®)
- 1 tablespoon oil (I use Crisco®)
- One 7.75-ounce can tomato sauce (I use El Pato®)
- One 14-ounce can beef broth (I use Swanson®)
- Two 14-ounce cans chicken broth (I use Swanson®)
- Garlic powder, to taste
- 6 tablespoons chili powder (I use Chili Man® seasoning mix)
- 4 tablespoons chili powder (I use Tone's®)
- 3 tablespoons cumin (I use Tone's®)
- 2 teaspoons cayenne pepper
- 1 tablespoon Spanish paprika (I use Tone's®)
- 2 small onions, chopped
- One 4-ounce can chopped green chiles (I use Old El Paso®)
- One 8-ounce can tomato sauce (I use Hunt's®)
- 2 tablespoons brown sugar
- 1 teaspoon Tabasco® sauce
- Salt, to taste
- White pepper, to taste
- Arrowroot, to taste

Directions

1. Brown the beef and sausage using the oil.

2. Mix the following spices in a separate bowl: garlic powder, chili powders, cumin, cayenne pepper, and Spanish paprika. Set aside.

3. To a large pot, add the can of El Pato® tomato sauce, beef broth, chicken broth, and three-quarters of the spice mixture. Bring to a boil.

4. Add half of the browned meat to the pot along with the chopped onions. Add the second half of the browned meat with the green chiles. Simmer for 2 hours, stirring when needed.

5. Add the remaining spice mixture, the can of Hunt's® tomato sauce, and the brown sugar. Cook for another 30 minutes or until the meat is tender.

6. At the end, add the Tabasco® sauce. Adjust the chili with additional chicken broth or arrowroot, salt, and white pepper to taste.

Chili Recipe Awards

- 1st in Southern Nights in July 2021 in Shelbyville, TN
- Won in other states in the past 10 years

GEORGE RIVES,
Eolia, Missouri

George Rives was skeptical about entering his first ICS cook-off in Clarksville, MO, in 1993. To his surprise, he won and qualified for the Last Chance Cook-off at the WCCC in Reno that year! Since 1993, he and the love of his life/chili-cooking partner, Mary Cannon, have competed in ICS cook-offs all over the Midwest. Over the years, they've each won several cook-offs in Missouri, Nebraska, Louisiana, Tennessee, and Arkansas.

COOK TIME

2 hrs. 30 mins.

Makes 6 servings

Scorpion Breath Chili

I attended my first chili cook-off in 1974. I got hooked, and I started cooking competitively a few years later in Houston, Texas. The chili newspaper, called *The Goat Gap Gazette*, was run by Hal John Wimberly, and he asked me to write a column, which l have done since 1980.

INGREDIENTS

- 2 pounds cubed beef
- One 14.5-ounce can beef broth
- 6 tablespoons chili powder
- 1 tablespoon cayenne pepper
- 1 tablespoon cumin
- 1 teaspoon Mexican oregano
- 1 teaspoon sea salt
- 1 packet Coriander & Annatto Goya® spice
- 1 jalapeño

Directions

1. Brown the cubed meat in a pot.
2. Add the broth and chili powder. Add the rest of the seasonings. Stir clockwise and well. Bring to a boil, then simmer for 2 hours 30 minutes.
3. While simmering, "float" a pricked jalapeño in the mixture.

RIGHT REV. MIKE SMITH, CHILI CLERGY,
Wimberley, Texas

Mike Smith is the founder of the "Texas Chili History Museum" Facebook group, a columnist for the chili publications *Goat Gap Gazette* and *Son of a Goat* since 1980. He is a competitive chili cook, promoter, official, and judge in Texas since the 1970s, and has been an original Terlingua International Chili Championship Final Judge since the early 1980s. Founder of the Terlingua World Championship B.E.AN. Cook-Off and P.E.A. Cook-Off, Mike has also been a Special Purveyor of Texas Bovine Residue since 1950.

Good-to-Know Info

While beans in chili are optional, most Texans will denounce it as no longer chili, but goulash or frijoles borrachos.

Chili Recipe Awards

- **3 first places in Texas**
- **Many top ten trophies**
- **Final Judge at Terlingua Original Cook-Off since 1983**

Cin Chili

COOK TIME

2 hrs.

Makes 6 servings

Cindy Reed Wilkins, aka "The Chili Queen," is a legend in the chili community. She's one of the greatest champions in the history of chili competition. Cindy has won an extraordinary fifteen first-place awards, more than 100 total, in the world of championship red chili. Her highest honor is winning the coveted Terlingua International Chili Championship not once, but twice, in 1992 and 1993. She's the only person ever to win it back-to-back. This recipe was passed down to Cindy from her mother and father. Her mother won the Tolbert Chili Cook-Off and her father won second in the same year.

INGREDIENTS

For Chili:
- 2 pounds beef chuck tender, cut into ⅜-inch cubes
- 1 teaspoon cooking oil
- 1 teaspoon seasoned salt
- One 14.5-ounce can beef broth
- One 8-ounce can no-salt tomato sauce
- 2 serranos

For First Spice Mix:
- 1 teaspoon chicken bouillon
- 1 teaspoon beef bouillon
- 1 tablespoon onion powder
- 1 teaspoon garlic powder
- 1 tablespoon chili powder
- ½ teaspoon jalapeño powder
- ½ teaspoon salt
- ¼ teaspoon black pepper

For Second Spice Mix:
- 5 tablespoons chili powder
- 1 teaspoon garlic powder
- ¼ teaspoon cayenne pepper powder
- 2 teaspoons cumin
- ¼ teaspoon brown sugar
- 1 teaspoon seasoned salt

For the Third Spice Mix:
- ⅛ teaspoon cayenne pepper
- ½ teaspoon garlic powder
- ½ teaspoon onion powder
- 2 teaspoons chili powder
- 1½ teaspoons cumin

Directions

1. In a 4-quart heavy saucepan, add the beef chuck, cooking oil, and seasoned salt. Brown the meat.
2. Combine the beef broth and tomato sauce and bring to a slight boil.
3. Combine the first spice mix and add it to the beef mixture. Return the mixture to a boil, then reduce the heat and simmer for 1 hour.
4. Sear and float the serranos in the mixture.
5. Combine the second spice mix and add it to the beef mixture. Bring to a boil, then reduce the heat and simmer for 30 minutes. You may add water or beef broth for consistency.
6. Remove the serranos when they become soft.
7. Combine the third spice mix and add it to the beef mixture. Simmer for 30 minutes.

CINDY REED WILKINS,
Houston, Texas

Cindy Reed Wilkins is the only back-to-back winner of the CASI International Chili Championship. She has won numerous awards for her products and was featured on *Throwdown with Bobby Flay: The Chili Challenge* on the Food Network. Who doesn't love a "good bowl of red"?
Facebook, Instagram:
@CinChili
Twitter:
@CindersosaChili

Chili Recipe Awards

- 1st Place two years in a row at Terlingua CASI International Chili Championship
- Tied Bobby Flay on Food Network's *Throwdown with Bobby Flay: The Chili Challenge*
- 1st Place Texas Ladies State
- 1st Place Chilympiad Chili Cook-Off
- 1st Place ICS Texas State Champion
- 1st Place Houston Pod Chili Championship
- 1st Place Czhilispiel Chili Cook-Off
- 1st Place VASA Pod Chili Cook-Off
- 1st Place SOT Pod Chili Cook-Off
- 1st Place Rio Grande Valley Regional ICS
- 1st Place Scovie Awards
- 1st Place Fiery Foods

Terlingua Championship Chili

COOK TIME
2 hrs. 30 mins.
Makes 6 servings

There is nothing better on a cold day than a hearty bowl of traditional red chili. This award-winning chili has no beans, as CASI chili rules require only meat and gravy. This recipe won the 2016 CASI 50th Anniversary Terlingua International Chili Championship, beating over 330 cooks.

INGREDIENTS

For Chili:
- 2 pounds 80% lean ground chuck
- 26 ounces beef broth
- One 8-ounce can tomato sauce

For First Spice Dump:
- 1 tablespoon onion granules
- 1 tablespoon beef granules
- 1 tablespoon chicken granules
- 2 teaspoons garlic granules
- 2 tablespoons chili powder (I use Mild Bill's San Antonio Original or Gebhardt®)
- 2 teaspoons chili powder (I use Mild Bill's Dixon®)
- ⅛ teaspoon cayenne pepper
- ⅛ teaspoon white ground pepper
- ⅛ teaspoon finely ground black pepper

For Second Spice Dump:
- 1 tablespoon cumin
- ½ teaspoon garlic granules
- 1 tablespoon chili powder (I use Mild Bill's San Antonio Original or Gebhardt®)
- 1½ teaspoons chili powder (I use Mild Bill's San Antonio Red®)
- 1 tablespoon chili powder (I use Mild Bill's Cowtown Light®)
- 1½ teaspoons Hatch® chile powder
- 1 packet Sazón Goya® Achiote or similar seasoning
- ⅛ teaspoon brown sugar

Directions

1. In a 3- or 4-quart pot, brown the ground chuck. As you are browning, leave the meat in big chunks or balls in your pot. Drain off the grease in a colander and set aside. Remove all the grease and clean out your pot with a paper towel. Add the meat chunks back into the pot.

2. Add the beef broth and tomato sauce and bring to a boil. Once it boils, turn down the heat to a low simmer with the lid on. Cook for about 45 minutes. This will tenderize the meat.

3. Mix the first spice dump and add it to the pot. Bring the mixture to a boil, being careful not to mash the meat. Instead, push the meat around with a spoon. Turn the heat down and let simmer for 30 minutes, keeping the lid on the pot.

4. After 30 minutes, break the meat into chunks down to about fingertip size. Then bring back to a boil and add the second spice dump. Hard boil for 5 minutes, then let simmer for 20 minutes.

5. Before serving, taste the chili for salt and heat and adjust if necessary. Check the gravy consistency—if it's too thick, you can add a little water or chicken broth.

Chili Recipe Awards
- 2016 Terlingua International Chili Championship, 50th Anniversary
- 2017 CASI Colorado State Chili Championship

LISA STONE,
Kempner, Texas

Lisa Stone won the 2016 Terlingua International Chili Championship Cook-Off in Terlingua, Texas, besting 330 cooks. Lisa has cooked competitively since 1983 along with her family who have won many awards. Their family motto is, "If one wins, we all win!" Their dad got them started in the chili world, so one could say cooking chili is in their blood. He is no longer with them, but they know he would be so proud of them and their accomplishments. Aside from cooking chili, Lisa enjoys traveling, boating, and fishing with her husband, children, and grandchildren.
Facebook, Instagram: @lisaedmonsonstone

Omaha Prime Chili Recipe

COOK TIME

3 hrs. 30 mins.

Makes 7+ servings

This is a basic competition chili. To compete, it can't be too hot or too spicy or have too many visible vegetables or beans. This recipe can be customized by adding more cayenne pepper, Tabasco® sauce, chopped tomato pieces, jalapeños, or whatever vegetables you may have around the house. I have seen people use celery, carrots, and even chopped potatoes. For competition, though, make sure you follow the protocol or you won't make it to any final rounds. Enjoy!

Note: You can cut this recipe exactly in half to make less.

INGREDIENTS

- 6 pounds premium beef (I recommend that you have the butcher coarse grind either chuck or pot roast or you can use 85%–15% premium hamburger)
- 4 medium yellow onions, diced as small as you can get them
- One 16-oz can Italian tomato sauce (I used Contadina)
- 3 tomatoes, pureéd in a blender
- 12 to 16 garlic cloves, pureéd in a blender (or you can use ⅓ cup of crushed garlic)
- 3 large poblanos
- 2 large red peppers

- 1 tablespoon hot sauce (I use Cholula® or sriracha)
- 1 teaspoon brown sugar
- 2 tablespoons ground cumin
- ⅓ cup of ordinary chili powder (add more depending on taste)
- 4 cups beef broth, low sodium is best
- 1 cup water (more if desired for thinner chili)
- 1 teaspoon black pepper
- Salt to taste
- 1 teaspoon chocolate powder
- 1 teaspoon cayenne pepper
- 3 or 4 tablespoons cooking oil
- 3 tablespoons vinegar

Directions

1. Cut off the stems of the peppers and remove the seeds without cutting up the peppers.

2. Boil the peppers in water for 45 minutes or until they are soft enough to remove the skin. Then mash the peppers with a spoon or fork. Set aside. You should have about a cup and a half of this mixture.

3. In a hot skillet, brown the beef 2 pounds at a time in hot oil and a little black pepper, salt, and a third of the onions. Make sure the beef is mashed so it's not in large clumps. Drain all but a few tablespoons of the fat, and set aside the meat in the chili pot. Repeat until all the meat is done.

4. With all the meat in the bottom of the pot, add the tomato sauce, tomato puree, pepper paste, and garlic. Then, add the water and beef broth. Add the rest of the ingredients and mix thoroughly.

5. Cook covered for 2 hours and stir every 15 minutes. Taste occasionally to see if it needs more chili spice or hot sauce to suit your taste.

DONN SEIDHOLZ,
Omaha, Nebraska

Donn played in the Chicago White Sox farm system for seven years. Playing and living in Mexico and Panama, he developed a taste for all kinds of chili-related foods and condiments. He got involved with the ICS after attending multiple events in Phoenix and worked with Jim West to move the 1992 World Championship to Rawhide in Scottsdale. One of his fondest memories was meeting Orville Redenbacher and Senator Barry Goldwater, who were judges. Donn has judged multiple regional events and finals in Omaha, Reno, and St. Louis, and looks forward to the next round.

Kevin's Biggest Fan's Chili

I was inspired to concoct my own chili recipe while watching *The Office*. I have been developing this recipe for 10 years and have found it to be the best chili I've ever had. In addition to beans and beef, I add spicy Italian sausage. A diced fresh jalapeño added after the sautéing process, along with some cayenne pepper, gives the medley of other spices an edge and a subtle heat that is pleasurable to most palates.

COOK TIME

2 hrs.

Makes 7+ servings

INGREDIENTS

- 1 pound ground beef
- 1 pound spicy Italian sausage
- 1 yellow onion, diced
- 1 red bell pepper, chopped
- 3 cloves garlic, minced
- 1 teaspoon cumin
- 2 tablespoons chili powder
- 1 teaspoon paprika
- ¼ teaspoon cayenne pepper
- ½ teaspoon salt
- ½ teaspoon black pepper
- 3 ounces tomato paste
- 29 ounces diced tomatoes
- 1 cup beef broth
- One 8-ounce can tomato sauce
- Two 15-ounce cans kidney beans, drained and rinsed
- One 15-ounce can pinto beans, drained and rinsed
- 2 tablespoons Worcestershire sauce
- 1 jalapeño, chopped
- 1 tablespoon brown sugar
- Garnishes: sour cream, green onions, freshly grated Monterey Jack cheese

Directions

1. Brown the meat and set it aside.
2. Sauté the onions, red bell pepper, and garlic.
3. Transfer the sautéed vegetables to a large pot. Add all the spices to the pot and continue to cook for a couple of minutes.
4. Add the tomato paste and cook for a couple more minutes.
5. Add the diced tomatoes, bring to a simmer, and cook for a few minutes.
6. Add the meat, beef broth, tomato sauce, and beans.
7. Bring the mixture to a simmer. Add the Worcestershire sauce, jalapeño, and brown sugar. Cook for at least 45 minutes to reduce the broth.
8. Serve however you want. I prefer a dollop of sour cream with green onion and freshly grated Monterey Jack cheese.

WATCH HOW TO MAKE THIS RECIPE

BEN GRANT,
Chesterfield, Michigan

Ben Grant is from Iowa, but now lives in Michigan with his family. His days on the job are spent jetting all over the United States, Central and South America, and the Caribbean as a captain for a major airline. When he is home, he enjoys spending time with his wife and kids, playing music for whoever will listen, flying his vintage 1959 Beechcraft Bonanza, and cooking. Instagram: @a320_captain_ben

COOK TIME

4 hrs.

Makes 7+ servings

Shotgun Willie Chili

This is my winning World Championship recipe . . . the culmination of trial-and-error competition cooking in International Chili Society cook-offs from 1979–1985. I'm frequently asked, "What's your secret?" I have several: quality ingredients, consistency in cooking the exact recipe, and my own blend of spices. Prior to winning the World title in 1985, I won first place in 15 ICS cook-offs, including 5th place in the World Championship in 1984. This recipe was created from prep to completion in 4 hours. You can also do a quick fix version in just 1 hour.

INGREDIENTS

- 6 pounds prime beef
- ½ pound kidney suet
- 1 tablespoon black pepper
- 4 medium onions, chopped
- 6 New Mexico chiles
- 6 pasilla chiles
- 1½ tablespoons oregano leaves
- One 15-ounce can tomato purée
- 2 tablespoons apple cider vinegar
- 1 teaspoon Tabasco® sauce
- 1 cup chili seasoning
- 2 tablespoons ground cumin
- 1 teaspoon cayenne pepper
- ½ teaspoon sugar
- 14 cloves garlic
- 4 cups beef broth
- Salt, to taste

Directions

1. Cut the beef into ¼-inch cubes. Render just enough kidney suet to slightly coat the bottom of a hot skillet. Brown the beef in about four batches, adding onions and black pepper to each batch. Combine all the finished beef and onions in a single large pot as you complete each batch. Set aside.

2. Remove the seeds and stems from the chiles. Cover the chiles with water and boil until the pulp parts from the skin. Put the cooked chiles into a blender to make a smooth paste. You will need about 1½ cups of the paste. Set aside.

3. Crush the oregano leaves and steep them in boiling water, straining after 12 minutes. Set aside.

4. In a large bowl, combine the chile paste, oregano "tea," tomato purée, vinegar, Tabasco® sauce, chili seasoning, cumin, cayenne, sugar, and garlic. Add this mixture to the browned beef. Simmer for 2 hours. Add beef broth as needed to maintain the desired consistency. Salt as desired.

CAROL ANN HANCOCK,
Coto de Caza, California

Carol competed in International Chili Society cook-offs beginning in 1979. She won first place in 15 events, including qualifying for the 1984 ICS's World Championships, placing fifth. In 1985, she won the World Championship and $25,000. Carol has appeared on numerous network TV shows, was selected as Hunt's Great American Chef, was a spokesperson for Frito-Lay, won a coast-to-coast one-on-one competition against a famous New York restaurateur, judged ICS-sanctioned chili cook-offs from 1983 to present, and cooked chili for numerous celebrities and musicians. In 2000, ICS founder, Carroll Shelby, asked her to take over the ICS as new CEO and owner. Carol retired in 2017.

Chili Recipe Awards

- **Fifth place in World's Championship Chili Cook-Off 1984**
- **First place in World' Championship Chili Cook-Off in 1985**
- **Dozens of first place District and Regional Cook-Offs**

Pools Brew Chili

Technically a Texas red chili. A culmination of 42 years of cooking competitively in chili cook-offs, this recipe has been tweaked many times. It will evolve again in the future, but prunes will always be the "secret ingredient."

COOK TIME

3 hrs.

Makes 4 "Texas-sized" servings

INGREDIENTS

For Chili:
- 2¼ pounds cubed tri-tip roast, trimmed of fat
- 2 tablespoons shortening (I use Crisco®)
- One 14.5-ounce can beef broth (I use Swanson®)
- One 14.5-ounce can chicken broth (I use Swanson®)
- One 8-ounce can tomato sauce (The brand is secret!)
- 2 pitted prunes (I use Sunsweet®)
- Water as needed
- Seasoned salt, to taste
- Tabasco® sauce (as needed for heat)

For First Spice Mixture:
- 1 tablespoon American paprika
- 1½ teaspoons onion powder
- 1 teaspoon garlic powder
- 2 teaspoons beef granules

- 1 teaspoon chicken granules
- ½ teaspoon seasoned salt
- ½ tablespoon New Mexico chile powder

For Second Spice Mixture:
- 3 teaspoons ground cumin
- ½ teaspoon garlic powder
- ½ teaspoon seasoned salt
- 1½ tablespoons chili powder (I use Gebhardt®)
- 1½ tablespoons Texas-style chili powder
- ½ tablespoon New Mexico Hot ground chile pepper
- ½ tablespoon New Mexico Light chile powder

For Third Spice Mixture:
- 2 teaspoons Texas-style chili powder
- 1 teaspoon ground cumin
- ¼ teaspoon garlic powder

Directions

1. Brown the meat in the shortening. Place the browned meat in a colander and drain off the shortening. Rinse the meat with water and return it to the pot.

2. Add the broths, tomato sauce, prunes, and first spice mixture. Cook for approximately 2 hours, removing the prunes after the first hour. (Let the prunes cool and enjoy them as an appetizer.) Add water to the chili if necessary. Cook longer if the meat is not tender.

3. Thirty minutes before serving, add the second spice mixture.

4. Fifteen minutes before serving, add the third spice mixture.

5. Add seasoned salt to taste. For heat, add Tabasco® sauce to taste.

Chili Recipe Awards

- The ONLY 5-time World Chili Champion
- Three-time (1996, 1998, 2006) Original Tolbert International Chili Championship (OTICC) in Terlingua, Texas
- The ONLY International Chili Society (ICS) back-to-back World Chili Champion in 2012 and 2013
- The ICS 2016 (50th Anniversary), Champion of Champions, Best Chili Cook in the World Award

BOB PLAGER,
Littleton, Colorado

Bob Plager has been cooking competition chili since 1980 and has done very well. Everyone wants to know his "secret," which is floating two prunes in his chili for one hour. They give the chili a little sweetness and the gravy a beautiful gloss. He is proud that his chili looks good and tastes great, as proven by his five World Championship wins.

Afro-Texan Brisket Chili

To create an American chili, I decided to take a deep dive into South Africa's cultural diversity and harmonize that with the traditional (Texas-style) chili. I'm excited to share the result. Here in South Africa, we are no strangers to stews and cooking what we call "bredie" (the Afrikaans word for a slow-cooked stew) for hours. We often pair this with interesting bases to absorb all those delicious juices and gravy. We especially love how chutney introduces sweet, spicy, and acidic flavor notes to elevate our dishes. This chili is prepared with precooked beef brisket and doesn't include any beans (in line with Texas-style chili). It is served with a traditional South African slap pap, which is a soft porridge made from maize meal, and a topping that is flavored with a well-loved African relish called chakalaka. The chakalaka adds another layer of pepper heat. This all may sound like a mouthful, but we are a nation that believes we can harmoniously combine what seems to be contradicting. The result is unique and fantastically delicious!

COOK TIME

30 mins.

Makes 6–8 servings

INGREDIENTS

- 2 tablespoons vegetable oil
- 2 yellow onions, diced
- Half of 1 jalapeño, minced
- ½ chipotle pepper, chopped
- 4 cloves garlic, minced
- ¼ cup chili powder
- 2 tablespoons rice vinegar
- 3 tablespoons paprika
- 1 tablespoon ground cumin
- 2 teaspoons Kosher salt
- 2 tablespoons dark brown sugar
- ½ teaspoon coarsely ground black pepper
- 28 ounces crushed tomatoes
- 4 cups beef broth
- 3 pounds beef brisket, cooked and chopped (preferably smoked low and slow)
- Slap pap or polenta (see recipe at right)
- Chakalaka (see recipe at right)
- Garnishes: young cilantro leaves, onion or leek ash

Directions

1. Add the oil to a deep and wide-based pot on high heat. Add the onions, jalapeño, and chipotle. Cook for about 5 minutes until the onions become translucent.

2. Add all of the other ingredients and mix well, making sure that all the chili powder is evenly distributed. Bring the liquid to the boil and cook on medium heat for about 2 hours, stirring occasionally.

3. To serve, add a large spoonful of the slap pap on the plate. Add a generous helping of the chili next to the pap. Pipe small rounds of the chakalaka on the chili and garnish with young cilantro leaves and a dusting of onion or leek ash.

CHARL MARAIS,
Cape Town, South Africa

Charl Marais is a food lover in heart and soul. He is a passionate home cook and holds a BSc in Food Science, as well as an MBA in the food and beverage industry. Shortly after the COVID-19 pandemic hit, Charl created a food enthusiasts platform page on Instagram called @fine_food_collective that rapidly grew its follower base to more than 30k. FFC is now supported by the website www.myfinefoodcollective.com that offers collaboration opportunities to restaurants, chefs, and food industry suppliers. MyFineFoodCollective is also launching a shop that supplies scarce molecular gastronomy ingredients and unique food products.
Website: www.myfinefoodcollective.com
Facebook, Instagram: @fine_food_collective

Chakalaka

INGREDIENTS

- 3 tablespoons oil
- 1 onion, finely chopped
- 2 green bird's eye chiles (Thai chiles), seeded and chopped
- 2 cloves garlic, crushed
- 2 ounces ginger, finely grated
- 2 tablespoons mild curry powder
- 1 green bell pepper, finely chopped
- 1 red bell pepper, finely chopped
- 1 yellow bell pepper, finely chopped

- 5 large carrots, scrubbed, topped, tailed, and grated
- One 14-ounce can chopped tomatoes
- 2 tablespoons tomato paste
- 2 sprigs fresh thyme, leaves only
- ½ teaspoon fennel seeds, ground
- Salt
- Freshly ground black pepper
- 1 cup extra creamy mayonnaise (I use Hellmann's®)
- 1 cup smooth full fat cream cheese

Directions

1. Add the oil to a warm pot. Fry the onions on medium heat until they start to turn translucent.
2. Add the chiles, garlic, and half of the ginger (the rest will be added right before the end). Add the curry powder and ground fennel seeds and stir well.
3. Add the bell peppers and sauté for a few minutes before adding the carrots. Combine well.
4. Add the tomatoes and tomato paste and cook for a good 10 minutes on medium heat, stirring occasionally.
5. Remove the mixture from the heat before adding the thyme and the rest of the ginger. Season with salt and pepper and allow to cool to room temperature. This mixture can be kept in an airtight container for 1–2 weeks in the fridge; it pairs well with meat, fish, or pap.
6. When ready to serve, combine the mayonnaise and cream cheese until smooth. Add 3–4 tablespoons of the cooled chakalaka, creating a ripple effect. Reserve for plating in a small piping bag.

Slap Pap

INGREDIENTS

- 3 cups boiling water
- 1 teaspoon salt
- ¾–1 cup maize meal
- 1 cup cold water
- 3 tablespoons butter
- 1 cup grated Parmigiano Reggiano cheese
- Salt and pepper, to taste

Directions

Note: This recipe is basically like making a really rich and creamy polenta. If you can't get your hands on the real thing, you can substitute with polenta. Slap pap is traditionally served with milk and sugar and enjoyed for breakfast, but in this case we are going to make it savory to complement and balance out the strong and rich flavor of the chakalaka and the chili.

1. Boil the water and salt in a pot with a lid.
2. Mix the maize meal with the cold water. Stir this mixture into the boiling water, and simmer for at least 30 minutes with the lid on.
3. Add the butter and cheese; allow them to melt completely into the mixture. Season with salt and pepper.

Mike's Texas-Style Chili

This Texas chili is meaty, just the right amount of spicy, and with not a chili bean in sight. I use a trio of dried chiles and lots of seasonings for maximum flavor, along with beef chuck that is incredibly tender from the low and slow cooking. You will love this version.

COOK TIME

2 hrs. 45 mins.

Makes 6 servings

INGREDIENTS

- 3 ancho chiles
- 3 pasilla chiles
- 3 dried New Mexico chiles
- 3 cups water, plus more as needed, or use chicken or beef stock or beer
- Salt, to taste
- 2½ pounds beef chuck, cut into bite-sized cubes
- 2 teaspoons cumin
- Pepper, to taste
- 2 tablespoons olive oil
- 3 jalapeños, chopped
- 2 serranos, chopped
- 1 medium white onion, chopped
- 4 cloves garlic, chopped
- 2 cups beef stock, or a dark beer
- 1 tablespoon brown sugar
- 1 tablespoon Worcestershire sauce
- 2 tablespoons masa harina (corn flour) (optional)
- Garnishes: chopped onion, spicy chili flakes, chopped fresh cilantro, lime wedges, crema or sour cream, Fritos® corn chips or tortilla chips, whatever else you desire

Directions

1. Start your chile paste first by lightly toasting the dried chiles in a dry pan about a minute or two per side. This will help to release the oils.

2. Remove the chiles from the heat and cool them down enough to handle. Remove the stems and pour out the seeds. Soak the chiles in hot water for 20 minutes, or until they are nice and soft.

3. Add the chiles to a food processor with ½–1 cup of water and a bit of salt to taste. Process until the paste is nice and smooth. Set aside.

4. Add the cubed beef to a large bowl and toss with the cumin and a bit of salt and pepper. Make sure everything is nice and coated.

5. Heat 1 tablespoon of oil in a large pot and add the seasoned beef. Cook for 6–7 minutes, searing the beef all over. Remove the beef and set aside.

6. Add the remaining olive oil along with the jalapeños, serranos, and onion. Cook them down for about 5 minutes.

7. Add the garlic and stir. Cook another minute.

8. Return the beef to the pot and stir in the chile paste. Cook it for 2–3 minutes to let the flavor develop a bit.

9. Stir in the beef broth (or beer), 2 cups of water, the brown sugar, the Worcestershire sauce, and the masa, and bring to a quick boil.

10. Reduce the heat, cover, and simmer for about 2 hours, or until the beef is very tender. It could take longer if you are using tougher cuts of beef. Give it a stir once about every 30 minutes. If it becomes too thick, add in ¼ cup of water and stir. Thicken with more masa.

11. Serve with your favorite fixin's!

WATCH HOW TO MAKE THIS RECIPE

MICHAEL J. HULTQUIST,
Huntersville, North Carolina

Mike Hultquist is the author of *The Spicy Dehydrator Cookbook* and *The Spicy Food Lovers' Cookbook*. You can find more of his culinary work at the popular food blog, Chili Pepper Madness (www.chili peppermadness.com). Facebook, Instagram, YouTube: @chilipeppermadness

Old Texas-Style Chili

Chili was a complimentary dish served at cantinas for outsiders who wanted something spicy and cheap. Chili was prepared from the leftover meals and often served free to drinking customers.

COOK TIME

3 hrs.

Makes 10–12 servings

INGREDIENTS

- 2 pounds lean beef, trimmed and cut into ½-inch cubes
- Salt and black pepper, to taste
- Granulated garlic, to taste
- ¼ cup olive oil
- 1 cup onions, diced
- ¼ cup garlic, minced
- 2 jalapeños, cored, seeded, and diced
- 1 quart beef stock
- 6 ancho chiles
- 1 tablespoon chili powder
- ½ teaspoon red pepper flakes
- 1 tablespoon ground cumin
- 1 tablespoon ground oregano
- Serve with: toasted French bread or crackers

Directions

1. Season the beef well with salt, pepper, and granulated garlic. In a large Dutch oven, heat the olive oil over medium-high heat. Add the beef and cook for 4–6 minutes or until browned on all sides, stirring occasionally.

2. Add the onions, minced garlic, and jalapeños. Sauté for 3–5 minutes or until wilted.

3. Add the beef stock and stir to incorporate. Bring to a boil, then add the ancho chiles and turn off the heat. Cover and allow the chiles to soak for 20–30 minutes. When the chiles have softened, remove the beef from the pot and set aside.

4. Transfer the remaining liquid and vegetables to a blender and blend until smooth. Return the meat and liquid to the pot and bring to a simmer over medium heat. Cover and simmer for 1 hour to 1 hour 30 minutes or until tender, stirring occasionally.

5. Remove the cover and continue simmering until the chili is slightly thickened. Add the chili powder, red pepper flakes, cumin, and oregano, then season to taste with more salt, pepper, and granulated garlic.

6. Ladle into serving bowls and serve hot with toasted French bread or crackers.

Good-to-Know Info

Chili was officially titled the State Food of Texas in 1977.

CHEF JOHN FOLSE,
New Orleans, Louisiana

Chef John Folse, Louisiana's Culinary Ambassador to the World, is proud to share his passion for Louisiana's swamp floor pantry around the world. As an entrepreneur, his interests range from restaurateur to manufacturer, author to educator. Some of his national and international accolades include being named Louisiana Restaurateur of the Year, National Chef of the Year, and several others. Author of 10 cookbooks, his *Can You Dig It* vegetable cookbook won the Benny Award for Best Cookbook. Folse hosts a national PBS television cooking show, *A Taste of Louisiana*. He was recently inducted into the American Academy of Chefs Culinary Hall of Fame and the Chef John Folse Culinary Institute at Nicholls State University is named in his honor.

COOK TIME
3 hrs. 30 mins.
Makes 10–12 servings

Doc's Primo Chili

There are few things better than a big pot of chili! While this recipe has many traditional ingredients, it also has a flavor unlike any other chili because of the apple pie spice and cocoa powder. Your family and friends will enjoy this dish that is perfect for feeding a small crowd!

This recipe is from Chef John Folse's *The Encyclopedia of Cajun & Creole Cuisine.*

INGREDIENTS

- ¼ cup vegetable oil
- 2 pounds ground pork
- 2 pounds ground beef
- 2 cups onions, diced
- 1 cup celery, diced
- 1 cup bell peppers, diced
- ½ cup garlic, sliced
- One 28-ounce can diced tomatoes and green chiles (I use Rotel®)
- One 8-ounce can tomato sauce
- 2 cups beef stock
- 1 teaspoon liquid smoke
- ½ cup beer

- 1 tablespoon ground cumin
- ¼ cup chili powder
- 2 teaspoons paprika
- 2 tablespoons apple pie spice
- 2 tablespoons ground fennel seeds
- 1 teaspoon cocoa powder
- Salt and black pepper, to taste
- Granulated garlic, to taste
- 1 jalapeño, seeded and diced
- One 15-ounce can red kidney beans (optional)

Directions

1. In a 12-quart cast iron pot, heat the oil over medium-high heat. Add the ground pork and ground beef, then cook until golden brown, stirring occasionally.

2. When the meat is golden brown, add the onions, celery, bell peppers, and garlic to the pot and sauté until the vegetables are wilted, stirring occasionally.

3. Blend in the diced tomatoes and green chiles, tomato sauce, beef stock, liquid smoke, and beer. Bring to a rolling boil, then reduce to a simmer.

4. Stir in the cumin, chili powder, paprika, apple pie spice, fennel seeds, and cocoa. Season lightly with salt, pepper, granulated garlic, and jalapeño. Allow to simmer for 3 hours, stirring often. The longer chili cooks, the better it will taste.

5. If desired, add red kidney beans 10 minutes prior to serving.

CHEF JOHN FOLSE,
New Orleans, Louisiana

Chef John Folse, Louisiana's Culinary Ambassador to the World, is proud to share his passion for Louisiana's swamp floor pantry around the world. As an entrepreneur, his interests range from restaurateur to manufacturer, author to educator. Some of his national and international accolades include being named Louisiana Restaurateur of the Year, National Chef of the Year, and several others. Author of 10 cookbooks, his *Can You Dig It* vegetable cookbook won the Benny Award for Best Cookbook. Folse hosts a national PBS television cooking show, *A Taste of Louisiana*. He was recently inducted into the American Academy of Chefs Culinary Hall of Fame and the Chef John Folse Culinary Institute at Nicholls State University is named in his honor.

109

Beef Mushroom Quinoa Chili

I put a spin on classic Texas beef chili by adding mushrooms and quinoa. It's admittedly unconventional, but I'm from Austin, and darn if it isn't just as spicy, satisfying, and downright delicious as old-school chili. Why did I put this combo in classic Texas-style beef chili? I'll admit, at first it was practical necessity—I thought there was more ground beef in the freezer than there actually was! I figured mushrooms and beef pair well, plus the mushrooms sneak in more nutrients for picky eaters and stretch the food budget.

COOK TIME

1 hr.

Makes 8 servings

INGREDIENTS

- 1½ pounds 90% or leaner ground beef
- 1 tablespoon olive oil
- 1 cup white or yellow onion, chopped
- 8 ounces cremini or white button mushrooms, finely chopped
- 1 tablespoon garlic, minced
- ½ cup dry (uncooked) quinoa

- 1–2 tablespoons chili powder
- 2 teaspoons chipotle powder
- 2 teaspoons ground cumin
- ½ cup red wine
- One 15-ounce can fire-roasted diced tomatoes, with juice
- One 8-ounce can tomato sauce
- 16 ounces beef broth (2 cups)
- 2 tablespoons Worcestershire sauce

Directions

1. Heat a large Dutch oven (or approximately a 3-quart pot with lid) over medium heat. Add the ground beef and cook for 8–10 minutes, breaking the beef into small crumbles and stirring occasionally. Remove the beef and pour it into a large strainer or colander to drain off excess liquid.

2. In the now-emptied pot (no need to wash it after the beef browning step), add the olive oil, onion, and mushrooms and sauté until softened, approximately 3–4 minutes. Add the garlic and stir around for another minute.

3. Add the dry quinoa to this mixture. Toast for 2–3 minutes by stirring around constantly with the other ingredients. In the last minute, add the chili powder, chipotle powder, and cumin, stirring around to "bloom" the flavor.

4. The bottom of pot may look like it's starting to brown or burn, but don't worry—these are all the beef and spice residues. Simply pour in the red wine to deglaze the pan, stirring around quickly to pull of the bits.

5. Add back in the beef that had been drained and set aside. Add the diced tomatoes (including juice), tomato sauce, Worcestershire sauce, and beef broth.

6. Bring to a simmer for a few minutes and then cover with a lid and continue to simmer until the sauce reduces and thickens and the flavors intensify—approximately 20–25 minutes.

JENNIFER FISHER,
Austin, Texas

Jennifer Fisher, the voice behind www.TheFitFork.com, is an award-winning recipe developer, a healthy-living content creator and spokesperson, and a lifelong competitive athlete. As a longtime member of the athletic group Texas Beef Team, Jennifer is a passionate advocate for the beef industry and shares with her communities how eating beef can help support an active and healthy lifestyle. A mom of three young men, she is an expert in making hearty food that tastes great and sneaks in extra nutrition.
Website: www.thefitfork.com
Facebook, Instagram, Pinterest: @thefitfork

COOK TIME

30 mins.

Makes 6 servings

Chouriço and Red Bean Portuguese Chili

My chili is one of family's favorite dishes. It only takes 20 minutes to prepare and can be made with Portuguese sausage or substituted with Spanish chorizo. The savory, slightly spicy paprika flavor adds a new twist for those Sunday game days or any day of the week. This will be a perfect dish for chili lovers looking for something new to try.

INGREDIENTS

- 1 small onion, diced
- 2 cloves garlic, diced
- 1 bay leaf
- 2 teaspoons olive oil
- 1 large Portuguese chouriço or Spanish chorizo sausage, cut into ¼-inch slices
- Two 28-ounce cans red kidney beans
- 1 teaspoon paprika
- 1–2 teaspoons piri piri sauce or hot sauce (optional for added spice)
- ¼ cup water
- ½ cup red wine
- 1 cup crushed red tomatoes
- 2 teaspoons parsley flakes

Directions

1. In a large, deep saucepan on medium heat, sauté the onions, garlic, and bay leaf in the olive oil for 1–2 minutes until translucent.
2. Add the chouriço. Let the sausage cook until slightly browned.
3. Add all the remaining ingredients except for the parsley flakes. Let the chili come to a boil. Reduce the heat and simmer on low for 15–20 minutes, stirring occasionally.
4. To thicken the chili, simply remove and mash about 1 cup of the beans with a fork, stir the mash back into the chili, and continue to cook until the chili reaches your desired consistency.
5. When you're ready to serve, garnish with parsley flakes.

MARIA D. DIAS,
Ludlow, Massachusetts

Maria Dias is a cook, author, and blogger who was born in Portugal and migrated to the US as a young girl. Currently, she writes and prepares recipes for Tia Maria's Blog and her social media channels, which have received millions of international visitors. Her cookbooks *Taste Portugal 101: Easy Portuguese Recipes* and *Taste Portugal: More Easy Portuguese Recipes* have sold thousands of copies around the world. Website: www.portuguesediner.com Facebook, YouTube, Instagram: @tiamariasblog

WATCH HOW TO MAKE THIS RECIPE

Cincinnati Chili

A savory, saucy mixture of beef, beans, onions, and lots of cheese,
Cincinnati chili is always served on a pile of spaghetti.

Please note: This is not officially considered "Italian Food" by Italians.

The Recipes

Good-to-Know Info

Add in your spices when you melt any butter or oil, brown the meat, or soften the onions so they're more potent, fragrant, and get infused into the dish.

Electric Pressure Cooker Cincinnati Chili

Vegetarian Cincinnati Chili

Alligator Chili

Heather's Cincinnati Chili

Vegetarian Cincinnati Chili

Vegetarian Cincinnati chili has become a lot easier in a world where plant-based proteins are increasingly prevalent. This recipe for a vegetarian version of Cincinnati chili also has some extra veggies and a little spice for kick. No worries, though—we didn't lose any of the cheese!

COOK TIME

1 hr. 15 mins.

Makes 6 servings

INGREDIENTS

- 1 pound plant-based meat substitute
- 5 cups water
- 1 cup carrots, finely diced or shredded
- 1 tablespoon cinnamon
- 1 teaspoon cocoa powder
- ½ teaspoon cumin
- 1 teaspoon soy sauce
- ½ teaspoon onion powder
- 1 tablespoon garlic, minced

- 1½ teaspoons chili powder
- ½ teaspoon black pepper
- 1 teaspoon salt
- ¾ teaspoon allspice
- 3 ounces tomato paste
- 1½ teaspoons cider vinegar
- ½ teaspoon liquid smoke
- 2 bay leaves
- Garnish and serve with: see options in directions

Directions

1. Crumble the raw meat into the water (do not brown it beforehand) in a large pot. Mix together a bit and cook for about 5 minutes as the mixture comes to a boil/simmer.

2. Add the remaining ingredients and bring the mixture to a boil.

3. Simmer for 1 hour, stirring and mashing with a meat chopper or potato masher every 30 minutes.

4. After the chili has finished simmering, remove the bay leaves.

5. Now it's time to serve! For a three-way, serve over spaghetti and top with shredded mild cheddar cheese. For a four-way, add drained kidney beans or diced onions. For a five-way, add all of the above!

HEATHER JOHNSON,
Blanchester, Ohio

Heather Johnson is the hussy behind TheFoodHussy.com! She is a food and travel blogger that covers restaurants, recipes, and road trips. She is also a huge fan of *The Office* and is hopeful that you might see her on the Food Network (someday)!
Facebook:
@TheFoodHussy
Instagram, Pinterest:
@foodhussy

Electric Pressure Cooker Cincinnati Chili

This recipe is inspired by childhood vacation memories. We traveled to Myrtle Beach, South Carolina, every year when I was a kid, and there was this small diner named Ritzy's run by a family from Cincinnati. They served Cincinnati chili, and we absolutely loved it! We went every year and looked forward to this simple and homey meal. It was the ultimate comfort food!

COOK TIME
1 hr. 15 mins.
Makes 6 servings

INGREDIENTS

- 1 tablespoon canola oil
- 2 pounds lean ground beef
- 1 onion, finely diced
- 3 cloves garlic, minced
- 6 ounces tomato paste
- One 15-ounce can tomato sauce
- 3 cups beef stock
- 3 tablespoons chili powder
- 1 tablespoon cumin

- 2 tablespoons cocoa powder
- 1 teaspoon oregano
- ½ teaspoon cinnamon
- ½ teaspoon allspice
- ¼ teaspoon cloves
- Salt and pepper, to taste
- Garnishes: onions, cheddar cheese
- Serve with: spaghetti

Directions

1. Turn your electric pressure cooker (I use an Instant Pot®) to "sauté." Once it reads "hot," add the oil, then the ground beef and onion. Cook the beef until browned.

2. Once the meat is brown, use a potato masher or wooden spoon to break the meat up into very fine pieces. Add the garlic and cook for 1 minute, or until fragrant.

3. Turn the "sauté" function off. Add all the remaining ingredients (except for the garnishes) and stir well. Put the lid on the cooker and turn set it to "manual" or "high pressure." Set the timer to 25 minutes. Let the mixture cook. When the timer beeps, let the pressure out with a quick release.

4. Serve over spaghetti and top with desired toppings. I recommend onions and cheddar cheese.

AMANDA DORICH,
Windber, Pennsylvania

Amanda Dorich is a wife, a high school Spanish teacher, a mom to two beautiful girls, and a food blog owner. She blogs at Old House to New Home, where she shares easy, family-friendly recipes and home decor ideas from her 105-year-old historic home.
Amanda loves cooking because food truly is love!
Website: www.oldhouse tonewhome.net
Facebook, Instagram: @oldhousetonewhome

Alligator Chili

The Spanish introduced many wonderful flavors and cooking techniques to Louisiana. This vegetable chili with its green chiles and various beans is a great example of Spanish-influenced cooking. In Louisiana, alligator is often used as a substitute for other meats, giving us great dishes such as alligator sauce piquante, alligator spaghetti, fried alligator tail, and alligator sausage. Here is an old camp recipe for alligator chili that I love.

This recipe is from Chef John Folse's *After the Hunt: Louisiana's Authoritative Collection of Wild Game & Game Fish Cookery.*

COOK TIME
2 hrs.

Makes 6 servings

INGREDIENTS

- ½ cup vegetable oil
- 3 pounds alligator meat, diced
- 2 cups onions, diced
- 1 cup celery, diced
- 1 cup bell peppers, diced
- 2 tablespoons garlic, minced
- 2 tablespoons jalapeños, diced
- One 16-ounce can pinto beans
- Three 8-ounce cans tomato sauce
- 1 cup fish stock
- 1 tablespoon chili powder
- 1 teaspoon ground cumin
- Salt and cracked black pepper, to taste
- Granulated garlic, to taste
- Serve over pasta

Directions

1. In a large Dutch oven, heat the vegetable oil over medium-high heat. Add the alligator and sauté for 20 minutes to render the juices.
2. Add the onion, celery, bell peppers, minced garlic, and jalapeño. Sauté for 3–5 minutes or until the vegetables are wilted, stirring occasionally.
3. Add the pinto beans, tomato sauce, and fish stock, stirring to incorporate. Bring to a low boil, then reduce to a simmer.
4. Stir in the chili powder and cumin and cook for approximately 1 hour or until the alligator is tender, stirring occasionally.
5. Season to taste using salt, pepper, and granulated garlic.
6. Serve hot over pasta.

CHEF JOHN FOLSE,
New Orleans, Louisiana

Chef John Folse, Louisiana's Culinary Ambassador to the World, is proud to share his passion for Louisiana's swamp floor pantry around the world. As an entrepreneur, his interests range from restaurateur to manufacturer, author to educator. Some of his national and international accolades include being named Louisiana Restaurateur of the Year, National Chef of the Year, and several others. Author of 10 cookbooks, his *Can You Dig It* vegetable cookbook won the Benny Award for Best Cookbook. Folse hosts a national PBS television cooking show, *A Taste of Louisiana.* He was recently inducted into the American Academy of Chefs Culinary Hall of Fame and the Chef John Folse Culinary Institute at Nicholls State University is named in his honor.

Heather's Cincinnati Chili

I moved to Ohio 17 years ago, and my first taste of Cincinnati chili did not go well. But now I'm addicted to it! Cincinnati chili is one of the most interesting dishes you'll ever taste. It's not like any chili you've ever had—it incorporates cinnamon, cocoa powder, and tons of other spices, and it's served on spaghetti with a whole lotta cheese! I love it.

INGREDIENTS

- 3½ cups water
- 1 pound lean hamburger
- 1 teaspoon cinnamon
- 1 teaspoon cocoa powder
- ½ teaspoon ground cumin
- 1 onion, minced
- ½ teaspoon onion powder
- ½ teaspoon Worcestershire sauce
- 1 teaspoon garlic, minced
- 3 teaspoons chili powder

- ½ teaspoon black pepper
- ¼ teaspoon red pepper flakes
- 1 teaspoon salt
- ¾ teaspoon allspice
- One 3-ounce can tomato paste
- 1½ teaspoons cider vinegar
- ½ teaspoon liquid smoke
- 2 large bay leaves
- Garnish and serve with: see options in directions

Directions

1. Crumble the raw hamburger into the water (do not brown it beforehand) in a large pot. Add all the remaining ingredients and mix well.

2. Bring the mixture to a boil, then simmer for 2 hours, stirring and mashing with a potato masher every 30 minutes.

3. After the chili has finished simmering, remove the bay leaves.

4. Now it's time to serve! For a three-way, serve over spaghetti and top with shredded mild cheddar cheese. For a four-way, add drained kidney beans or diced onions. For a five-way, add all of the above! This chili can also be served over hot dogs and buns to make a Cincinnati Coney!

HEATHER JOHNSON,
Blanchester, Ohio

Heather Johnson is the hussy behind TheFoodHussy.com! She is a food and travel blogger that covers restaurants, recipes, and road trips. She is also a huge fan of *The Office* and is hopeful that you might see her on the Food Network (someday)! Facebook: @TheFoodHussy Instagram, Pinterest: @foodhussy

Turkey Chili

A spin on chili con carne, turkey chili replaces ground beef with ground turkey for a healthier option that's still full of flavor.

The Recipes

The Perfect Turkey Chili with Pasta

Slow Cooker Pumpkin Turkey Chili

Turkey and Quinoa Chili

Zero-Point Turkey Chili

Slow Cooker White Turkey Chili with Salsa Verde

This quick and easy slow cooker turkey chili is one of my favorite ways to use up leftover holiday turkey. It freezes beautifully and makes a comforting meal to come inside to on a crisp fall day.

COOK TIME
3 hrs. 15 mins.
Makes 6 servings

INGREDIENTS

- 1 tablespoon olive oil
- 1 onion, chopped
- 1 tablespoon garlic, minced
- 2 strips bacon, chopped
- Two 15-ounce cans white beans
- One 8-ounce can corn
- 2 cups leftover cooked turkey, chopped
- One 3-ounce can salsa verde
- 5 cups chicken or turkey broth
- 2 teaspoons cayenne pepper
- 1 teaspoon paprika
- 1 teaspoon dried oregano
- 1 teaspoon dried thyme
- Salt and pepper, to taste

Directions

1. Place the oil, onion, garlic, and bacon in a large slow cooker. Cover and heat on high for approximately 10 minutes, until the onions are translucent.

2. Add the beans, corn, turkey, salsa verde, and broth. Stir and cover to cook on high for about 45 minutes to 1 hour, on low for 2–3 hours. If using raw turkey, cook in a skillet before adding to slow cooker.

3. Season to taste with all the spices, and then cover and allow to cook for 15 more minutes before serving.

WATCH HOW TO MAKE THIS RECIPE

JENNIFER TAMMY,
London, Ontario, Canada

Jennifer Tammy is the blogger behind www.SugarSpiceAndGlitter.com where she shares delicious recipes, fun kids' activities, and travel tips to make family life easier and add a bit of magic to your day. Her recipes have been enjoyed by millions of people all over the world and have been featured in cookbooks and magazines, from *Southern Living* to the BBC.
Website: www.sugarspice andglitter.com
Facebook, Instagram: @sugarspiceandglitter
Pinterest: @jennifertammy
Twitter: @sugarspiceglitr

COOK TIME

6 hrs.

Makes 7+ servings

Ozzy's Beanless Chili

My chili recipe is one that I developed years ago and has won many awards within my family. I start the chili at 10 a.m. on football Sundays and it's ready for the 4 p.m. games. Instead of beans, I use corn, and you can substitute various meats. I recommend serving it with a side of fresh maple or cheddar cornbread.

INGREDIENTS

- 1 tablespoon olive oil
- 2 pounds ground turkey
- 1 yellow onion, diced
- 4 cloves garlic, sliced
- 1 yellow bell pepper, diced
- 1 orange bell pepper, diced
- 2 jalapeños with seeds, sliced
- One 15-ounce can Mexican corn
- One 14-ounce can diced tomatoes, drained
- One 29-ounce can tomato sauce
- One 6-ounce can tomato paste
- 2 tablespoons chili powder, or to taste
- 2 tablespoons cumin, or to taste
- 2 tablespoons paprika
- Salt and pepper, to taste
- 1 tablespoon honey (optional)
- Garnishes: freshly grated cheese, sour cream
- Serve with maple or cheddar cornbread

Directions

1. Heat the pan to medium-high heat. Add the olive oil and meat. Cook until brown.
2. Drain the meat of grease and add all the vegetables—do not clean the pot. Cook until just tender.
3. Add the meat back to pot. Add all the canned items to the pot and stir until everything is together like one happy family.
4. Add the seasonings and stir. Adjust the spices to taste. Add the honey to offset the heat (if you're into that).
5. Serve on homemade cornbread with freshly grated cheese and sour cream.

JASON OSTROUT,
New Britain, Connecticut

Jason Ostrout is a husband and father of three wonderful kids. When he is not making chili on football Sundays, he is making great coffee, going to concerts, and traveling to every MLB baseball stadium with his wife. Instagram: @newenglandcoffeeguy

Chili Recipe Awards

- **Ostrout Family Chili Cook-Off, 3 years in a row.**

123

Capobianco Turkey Chili

This super-simple, family-friendly turkey chili is a hit in my house from my kids to my husband. It's not too spicy, but it has just the right amount of kick. It's perfect for an on-the-go family meal. Include some fresh Italian bread (crunchy, of course) to dunk!

COOK TIME

1 hr.

Makes 6 servings

INGREDIENTS

- 2 teaspoons olive oil
- 1 yellow onion, chopped
- 5 gloves garlic, minced
- 1 medium red bell pepper, chopped
- 1 medium green bell pepper, chopped
- 1 pound lean turkey, ground
- 4 tablespoons chili powder
- 2 teaspoons ground cumin
- 1 teaspoon dried oregano
- ¼ teaspoon cayenne pepper
- ½ teaspoon salt, or to taste
- One 28-ounce can diced or crushed tomatoes
- 1¼ cups chicken stock
- Two 15-ounce cans dark kidney beans, drained and rinsed
- One 15-ounce can sweet corn, drained and rinsed
- Garnishes: avocado, cheese, sour cream, tortilla strips

Directions

1. Heat the oil in a large pot over medium-high heat. Add the onion, garlic, and chopped peppers. Sauté for 5–7 minutes, stirring frequently.
2. Add the ground turkey and break it up as it cooks. Cook until it's no longer pink.
3. Add the chili powder, cumin, oregano, cayenne pepper, and salt. Stir.
4. Add the tomatoes, chicken stock, beans, and corn. Bring the mixture to a boil.
5. Reduce the heat and simmer for about 30–45 minutes or until the chili thickens and the flavors come together. Adjust the seasonings to taste.
6. Garnish as desired or serve with bread to dunk.

AMANDA CAPOBIANCO,
Cranston, Rhode Island

Amanda Capobianco is a mom of two wonderful children, KJ and Evelina. Her husband, Kenny, and their family reside in Cranston, RI. They are blessed with a beautiful, healthy family and are truly looking forward to each day we have with one another. Amanda likes cooking quick, simple, and tasty meals that her whole family can enjoy. Her turkey chili is a great meal for any night of the week!

COOK TIME
4 hrs. 15 mins.
Makes 6 servings

Slow Cooker Pumpkin Turkey Chili

This chili is *the* fall comfort food you need to turn to when the weather turns cool. Full of pumpkin, warming spices, and ground turkey, this is a lightened-up chili that you won't be able to get enough of. It tastes like a bite of fall in every spoonful! It's the simplest recipe to make in the slow cooker, and if you have an electric pressure cooker, I swear it's that much easier.

INGREDIENTS

- ½ teaspoon olive oil
- Half of 1 white onion, diced
- 1 pound ground turkey
- One 16-ounce can hot chili beans
- One 16-ounce can kidney beans
- One 14.5-ounce can fire-roasted tomatoes
- ⅓ cup tomato paste
- ¼ cup pumpkin purée
- 1⅓ cups chicken stock
- 1 teaspoon salt

- 1 teaspoon pepper
- 1 teaspoon cocoa powder
- 1 teaspoon chili powder
- ½ teaspoon paprika
- ¼ teaspoon cayenne pepper
- ½ teaspoon garlic powder
- ½ teaspoon onion powder
- ¼ teaspoon cinnamon
- 1 teaspoon pumpkin spice
- Garnishes: sour cream, shredded sharp cheddar cheese, cilantro

Directions

1. In a large skillet, heat the olive oil over medium-high heat. Once the oil is hot, add the diced onions and cook until they begin to soften, approximately 3 minutes.
2. Add the turkey and cook until browned, approximately 4–5 minutes.
3. Remove the mixture from the heat and add it to a slow cooker.
4. Add the remaining ingredients to the slow cooker. Stir to combine. Slow cook on high for 4 hours. If instead you're using an electric pressure cooker (I use an Instant Pot®), cook on "manual" on "high" for 25 minutes. Natural release.
5. Serve warm.

MEGHAN YAGER,
Denver, Colorado

Food addict turned food blogger, Meghan Yager is the author of Cake 'n Knife where she teaches readers to celebrate life's everyday moments with her favorite recipes. With a focus on seasonal ingredients and adventurous flavors, she imparts her years of experience in the kitchen with a passion that brings everyone to the table. Meghan has been featured on Buzzfeed, *The Huffington Post, Good Housekeeping, Oprah Daily, Southern Living,* and more.
Website: www.caken knife.com
Facebook, Instagram, Pinterest, TikTok: @cakenknife

2Chefs Turkey Chili

As married private chefs, when we're cooking for families, when we're cooking for families, we only have a few hours in their home to prepare all of our menu items, so any soup or chili has to have a fast cook time. We developed this quick chili recipe so that it has a ton of flavor and is super healthy with lots of beans, veggies, and just the right amount of chili spice without being too spicy for the kiddos. It continues to be one of our most highly requested recipes from all our clients.

COOK TIME

1 hr. 30 mins.

Makes 4 servings

INGREDIENTS

- 1 tablespoon olive oil
- 1 red onion, finely diced
- 1 pound ground turkey
- 2 cloves garlic, minced
- 1 red bell pepper, medium diced
- 3 cups fresh corn kernels, cut off the cob (reserve the cobs on the side)
- 2 teaspoons cumin
- 1 teaspoon smoked paprika
- 2 teaspoons chili powder

- 2½ teaspoons salt
- ½ teaspoon chipotle powder
- 4 cups chicken broth
- One 14.5-ounce can diced tomatoes
- 2 large limes, zest and juice
- One 15-ounce can black beans
- One 15-ounce can kidney beans

Directions

1. Place a pot over medium-high heat. Add the olive oil and onion and sauté for 3 minutes.
2. Add the turkey and sauté for 5 minutes.
3. Add the garlic, bell pepper, corn, cumin, smoked paprika, chili powder, salt, and chipotle powder. Sauté for 5 minutes.
4. Stir in the chicken broth, tomatoes, lime juice and zest, kidney beans, black beans, and corn cobs. Return to a boil, then lower the heat to a simmer and simmer for 60 minutes.
5. Discard the corn cobs. Using an immersion blender, give the chili a few quick pulses to thicken it, then mix well with a spoon.

WATCH HOW TO MAKE THIS RECIPE

CHEF MARA AND RYAN WOLLEN,
Austin, Texas

2Chefs are a husband-and-wife private chef team who prepare healthy weekly meals for their clients using quality seasonal ingredients. Additionally, they teach online cooking classes, for all levels of skill, from beginners seeking some cooking basics to seasoned home cooks who are looking for pro tips to up their game.
Instagram, Facebook: 2chefs.food
YouTube: Cooking with 2chefs

COOK TIME
30 mins.
Makes 6 servings

Turkey and Quinoa Chili

This recipe is packed with hearty black beans, delicious veggies, lean ground turkey, and a little quinoa. I created it because I was looking for a healthier version of chili than my normal, easy chili recipe.

INGREDIENTS

- 1 tablespoon vegetable oil
- 1 small onion, finely diced
- One 16-ounce package lean ground turkey
- 3 cloves garlic, minced
- 1 tablespoon chili powder
- 1 tablespoon ground cumin
- 3 cups low-sodium chicken broth
- One 14.5-ounce can diced tomatoes, undrained
- One 16-ounce can black beans, drained and rinsed
- One 10-ounce can mild diced tomatoes and green chiles, undrained (I use Rotel®)
- ½ cup dry (uncooked) quinoa
- Garnishes: chopped avocado, lime wedges, plain yogurt or sour cream, chopped fresh cilantro

Directions

1. Add the oil and onion to a pot and cook over medium heat until the onion is translucent and softened.
2. Add in the turkey, garlic, chili powder, and cumin. Cook the turkey as specified on the package. Always cook to well-done: 165 degrees Fahrenheit as measured by a meat thermometer.
3. Add the broth, tomatoes, beans, diced tomatoes and green chiles, and quinoa. Then simmer the mixture for about 30 minutes, until the quinoa cooks all the way.
4. This chili will thicken over time. Ladle the chili into bowls and serve with your desired toppings.

JENNIFER SIKORA,
Calvert City, Kentucky

Jennifer Sikora is a food and travel blogger living her best life in Western Kentucky. She spends her days making delicious recipes to share with her friends and family. Her recipes are inspired by her Southern background, where she learned that a sprinkle of this and a pinch of that can make any dish sing. When Jennifer is not in the kitchen cooking, you can find her exploring and traveling with her family and her two Australian Shepherds.
Website: www.jenaround theworld.com
Instagram: @JenniferSikora
Facebook: @Jen AroundTheWorld

The Perfect Turkey Chili with Pasta

This is my go-to chili recipe and has been a fall tradition in my family for years! It is my all-time favorite comfort food. The cinnamon always catches people by surprise in the best way. I think it is the perfect complement to this classic dish. Not only is this chili cozy and warm, but it also freezes well and makes amazing leftovers!

COOK TIME
45 mins.
Makes 5 servings

INGREDIENTS

- 1 pound ground turkey
- 1 large onion, chopped
- 4 tablespoons chili powder
- 3 teaspoons cumin
- 2 teaspoons cayenne pepper
- 1 teaspoon oregano
- 2 teaspoons paprika
- 2 teaspoons red pepper flakes (optional if you want it spicier)
- ½ teaspoon cinnamon

- 1 teaspoon sea salt, plus more as needed
- 1 teaspoon black pepper
- 4 cloves garlic, minced
- 4 cups beef bone broth
- One 18-ounce jar crushed tomatoes
- Two 15-ounce cans kidney beans, drained
- 1 pound gluten-free shell pasta

Directions

1. In a large soup pot over medium-high heat, add the ground turkey, onion, and all the spices. Break apart the meat with a wooden spoon and cook until the turkey is browned.

2. Add the garlic and sauté for 30 seconds, then pour in the bone broth and crushed tomatoes. Bring to a boil.

3. Reduce the heat to low and cook for 20 minutes, covered.

4. Add the kidney beans and adjust the seasoning as needed. Simmer for an additional 20 minutes, until the chili starts to thicken.

5. While the chili is simmering, cook the shell pasta. Serve the chili with the pasta and enjoy!

ASHLEY ROMEO,
Las Vegas, Nevada

Ashley Romeo is an Integrative Health Coach born and raised in Las Vegas, Nevada. She has always had a passion for health and wellness, both in and out of the kitchen. She started Wellness Kitchen Makeover in 2018 in hopes of changing the conversation around food and to give people the tools they need to build healthy, sustainable habits. Ashley believes that eating delicious, nutrient-dense food is one of the highest forms of self-care. Instagram @ashromeo

Best Turkey Chili Ever

I am a mom to "5 under 5," so I do not have a ton of time. That is why I love this chili recipe that my grandmother taught me. It's simple and yummy! Plus, you can keep it on low heat and let it simmer all day. I use a Dutch oven on the stovetop. This recipe is also naturally gluten free.

COOK TIME

2 hrs.

Makes 6 servings

INGREDIENTS

- 3 tablespoons olive oil
- 2 cloves garlic, minced
- 1 pound ground turkey
- 1 red bell pepper, chopped
- 5 tablespoons chili powder
- 2 teaspoons ground cumin
- 1 teaspoon dried oregano
- ½ teaspoon cayenne pepper
- ½ teaspoon salt
- ½ teaspoon pepper
- One 28-ounce can diced tomatoes; do not drain
- 1½ cups chicken broth
- One 15-ounce can black beans, rinsed
- One 15-ounce can red kidney beans, rinsed
- One 14.5-ounce can corn
- Garnishes: cheese, avocado, cilantro, sour cream

Directions

1. In a large pot or Dutch oven, add the oil over medium heat. Add in the garlic, then the turkey. Cook until the meat is done.

2. Add in all the rest of the ingredients except the garnishes. Lower the heat to low and cover. Cook for 1 hour. If you want your chili to be thicker, leave uncovered instead.

3. Serve with toppings and enjoy.

SARA LUNDBERG,
Portland, Oregon

Sara Lundberg is a cookbook author and founder of the lifestyle blog BudgetSavvyDiva.com. She is a wife and a mother to five children, and she loves cooking and getting messy in the kitchen with her two oldest.
Facebook: @thebudgetsavvydiva
Instagram, TikTok: @budgetsavvydiva

COOK TIME
45 mins.

Makes 4 servings

Zero-Point Turkey Chili

This turkey chili packs a lot of flavor and so many tastes in each bite—but the best part is that it has zero points. Now what does that mean? If you're on Weight Watchers, it means you're very happy! If you're not, it basically means eat up, because it's really healthy!

INGREDIENTS

- 1 pound fat-free ground turkey breast
- 1 yellow onion, diced
- 1 green bell pepper, diced
- 1 package taco seasoning
- 1 tablespoon garlic, minced
- 1 tablespoon salt
- One 15-ounce can kidney beans, drained
- One 15-ounce can black beans, drained
- One 14.5-ounce can fire-roasted diced tomatoes
- One 4-ounce can diced green chiles
- One 8-ounce can tomato sauce
- One 15.25-ounce can corn, drained
- Garnishes: Greek yogurt, cilantro

Directions

1. Brown the ground turkey, onion, and green pepper in a large pot until cooked through.
2. Add the taco seasoning, garlic, and salt, and stir until all the meat is coated.
3. Add all the remaining ingredients and stir. Cook over medium heat, simmering, for 15 minutes.
4. When ready to serve, top with a dollop of plain Greek yogurt and cilantro if desired.

WATCH HOW TO MAKE THIS RECIPE

HEATHER JOHNSON,
Blanchester, Ohio

Heather Johnson is the hussy behind TheFoodHussy.com! She is a food and travel blogger that covers restaurants, recipes, and road trips. She is also a huge fan of *The Office* and is hopeful that you might see her on the Food Network (someday)! Facebook: @TheFoodHussy Instagram, Pinterest: @foodhussy

Slow Cooker Turkey Pumpkin Chili

My chili is easy to make and a tasty mix of sweet and savory. It's the first thing I want to make when fall arrives. I saw a few recipes online for turkey chili that were too spicy or too sweet, so this is the one I created on my own. It's important to get the fall spices in!

COOK TIME
2 hrs.
Makes 6 servings

INGREDIENTS

- 1 pound ground turkey
- ½ cup onion
- One 15-ounce can diced tomatoes
- One 15-ounce can pumpkin purée
- One 16-ounce can kidney beans
- 2 teaspoons chili powder
- ¼ cup brown sugar
- Dash salt
- 1 teaspoon pumpkin pie spice

Directions

1. Turn the slow cooker to high and allow it to heat up for 10 minutes.
2. Add the turkey and onion to the slow cooker. Cook for 15 minutes.
3. Break the turkey up into chunks—it will be partially browned.
4. Add the remaining ingredients to the slow cooker in order. Stir to mix everything.
5. Cook the chili on high for 2 hours or low for 4 hours.

MARCIA FROST,
Champaign, Illinois

Marcia Frost is a lifestyle journalist who slowed down her food and wine travel when faced with multiple chronic illnesses. She still loves to cook and has done food demonstrations on *CI Living*, an afternoon lifestyle show on her local CBS affiliate. Her articles have appeared in *The Daily Meal*, *USA Today*, and *Yahoo!*. She currently writes regularly for *Medium*. Facebook, Twitter, Instagram: @Spiritstraveler

COOK TIME
30 mins.
Makes 4 servings

Signature Turkey Chili

The very first meal I ever made was chili. My parents taught me at a very young age how to cook and enjoy being in the kitchen. I have entered more chili cook-offs than I can count, including some I have personally hosted. I'm not a chef, nor have I ever taken culinary classes—everything I've learned has been through trial and error and taste testing. This recipe is simple and delicious, but, more importantly, it has been approved by the pickiest of eaters!

INGREDIENTS

- 1 tablespoon olive oil
- 1 yellow onion, finely diced
- 2 tablespoons garlic, minced
- 1 green pepper, finely diced
- 1 pound lean ground turkey or beef
- One 16-ounce can mild chili beans, do not drain
- Two 14.5-ounce cans petite diced tomatoes, do not drain
- 2 cups low-sodium tomato juice
- ½ teaspoon Cajun seasoning
- 2 tablespoons pure maple syrup
- 4 teaspoons chili powder
- ½ teaspoon cayenne pepper
- ½ tablespoon onion powder
- ½ tablespoon garlic powder
- 1 teaspoon cumin
- ¼ teaspoon black pepper

Directions

1. Heat a large skillet with olive oil. Add the onion, garlic, and green pepper. Cook until the veggies are soft and the onion is translucent.

2. Add the ground turkey or beef to the skillet. Cook until brown and crumbled. Drain the excess grease.

3. In a large stockpot or slow cooker, place the meat mixture. Add all the remaining ingredients. If you prefer, you can replace the seasoning mix (the chili powder through the black pepper) with a store-bought chili seasoning mix instead, such as McCormick® Mild Chili Seasoning.

4. If you're using a slow cooker, cook on high for 2–4 hours or low for 6–8 hours. This is the method I recommend. If you're cooking on the stovetop in a pot, bring the chili to a boil and allow it to simmer for 30 minutes.

SHANNON BURRS,
Madison, Wisconsin

Shannon is an American cookbook author, food blogger, and podcast host. She is a Wisconsin native with a love for all things cheese and dairy. Shannon aims to simplify recipes while maintaining a balance between healthy eating and delicious food. She published her first book *A Healthy Balance: In Life and In the Kitchen* in 2021 and is currently working on her second book. Shannon's chili has earned several first-place awards and a people's choice award.
Website: www.faith foodfarm.com
Facebook, Instagram, Pinterest, TikTok: @faith.food.farm

Chili Recipe Awards

- **Best Chili Award (4)**
- **People's Choice Award**

White Bean Turkey Chili

This recipe is so easy and made with simple ingredients. Double the amount of beans and use veggie broth for a vegan version of this chili! It incorporates the perfect blend of flavors and is loved by kids and adults alike. My daughter Becca and I recently made it on our livestream show *Cooking with Katie & Becca*, and she and her friends devoured it after we wrapped! This recipe was submitted by Cynthia Sutter, founder and editor of Spirited Table®, which provides seasonal and holiday lifestyle tips, epicurean news, and recipes.

COOK TIME
2+ hrs.

Makes 6 servings

INGREDIENTS

- 2 tablespoons extra virgin olive oil
- 1 clove garlic, minced
- 1 cup white onion, chopped
- 3 poblanos, ribs removed, seeded, and finely chopped
- 1 pound ground turkey
- 1 teaspoon salt
- 1 teaspoon ground cumin
- ¾ teaspoon ground oregano
- ½ teaspoon ground coriander

- ½ ground black pepper
- ½ teaspoon cayenne pepper
- 2 celery stalks, chopped
- Two 15-ounce cans white beans (cannellini or white kidney), drained and rinsed
- One 15-ounce can white or yellow hominy, drained and rinsed
- 4 cups chicken broth
- Garnishes: sour cream, fresh cilantro, lime wedges, avocado cubes, chopped scallions, shredded cheese

Directions

1. Heat a pot over medium-high heat. Add the oil and swirl to coat. Add the garlic and onions and sauté until fragrant and translucent, about 2–3 minutes.

2. Add the poblanos, turkey, salt, cumin, oregano, coriander, black pepper, and cayenne pepper. Break up the turkey with a spatula and sauté for 3–4 minutes until it is no longer pink.

3. Add the celery and sauté for 4–5 minutes.

4. Stir in the beans, hominy, and broth. Bring the mixture to a boil over high heat. Reduce the heat to medium and allow the mixture to boil for 50–75 minutes or until most of the liquid is reduced.

5. Lower the heat and allow to simmer for 10 minutes.

6. Serve immediately with your desired toppings.

KATIE CHIN

Celebrity Chef Katie Chin is an award-winning cookbook author, caterer, blogger, and culinary ambassador to the National Pediatric Cancer Foundation. Katie has been featured in many publications, such as *O* magazine, *Cooking Light*, *Bon Appetit*, *Elle*, *Real Simple*, *The Wall Street Journal*, HuffPost, and *Family Circle*. Her numerous appearances on national television include *Live with Kelly & Ryan*, *The Real*, *The Today Show*, Hallmark Channel, Cooking Channel, *Cutthroat Kitchen*, *Beat Bobby Flay*, ABC's *Localish*, and *Iron Chef America*. In 2013, Katie was a featured chef at the annual Easter Egg Roll at the White House.

COOK TIME

2 hrs. 30 mins.

Makes 7+ servings

Chipotle Apple Turkey Chili

Can I tell you a secret? I made this chili for my husband (a self-proclaimed chili expert as a winner of at least one chili cook-off), and he couldn't tell it was turkey chili. Nor could he tell it had apples in it. He gave it a thumbs-up and still believes it was made with beef!

INGREDIENTS

- 1 tablespoon olive oil or avocado oil
- 1 pound ground turkey
- 4 cloves garlic, minced
- 1 large onion, diced
- 1 bell pepper (any color), diced
- 1 medium apple, cored and diced
- 2 cups beef broth
- 2 tablespoons apple cider vinegar
- 3 tablespoons chili powder
- 2 teaspoons ground cumin
- 1 teaspoon smoked paprika
- 1½ teaspoons chipotle powder
- 1 teaspoon Mexican oregano
- ½ teaspoon ground nutmeg
- ½ teaspoon salt
- One 15-ounce can black beans, drained
- One 15-ounce can kidney beans, drained

Directions

1. Heat the oil in a large pot over medium-high heat.
2. Add the ground turkey and cook until browned, using a wooden spoon to break the turkey into small pieces.
3. Add the garlic, onions, bell pepper, and apple. Cook, stirring, until the vegetables are softened.
4. Add the remaining ingredients and stir well to combine.
5. Cover the pot and reduce the heat to low. Simmer the chili, stirring every once in a while, until it has thickened and the vegetables are cooked down.
6. Serve with any toppings you like.

KALEIGH MCMORDIE,
Abilene, Texas

Kaleigh McMordie is a registered dietitian, recipe developer, food photographer, and creator of the blog Lively Table. She is passionate about making healthy eating delicious and approachable. She lives in west Texas where she is always cooking up something new for her husband and two young daughters. Website: www.livelytable.com Facebook, Instagram, Pinterest, Twitter: @livelytable

Vegetarian Chili

Options abound—there are many ways to make chili without meat. Some use sweet potatoes or beans in place of meat. You'll also find a number of vegan options in this section, indicated by the 🌱.

The Recipes

White Bean Swamp Chili

Vegan Pumpkin Lentil
Quinoa Chili

Veggie Chili with
Marinara Sauce

Three Bean Chili

2Chefs Vegan Chili

Working as private chefs, we specialize in cooking menus with each client's likes, dislikes, and dietary needs in mind. Some of our clients are vegetarian or vegan, so we've created this vegan chili to please everyone. This recipe is so delicious that even our meat-loving clients don't notice that it's completely meat-free, since the quinoa adds that thick richness of a protein-based chili. Serve this on your next meatless Monday or on any cold night of the week.

COOK TIME
1 hr. 30 mins.
Makes 4 servings

INGREDIENTS

- 1 tablespoon olive oil
- 1 red onion, finely diced
- 2 cloves garlic, minced
- 1 red bell pepper, medium diced
- 3 cups fresh corn kernels, cut off the cob (about 4 ears) (reserve the cobs on the side)
- 2 teaspoons cumin
- 1 teaspoon smoked paprika
- 2 teaspoons chili powder
- 2½ teaspoons salt
- ½ teaspoon chipotle powder
- 4 cups vegetable broth
- One 14.5-ounce can diced organic tomatoes
- 2 large limes, zest and juice
- One 15-ounce can kidney beans
- One 15-ounce can black beans
- 3 cups cooked quinoa
- Garnishes: cilantro, scallions

Directions

1. Heat a pot over medium-high heat. Add the olive oil and onion and sauté for 3 minutes.

2. Add the garlic, bell pepper, corn, cumin, smoked paprika, chili powder, salt, and chipotle powder. Sauté for 5 minutes.

3. Add the vegetable broth, tomatoes, lime juice and zest, kidney beans, black beans, and corn cobs and stir it all together. Return the mixture to a boil, then lower the heat to a simmer and simmer the chili on low for 60 minutes.

4. Discard the corn cobs, then stir in the quinoa. If desired, garnish with cilantro and scallions.

WATCH HOW TO MAKE THIS RECIPE

CHEFS MARA AND RYAN WOLLEN,
Austin, Texas

2Chefs are a husband-and-wife private chef team who prepare healthy weekly meals for their clients using quality seasonal ingredients. Additionally, they teach online cooking classes, for all levels of skill, from beginners seeking some cooking basics to seasoned home cooks who are looking for pro tips to up their game. Facebook, Instagram: 2chefs.food YouTube: Cooking with 2chefs

COOK TIME

2 hrs.

Makes 7+ servings

Veggie Chili Face Melter

Of all my favorite recipes I've perfected over the last 15 years producing The Takedown, I'm guessing veggie chili is the least respected. Some people will seriously lay an egg if chili's not a straight-up bowl of red (meat, chiles, garlic, cumin, and bacon fat). I've explored tons of different chile combinations, and I think maybe I've nailed it thanks to the super sweet Mexican market down the street from me that provides me with all the best ingredients. Chili, to me, is a kitchen sink recipe—and my veggie chili will melt your face.

INGREDIENTS

- 3 puya chiles (substitute guajillo chiles if needed)
- 3 pasilla chiles (substitute guajillo chiles if needed)
- 2 cups vegetable stock, divided
- 5 tablespoons vegetable oil
- 1 cup onions, finely chopped
- 6 cloves garlic, crushed
- 1 cup carrots, chopped
- 1 red bell pepper, diced
- 1 cup full-bodied red wine
- 1 cup dry (uncooked) red lentils
- 1 tablespoon kosher salt
- 2 teaspoons ground cumin
- 2 teaspoons Mexican oregano
- 1 tablespoon honey
- 2 cups cooked kidney beans
- 2 cups dry (uncooked) hominy
- 1 teaspoon freshly ground black pepper
- 1 tablespoon Carolina reaper sauce, to taste

Directions

1. Soak the chiles for 30 minutes in boiled water, then stem and seed them. Purée the chiles with 1 cup of vegetable stock and set aside.
2. In a large pot or Dutch oven, heat the oil, sauté the onions for 10 minutes, and then add the garlic and cook for another 3 minutes.
3. Add the carrots and red bell pepper and cook for another 5 minutes.
4. Add the chile purée, red wine, remaining vegetable stock, lentils, salt, cumin, oregano, and honey. Cook for 10 minutes.
5. Add the beans and hominy and cook for 15 minutes on low heat.
6. Finish with the black pepper and Carolina reaper sauce to taste.

MATT TIMMS,
Brooklyn, New York

Matt Timms brings home cooks together to compete at huge parties called "Takedowns" in cities across the country. Chili, Mac and Cheeze, Food on a Stick Takedowns . . . whatever. The emphasis is always on home cooking, with all its beautiful perfections and imperfections. Matt brings the party, while real people fight for prizes. He personally designed a ton of recipes, too, and thought he'd give you his favorite veggie chili. Think of chili as a diabolical adventure: throw the kitchen sink in a pot and don't fuss about it like a dang chemistry experiment. It better be spicy, though, and this chile combo is proven yummers. He also paints little paintings of cats. Instagram: @thetakedowns, @allthebadcats

Good-to-Know Info

The U.S. president who famously loved chili the most was Lyndon B. Johnson.

WATCH HOW I SAUTÉ GREEN BELL PEPPERS, ONIONS, AND GARLIC HERE.

VEGAN

White Bean Swamp Chili

Warm and comforting food has always been a staple when the seasons begin to change and the cold weather sets in. One of my favorite meals to eat during this time, especially when I was back home in Ohio, is a big bowl of chili! This recipe is filled with plant-based ingredients, including white beans, which are loaded with cancer-fighting dietary fibers, have a low glycemic index, and are a great source of protein as well as antioxidants. This meal will fuel you up in more ways than one, so give it a try when the weather turns chilly.

COOK TIME
2 hrs.
Makes 5 servings

INGREDIENTS

- ¼ cup olive oil
- 1 large white onion, chopped
- 6–8 cloves garlic, chopped
- 1 cup tomato sauce
- ½ cup tomato paste
- 1½ cups cooked cannellini beans, whole
- 1½ cups cooked navy beans, whole
- 1¾ cups cooked cannellini beans, puréed
- 2½ cups tomatoes, diced
- 2 cups whole corn

- 1 cup filtered water
- 1 tablespoon curry powder
- 2 teaspoons cayenne pepper
- 2 teaspoons ground coriander
- 4 tablespoons chili powder
- ½ teaspoon allspice
- 2–3 teaspoons Himalayan fine pink salt (I use Vitacost®)
- ¼ teaspoon ground black pepper (I use Spicely® Organics)
- 1 tablespoon organic sugar
- Garnishes: sour cream, chives, vegan cheddar cheese

Directions

1. In a large pot on medium heat, add the oil, onions, and garlic. Sauté until tender.

2. Add the tomato sauce, paste, beans, puréed beans, diced tomatoes, corn, water, and all spices. Bring to a slight boil and reduce the heat to low.

3. Cook for 1–2 hours minimum; I cook mine for 3 hours.

4. Serve topped with sour cream and chives or cheddar cheese of choice.

RYAN SHEPARD,
Boca Raton, Florida

Ryan, a self-made plant-based chef, can often be found experimenting in the kitchen with colorful whole-food ingredients. He enjoys promoting a healthy lifestyle and sharing accessible, vegan-friendly recipes (inspired by popular dishes from around the world) with the masses. When the apron's off, he's likely at the beach or kickin' it with close friends. Visit www.theveganrhino.com or follow him on Instagram @theveganrhino for tasty finds, eco-friendly tips, and updates on his upcoming cookbook, *From Roots to the Kitchen.*
Website: www.thevegan rhino.com
Instagram: @theveganrhino

Three Bean Chili

COOK TIME

2 hrs. 30 mins.

Makes 5 servings

This three-bean chili is great for serving to guests with different dietary preferences and is a splendid way to stretch your budget. Enjoy a bowl as is or use it as a topping for your favorite chili-garnished recipes.

INGREDIENTS

- 1 cup dry (uncooked) black beans
- 1 cup dry (uncooked) kidney beans
- 1 cup dry (uncooked) pinto beans
- 1 tablespoon cooking oil
- 1 onion, diced
- 2 jalapeños, diced, seeded if desired
- 4 cloves garlic, smashed and sliced
- 2–3 tablespoons southwestern seasoning
- 1 tablespoon Worcestershire sauce
- 3–4 cups vegetable broth or water
- One 32-ounce can tomatoes

Directions

1. Rinse the beans and combine in a large stockpot. Cover with water and bring to a boil over high heat.
2. Reduce the heat to medium-low and simmer the beans for 1 hour to 1 hour 30 minutes, until the beans are tender. Drain and rinse the beans and clean out the stockpot.
3. Place the oil in the stockpot and set over medium heat. Once the oil is hot, add the onion and diced jalapeños and cook for 3 minutes.
4. Add the garlic and continue cooking for 1 minute, stirring occasionally.
5. Add the cooked beans, seasoning, Worcestershire sauce, vegetable broth, and tomatoes. Increase the heat to medium-high and bring to a boil.
6. Reduce the heat to medium-low and cover, simmering, for 1 hour until all liquid is absorbed, stirring occasionally.

JENNIFER TAMMY,
London, Ontario, Canada

Jennifer Tammy is the blogger behind www.SugarSpiceAndGlitter.com where she shares delicious recipes, fun kids' activities, and travel tips to make family life easier and add a bit of magic to your day. Her recipes have been enjoyed by millions of people all over the world and have been featured in cookbooks and magazines, from *Southern Living* to the BBC.

Website: www.sugarspice andglitter.com
Facebook, Instagram: @sugarspiceandglitter
Pinterest: @jennifertammy
Twitter: @sugarspiceglitr

The Real Deal Red Chili

COOK TIME
3 hrs. 30 mins.

Makes 3 servings

This spin on an authentic Texas red chili is made with fresh cayenne peppers, mushrooms for the mock "meat," and tons of other seasonings and flavors. You'll also notice that I chose not to use beans! I've always been curious to see what an "authentic" chili would be like without the beans, so I decided to give it a go. (You can always add a cup of beans and corn to this recipe if desired, though!)

INGREDIENTS

- 6–8 red cayenne peppers
- 1½ tablespoons chili powder
- 1 tablespoon cumin
- ½ teaspoon ground black pepper
- 3 cloves garlic, minced
- 1 tablespoon tomato paste
- 2 cups vegetable stock
- 2 cups filtered water
- 2 tablespoons corn flour
- 1½ tablespoons brown sugar
- 1½ tablespoons white vinegar
- 4 tablespoons avocado oil
- ½ cup onion, finely chopped
- 2 pounds baby bella mushrooms, cubed
- 3–4 tablespoons hemp seeds
- 1 teaspoon Himalayan fine pink salt (I use Vitacost®)
- Garnishes: vegan sour cream, green onions, vegan cheese

Directions

1. Preheat the oven to 400 degrees Fahrenheit. Roast the cayenne peppers in the oven for 25–30 minutes, just until the outsides begin to blacken.

2. While wearing gloves, place the cayenne peppers in a bowl and cover with plastic wrap for 3–5 minutes. The trapped steam will help the skin loosen up. Remove the skin, de-seed, and toss the scraps away.

3. In a blender, combine the cayenne peppers, chili powder, cumin, pepper, garlic, tomato paste, vegetable stock, water, flour, brown sugar, hemp seeds, salt, and vinegar. Pulse until well mixed and combined. Set aside.

4. In a large pot, add the oil with the onions and turn to medium-high heat. Sauté for 3–5 minutes until translucent.

5. Add the mushrooms to the pan and cook for an additional 5 minutes.

6. Pour in the chili sauce mixture and bring to a boil. Reduce to a simmer on low heat, cover, and cook for 2 hours 30 minutes to 3 hours, stirring frequently.

7. Serve plain or top with vegan sour cream, green onions, and vegan cheese.

RYAN SHEPARD,
Boca Raton, Florida

Ryan, a self-made plant-based chef, can often be found experimenting in the kitchen with colorful whole-food ingredients. He enjoys promoting a healthy lifestyle and sharing accessible, vegan-friendly recipes (inspired by popular dishes from around the world) with the masses. When the apron's off, he's likely at the beach or kickin' it with close friends. Visit www.theveganrhino.com or follow him on Instagram @theveganrhino for tasty finds, eco-friendly tips, and updates on his upcoming cookbook, *From Roots to the Kitchen*.
Website: www.theveganrhino.com
Instagram: @theveganrhino

COOK TIME
45 mins.
Makes 6 servings

Vegan Harvest Chili

VEGAN

My chili is packed with veggies, pumpkin, and cozy fall flavors! It makes a super-healthy but filling meal for the whole family. The recipe comes together in less than 40 minutes with mostly low-cost pantry ingredients. I developed this recipe inspired by the famous Trader Joe's® Harvest Chili. As a bonus, this chili costs just about $2 per serving!

INGREDIENTS

- 2 tablespoons olive oil
- 1 small white onion, diced
- 1 medium sweet potato, diced
- 4 cloves garlic, minced
- 2 cups cauliflower, chopped
- One 14-ounce can black beans
- One 14-ounce can kidney beans
- 1 cup pumpkin purée
- One 14-ounce can crushed tomatoes
- 1 teaspoon sea salt
- 1 teaspoon chili powder (chipotle powder is best)
- 1 teaspoon oregano
- ½ teaspoon cumin
- ½ teaspoon maple syrup
- ¼–½ teaspoon pumpkin pie spice
- ⅛–¼ teaspoon cayenne pepper
- 1 cup cooked quinoa

Directions

1. Put a large soup pot over medium-high heat. Add the olive oil when it's hot, then add the onion and sweet potato. Sauté for 2 minutes, then add the garlic and cauliflower and stir.

2. Add the black beans and kidney beans (not drained), followed by the pumpkin, tomatoes, salt, chili powder, oregano, cumin, maple syrup, pumpkin pie spice, and cayenne. Stir well and reduce to medium-low heat. Simmer for 20 minutes.

3. Add the quinoa. Taste and adjust the spices if needed. Simmer for 10 more minutes.

MEGAN SADD,
Los Angeles, California

Megan Sadd is an LA-based artist and the author of *30-Minute Vegan Dinners* and *Vegan YUM*. She's also the founder of Carrots & Flowers, a popular plant-based lifestyle blog, and Lily's Show, a bitcoin podcast. Her work has been featured in *Forbes*, *The Washington Post*, *Women's Health*, *THRIVE Magazine*, and many more.
Facebook, Instagram: @carrotsandflowers
Tiktok: @MeganSadd
Twitter: @micro_d0se

Quick Vegetarian Chili

Chili is a favorite lunch of mine throughout the fall and winter, but I find it a little heavy sometimes, even when it's made with ground chicken instead of beef. This meatless version is super quick to make and doesn't skimp on taste. In fact, many of my taste testers didn't even seem to notice the absence of meat, and my vegetarian friends love it too. I like to make it ahead of time and let the flavors blend for a day or two in the fridge before serving; it freezes beautifully as well.

COOK TIME

45 mins.

Makes 4–6 servings

INGREDIENTS

- 2 tablespoons vegetable oil
- 1 medium onion, finely chopped
- 1 stalk celery, diced
- 1 green bell pepper, chopped
- 2 cloves garlic, minced
- 1 large carrot, shredded
- 1 medium zucchini, shredded
- ½ cup frozen corn niblets
- One 15-ounce can kidney beans, drained and rinsed
- One 28-ounce can diced tomatoes, with juice

- One 8-ounce can tomato sauce
- ½ cup water
- 1 teaspoon chipotle powder, or to taste
- 1 teaspoon ground cumin
- 1 teaspoon dried basil
- 1 teaspoon dried oregano
- ½ teaspoon salt
- ½ teaspoon freshly ground black pepper
- Garnishes: grated cheddar, sour cream, lime wedges

Directions

1. Heat the oil over medium heat in a very large saucepan or small stockpot.

2. Add the onion, celery, green pepper, garlic, carrot, zucchini, and corn. Sauté, stirring often, until the vegetables just begin to soften (3–5 minutes).

3. While the vegetables are cooking, drain the canned kidney beans and rinse them thoroughly under cold water. Pour them into a broad, shallow dish and mash lightly with a potato masher. This not only gives the chili a smoother consistency, it's also a great way to "hide" the beans from picky eaters!

4. Once the vegetables have softened, add the mashed kidney beans, diced tomatoes, tomato sauce, water, and all seasonings to the pot.

5. Cover the pot and increase the heat to bring the mixture to a boil, then reduce the heat to medium-low.

6. Let the chili simmer for 20 minutes. Taste the chili and adjust the seasonings to suit your preferences.

7. Garnish each serving with grated cheese and sour cream as desired; serve with lime wedges.

PAULA ROY,
Ottawa, Canada

A passionate home cook, recipe developer, and food photographer, Paula Roy lives in Ottawa, Ontario, Canada, where she is the host of the popular television show *Paula Roy's Favourite Foods*. Her delicious recipes can be found on her website, Constantly Cooking, and in the pages of *Ottawa At Home* magazine where she serves as food editor. A big supporter of local and sustainable food, one of her main goals is to encourage others to make their time in the kitchen, making eating as fun and flavorful as possible.
Website: www.constantly cooking.com
Facebook: @constantlycooking
Instagram, Twitter: @paulajroy

COOK TIME
45 mins.

Makes 6 servings

Mango Black Bean Chili

Mangos add a sweetness and complexity that's just right for a hearty chili, especially if it's a vegetarian black bean chili like this one. A little allspice and a squeeze of lime kick it up a notch!

INGREDIENTS

- ¾ cup dry (uncooked) quinoa
- 3½ cups water, divided
- 3 mangoes
- 2 tablespoons olive oil
- 1 large yellow onion, diced
- 4 cloves garlic, minced
- 1 green bell pepper, diced
- 1 tablespoon Worcestershire sauce
- One 6-ounce can tomato paste
- 2 tablespoons chili powder
- 1 tablespoon ground cumin
- ½ teaspoon allspice
- Two 15-ounce cans black beans, drained and rinsed (or 3 cups cooked black beans)
- One 28-ounce can crushed fire-roasted tomatoes
- One 28-ounce can diced fire-roasted tomatoes
- ½ cup cilantro, coarsely chopped
- 1½ teaspoons kosher salt
- Garnishes: extra mango, lime wedges, sour cream

Directions

1. Place the quinoa in a saucepan with 1½ cups of water. Bring to a boil, then reduce the heat to very low. Cover the pot and simmer so the water is just bubbling for about 15–20 minutes until the water has been completely absorbed (check by pulling back the quinoa with a fork to see if any water remains). Turn off the heat and let sit covered to steam for 5 minutes. You will want about 1½ cups of cooked quinoa for this chili.

2. Dice the mangos into chunks and set aside 2½ cups for the chili, then small dice the rest for the garnish.

3. In a large pot or Dutch oven, heat the olive oil, then sauté the onion for 5 minutes over medium-high heat.

4. Add the garlic and green pepper and sauté about 5 minutes.

5. Stir in the Worcestershire sauce, tomato paste, chili powder, cumin, and allspice. Cook for 2 minutes, stirring constantly so that the mixture does not stick to the bottom of the pot.

6. Add the black beans, cans of tomatoes, chopped cilantro, kosher salt, and 1½ cups of the cooked quinoa (reserve any remaining for future use). Pour in 2 cups of water. Bring to a boil, then simmer on low for 15 minutes. Stir in the diced mango, then remove from the heat.

7. Serve warm topped with reserved mango garnish and a squeeze of lime juice. If desired, garnish with sour cream or nacho cheese.

SONJA AND ALEX OVERHISER, A COUPLE COOKS,
Indianapolis, Indiana

Alex and Sonja Overhiser are the writer and photographer behind the award-winning food blog ACoupleCooks.com, an online resource for home cooks. The couple has a worldwide following for their recipes, which range from healthy dinners to cocktails.

They are contributors to *The Washington Post* and authors of the acclaimed cookbook *Pretty Simple Cooking*. Website: www.acouple cooks.com
Instagram: @acouplecooks

Perfect Vegan Chili

This vegan, plant-based recipe is budget-friendly (about $10 for a whole batch!), easy to make, and super flavorful. It's thick and creamy, but still a little brothy for those who want their chili to be a bit more soup-like. I started testing this recipe in my college days and have recreated it more than 50 times since then. It's safe to say that it's perfection.

COOK TIME
30 mins.

Makes 6 servings

WATCH HOW TO MAKE THIS RECIPE

INGREDIENTS

- 1 tablespoon avocado oil (or any neutral oil)
- Half of 1 onion, diced
- 1 bell pepper or zucchini, chopped
- 3 cloves garlic, minced
- 1 jalapeño, chopped
- One 6-ounce can tomato paste
- 2 teaspoons cumin powder
- 1 teaspoon dried oregano
- ¼ cup guajillo or regular chili powder
- 3 cups vegetable broth

- One 28-ounce can fire-roasted crushed tomatoes
- 1 cup canned tomato sauce
- One 15.5-ounce can black beans, drained
- One 15.5-ounce can kidney beans, drained
- One 15.5-ounce can chickpeas, drained
- One 15.5-ounce can corn kernels, drained
- Salt and pepper, to taste
- Garnishes: tortilla chips, vegan sour cream, green onions, jalapeños, nutritional yeast

Directions

1. Put a large pot on medium heat. Add the oil and sauté the onion and bell pepper.

2. After about 5 minutes, add the minced garlic and jalapeño and sauté for another 2 minutes.

3. Add the tomato paste, spices, and a splash of the vegetable broth to the pot and cook for 5 minutes to release all the flavors of the spices. Stir frequently here to avoid sticking.

4. Add the canned tomatoes, the rest of the broth, the tomato sauce, and all the beans and corn. Add salt and pepper to taste. Bring to a boil and then reduce to a simmer for about 15 minutes.

5. Top with your choice of toppings and enjoy!

6. Note: This recipe is also slow cooker friendly. Make sure to dissolve the tomato paste and mix everything together well. Add all ingredients to the slow cooker and cook for 5 hours on low or 3 hours on high.

ANNA RIOS,
Guerneville, California

Anna is a Registered Dietitian Nutritionist (RDN) and food enthusiast from the northern California coast. Her goal is to share recipes, tips, and tricks to help you make healthy, affordable, easy, and yummy meals. She hopes to share these amazing plant-based recipes with other food lovers, just like her.

Website: www.healthy simpleyum.com
Instagram, TikTok: @healthysimpleyum

Wild Mushroom Chili

This vegetarian mushroom chili needs no meat for big flavor. The secrets to this recipe are the umami bombs: dried mushrooms, chipotles, smoked paprika, and soy sauce provide the chili with all the savory, smoky flavor that you'll need. Using fire-roasted tomatoes also layers on smokiness. Sautéing the fresh mushrooms, and then adding them into the chili at the end of cooking, ensures that the mushrooms retain their amazing flavor and texture.

COOK TIME

1 hr. 15 mins.

Makes 8 servings

INGREDIENTS

- 2 whole chipotle peppers in adobo sauce (from one can), chopped
- 1 cup water
- ½ cup dried mushrooms (such as shiitake, morel, porcini, chanterelle, cremini)
- 2 tablespoons cooking oil
- 1 small onion, chopped
- 2 stalks celery, chopped
- 2 medium carrots, chopped
- 3 cloves garlic, minced
- 2 tablespoons chili powder
- 2 teaspoons ground cumin
- 1 teaspoon smoked paprika
- Two 14-ounce cans diced fire-roasted tomatoes

- 2 cups vegetable broth
- 3 tablespoons soy sauce
- One 14-ounce can kidney beans, drained, rinsed, and drained again
- One 14-ounce can cannellini beans, drained, rinsed, and drained again
- ½ cup pearl barley
- 2 tablespoons butter
- 1 pound fresh mushrooms of choice, chopped into dice-sized pieces
- 1½ teaspoons kosher or sea salt
- Salt and pepper, to taste
- Garnishes: shredded cheese, chopped fresh cilantro, avocado slices, sour cream, diced red onion

Directions

1. Bring the water to a boil and pour it into a small heat-proof bowl. Add in the dried mushrooms and allow them to soak for 20 minutes. After 20 minutes, use your fingers to squeeze the mushrooms of liquid, letting the liquid fall back into the bowl. Reserve this soaking liquid. Transfer the mushrooms to a cutting board and chop them up.

2. Heat the oil in a heavy-bottomed stockpot over medium-high heat until shimmering. Add in the chopped chipotles, rehydrated chopped mushrooms, onion, celery, and carrots. Cook for 8 minutes, until the vegetables are softened.

3. Add in the garlic, chili powder, cumin, and smoked paprika. Cook for another minute, until the spices are fragrant.

4. To the pot, add in the reserved mushroom liquid (avoiding any grit at the bottom of the liquid) as well as the diced tomatoes, broth, soy sauce, kidney beans, cannellini beans, and pearl barley. Bring to a boil, cover with a lid, and then turn the heat to low to simmer for 40 minutes, or until the barley is tender.

5. While the chili is cooking, heat the butter in your largest skillet over medium heat. Cook the fresh mushrooms for 6–10 minutes, until browned. Season with a little salt.

6. When the chili has finished cooking, add in the sautéed mushrooms and cook for another 5 minutes.

7. Top with shredded cheese and other toppings of your choice just before serving.

*Note: This recipe calls for chipotles in adobo sauce. We'll only use two chiles from the can (NOT two cans!)—reserve the rest for another recipe. I like dividing the chipotles into little baggies of two chiles each and then freezing the bags. Most recipes will just call for a couple of chipotles.

THE STEAMY KITCHEN / JADEN RAE,
Las Vegas, Nevada

Jaden Rae is a television chef, amateur mycologist, author of two best-selling cookbooks, and award-winning publisher of SteamyKitchen.com. Celebrating its 16th year, Steamy Kitchen is one of the biggest blogs in the world with nearly half a billion pageviews and over 75 million unique users. Jaden is regularly featured on such syndications as *Daytime Show* and *The List*, and documents her at-home mushroom cultivation journey on www.JadenRae.com. Website: www.SteamyKitchen.com Facebook, Instagram: @SteamyKitchen

Whole Food Plant-Based Chili

This chili is as rich and delicious as any of the artery cloggers, but it doesn't have any of the animal products or saturated fat. We don't even use oil to cook this recipe—it's truly the healthiest chili you'll ever love. I make a batch of it and portion it into pint containers, freeze them, and have a quick and delicious meal ready whenever I don't feel like cooking. I make it a point to use the best ingredients available, which for me include Rancho Gordo® beans and posole and Muir Glen® tomatoes.

COOK TIME
2 hrs.

Makes 6 servings

INGREDIENTS

- 1 head garlic, halved and wrapped in aluminum foil
- 2 onions, diced
- Salt, to taste
- 2 tablespoons water, plus more as needed
- One 28-ounce can fire-roasted tomatoes (I use Muir Glen®)
- One 7-ounce can chipotles in adobo sauce
- 2 tablespoons cumin
- 2 tablespoons smoked paprika
- 1 tablespoon crushed red pepper flakes
- One 16-ounce bag dry (uncooked) Moro beans, soaked overnight (I use Rancho Gordo®)
- One 16-ounce bag prepared hominy, soaked overnight (I use Rancho Gordo®)
- 6 ounces tempeh, grated
- Garnishes: mashed avocado, tortilla chips

Directions

1. Heat the oven to 350 degrees Fahrenheit. Add the garlic and roast for 1 hour.

2. Heat a large pot on the stove. Add the onions with a punch (not a pinch) of salt and 2 tablespoons of water. Stir the onions and cook until caramelized, adding more water by the tablespoon as needed. Once the onions are caramelized, add the tomatoes and chipotles (including the adobo sauce), as well as the spices, to the pot. Let simmer.

3. Drain and rinse the beans and the hominy. Place them in a separate pot together and simmer for 1 hour.

4. Use an immersion blender to blend the tomato mixture into a sauce directly in the pot. (If you don't have an immersion blender, pour into a countertop blender, then return to the pot when blended.) Taste and adjust the seasoning.

5. Drain the (mostly) cooked beans and hominy and add them to the tomato mixture pot. Also add the tempeh. Let simmer for 45 minutes, adding water if it gets dry.

6. Taste your chili and adjust the seasoning as needed.

7. Top with mashed avocado and tortilla chips.

EDDIE MCNAMARA,
New York, New York

Eddie McNamara is a plant-based chef and the author of *Toss Your Own Salad: The Meatless Cookbook*. He lives in New York City. His work has appeared in *InStyle*, *Penthouse*, HGTV, *Yoga Journal*, and *People Magazine*. Lydia Bastianich liked his food. Instagram: @tossyourownsalad

Vegan Pumpkin Lentil Quinoa Chili

COOK TIME

1 hr.

Makes 7+ servings

This recipe uses canned pumpkin to lean into the fall feeling, while also thickening the chili without hours of simmering. I'm very much an omnivore and often feel let down by vegetarian chili recipes, so I set out to create a vegetarian chili that still has the stick-to-your-ribs feel of traditional beef chili. Using both quinoa and lentils lends the familiar texture of chili con carne while also adding plant protein that you may not always find in vegetarian versions.

INGREDIENTS

- 1 teaspoon olive oil
- 1 red bell pepper, diced
- 1 small onion, diced
- 2 carrots, diced
- 3 cloves garlic, minced
- 1 cup dry (uncooked) quinoa
- 1 cup dry (uncooked) lentils
- One 15-ounce can low-sodium black beans, drained and rinsed
- One 15-ounce can low-sodium diced tomatoes
- One 4-ounce can diced green chiles, mild or spicy
- 4 cups low-sodium vegetable stock
- One 15-ounce can pure pumpkin purée
- 1 tablespoon chili powder
- ½ tablespoon cumin
- 1 teaspoon freshly ground black pepper
- ½ tablespoon smoked paprika
- Garnishes: cheese, sour cream, avocado, cilantro, sliced jalapeño

Directions

1. In a large pot, heat the oil over medium heat.

2. Add the pepper, onion, carrots, and garlic. Cook for 1–2 minutes, stirring, until the veggies are slightly softened.

3. Add the remaining ingredients and stir to combine.

4. Cover the pot and reduce the heat to low. Let simmer for 30–45 minutes, stirring about every 15 minutes.

5. Serve the chili hot and garnish with any toppings you like, such as cheese, sour cream, avocado, cilantro, or sliced jalapeño.

KALEIGH MCMORDIE,
Abilene, Texas

Kaleigh McMordie is a registered dietitian, recipe developer, food photographer, and creator of the blog Lively Table. She is passionate about making healthy eating delicious and approachable. She lives in west Texas where she is always cooking up something new for her husband and two young daughters. Website: www .livelytable.com Facebook, Twitter, Instagram, Pinterest: @livelytable

COOK TIME
45 mins.
Makes 10+ servings

Sara's Award-Winning Vegetarian Chili

This chili won our neighborhood cook-off award! No one believed me that it was vegetarian. It tastes very hearty and the vegetarian meat crumbles really taste similar to ground beef.

INGREDIENTS

- Two 13.7-ounce packages vegetarian meat crumbles (I use Gardein®)
- 2 tablespoons olive oil
- 1 onion, chopped
- 1 red bell pepper, chopped
- 3 cloves garlic, minced
- 3 teaspoons salt
- 1 teaspoon pepper
- 2 cups water
- One 28-ounce can crushed tomatoes
- One 14-ounce can stewed tomatoes
- Two 14-ounce cans kidney beans, drained
- ⅓ cup chili powder
- 2 teaspoons cumin
- 1 teaspoon cinnamon
- 1 teaspoon cayenne pepper
- Garnish: vegan cheese

Directions

1. Heat up your pan until it is very hot. Add in the olive oil and let it get hot as well. Sauté your vegetarian meat crumbles for 3–4 minutes.

2. Add in the onions, bell pepper, and garlic. Sauté for another 3–4 minutes.

3. Add in all the rest of your ingredients (except for the garnish). Bring the mixture to a boil over medium-high heat. Then reduce the temperature and simmer gently for about 30 minutes. You can cook it longer to get it to thicken up more if desired.

4. To serve, top with some vegan cheese.

SARA LAFOUNTAIN,
Fairfax Station, Virginia

Sara LaFountain has been a food blogger for the past 11 years. She loves to cook with her children and runs a school lunch program. Sara's passion is to teach children how to enjoy healthy food, read food labels, and feel comfortable in the kitchen. Facebook, Twitter, Instagram, Pinterest, TikTok: @cookwith5kids

Chili Recipe Awards

- **My chili won our neighborhood chili cook-off against 25 other chilis!**

Hearty Mushroom Plant-Based Chili

Beans or no beans? Noodles or not? There's an ongoing debate about which ingredients "belong" and "do not belong" in chili. Good news for you and your hungry crew, you can easily settle the discussion with this fun build-your-own-bowl concept. Original recipe found on vitacost.com.

COOK TIME
30 mins.
Makes 6 servings

INGREDIENTS

- Half of 1 lemon, juiced
- 3¼ cups and 2 tablespoons vegetable broth, divided
- 1 small red onion, diced
- 8 portobello mushroom caps, diced
- 3–4 cloves garlic, minced
- 1 small habanero, seeded and chopped
- 18 ounces organic diced tomatoes
- 2 tablespoons organic light brown sugar
- 1 tablespoon organic maple syrup
- ½ teaspoon Himalayan pink salt

- Two 15-ounce cans organic kidney beans, rinsed and drained (optional)
- 1 tablespoon cocoa powder
- 1 tablespoon organic cumin
- 1 tablespoon dried oregano
- 4 tablespoons chili powder
- 2 teaspoons coriander powder
- ½–1 tablespoon miso (optional, for an umami flavor profile)
- Garnish and serve with: spaghetti, cornbread, tortilla chips, dairy-free cheese, dairy-free sour cream, green onions, parsley, or crispy onion straws

Directions

1. In a small bowl, mix the lemon juice and 2 tablespoons of vegetable broth. Set aside.

2. In a saucepot over medium-high heat, add the onions and mushrooms. Pour in the lemon juice/broth mixture as necessary to reduce sticking. Add a pinch of salt and sauté for around 5 minutes.

3. Add the garlic and pepper and continue cooking for 2 minutes.

4. In the same saucepot, stir in the tomatoes, brown sugar, maple syrup, salt, kidney beans, and remaining vegetable broth. Add the cocoa, cumin, oregano, chili powder, and coriander. Stir until well combined. Cook on medium-low heat for 20 minutes.

5. To prepare the DIY station, arrange all of your desired garnishes and accompaniments in bowls and surround them on a large board with dippers and scoopers. We suggest spaghetti, cornbread, tortilla chips, dairy-free cheese and sour cream, green onions, crispy onion straws, and parsley.

RYAN SHEPARD,
Boca Raton, Florida

Ryan, a self-made plant-based chef, can often be found experimenting in the kitchen with colorful whole-food ingredients. He enjoys promoting a healthy lifestyle and sharing accessible, vegan-friendly recipes (inspired by popular dishes from around the world) with the masses. When the apron's off, he's likely at the beach or kickin' it with close friends. Visit www.theveganrhino.com or follow him on Instagram @theveganrhino for tasty finds, eco-friendly tips, and updates on his upcoming cookbook, *From Roots to the Kitchen.*
Website: www.thevegan rhino.com
Instagram: @theveganrhino

Quick and Easy Spicy Vegan Chili

I have been making this recipe for years, and I've never come across anyone who didn't absolutely love it. It's one hundred percent vegan (even though you can't tell by tasting it) and has a spicy kick! It can be made in under 30 minutes and is the perfect cozy yet light weeknight dinner. I'm from Texas, so eating my chili with large scoop Fritos® corn chips is mandatory!

COOK TIME

30 mins.

Makes 5 servings

INGREDIENTS

- 2–3 red bell peppers, diced
- 6 cloves garlic, minced
- ½ ghost pepper, sliced
- One 10-ounce package meat substitute of choice (I use Abbot's Butcher Ground "Beef")
- 2 tablespoons chili powder
- 4 tablespoons cumin powder
- 1 tablespoon cacao powder
- 10 Roma tomatoes, diced
- 2 cups marinara sauce
- Two 15-ounce cans black beans
- ¾ cup veggie broth
- Salt and pepper, to taste
- Cilantro (optional)

Directions

1. Add the bell peppers to large, heavily oiled pot over medium heat and sauté, stirring often until soft, for about 5 minutes.

2. Add the garlic and ghost pepper and sauté for 1 minute.

3. Add the plant-based ground beef, chili powder, cumin, and cacao powder and stir until well combined.

4. Stir in the diced tomatoes, marinara sauce, black beans, and veggie broth. Bring to a boil, then reduce the heat. Cover and let simmer, stirring occasionally, until the beans are tender, about 20 minutes. Season to taste and top with cilantro if desired.

DELALI KPAKOL,
Dallas, Texas

Delali is a social media content creator born and raised in Dallas, TX. She is passionate about balancing a healthy, happy lifestyle all while showcasing a little style and flare along the way! She shares her homemade, *mostly* plant-based dishes and recipes daily along with healthy lifestyle and wellness tips. Her overall goal is to help women feel their best through healthy eating. Delali wants to inspire others to nourish themselves by increasing their intake of wholesome foods while still finding time to indulge in all the treats that life has to offer. Instagram: @dishydeets

COOK TIME
4 hrs.
Makes 6 servings

Easy Vegetarian Chorizo Chili

I love this super quick and easy recipe! It's so delicious and perfect for a cold winter night. My family likes to set up toppings for everyone to choose their favorites and eat it with cornbread slathered with honey butter!

INGREDIENTS

- 2 tablespoons oil
- 6 ounces vegan chorizo
- 1 large onion, chopped
- 2 cloves garlic, finely grated
- 1 teaspoon chili powder
- Two 15-ounce cans diced tomatoes with chiles
- 3 cups vegetarian broth
- One 14.75-ounce can corn
- One 15-ounce can black beans, rinsed
- One 15-ounce can pinto beans, rinsed
- Salt and pepper, to taste

Directions

1. Sauté the onion and chorizo in oil until the onions are translucent.
2. Add the sautéed mixture to a slow cooker, then add all of the remaining ingredients. Cook on low for 4 hours.
3. When you're ready to serve, add your desired toppings and enjoy!

VEGETARIAN CHILI

MICHELLE JAMES,
Richfield, Utah

Michelle James loves cooking, especially frugal and wholesome meals for her large family. She lives in the Mountain West and enjoys stunning views and clean air every day. She has been writing content online for many years for major corporations, including HP, Disney, and Walmart. You can find her website at www.CentsibleCooking.com.

Veggie Chili with Marinara Sauce

COOK TIME
1 hr.

Makes 7+ servings

Who doesn't love a good, hearty vegetarian chili? This recipe uses an electric pressure cooker (I use an Instant Pot®), and really any vegetable works in it. I usually raid my fridge veggie drawer to add whatever's on hand. Making it in the pressure cooker means I can get this on our dinner table in under 60 minutes. Top with sour cream and shredded cheddar for a delicious dinner that even picky kids will enjoy.

INGREDIENTS

- 1 tablespoon olive oil (or desired oil spray)
- 1–2 cloves garlic, minced
- 1 cup yellow onion, chopped
- 6 stalks celery, chopped
- 1 cup baby bella mushrooms, chopped
- Two 1-pound jars marinara sauce (I use Newman's Own®)
- Two 15.5-ounce cans small white beans (I use Goya®)
- Two 15-ounce cans low-sodium black beans
- 1 mild chili spice packet (I use Mrs. Dash® Chili Seasoning Mix)
- 2 cups vegetable stock or water
- One 15-ounce can corn
- 1 medium zucchini

Directions

1. Hit the "sauté" button on your electric pressure cooker. Add the olive oil to the cooker.

2. As the cooker is heating up, add the garlic cloves and the onions and keep stirring. After two minutes, add the celery and mushrooms. Keep stirring.

3. Turn off the cooker, then add the rest of the ingredients and mix well.

4. Turn on "manual pressure" for 14 minutes. Let the cooker natural release for 5–10 minutes (don't touch it). Quickly release the steam valve and serve with any optional toppings you desire.

NANCY JOHNSON HORN,
Kew Gardens, New York

Nancy Johnson Horn has been a content creator since February of 2007. She started The Mama Maven Blog in the fall of 2011 and hasn't stopped since. She is married and has three children, and she really didn't start cooking until her first pregnancy (despite working at the Food Network in her 20s) and loves to develop her own easy and healthy recipes for her blog. She adores her Instant Pot and Air Fryer.
Website: www.themamamaven.com
Facebook: The Mama Maven Blog
Instagram, Twitter, TikTok: @themamamaven

COOK TIME
2 hrs.
Makes 10–12 servings

Louisiana Vegetable Chili

The Spanish introduced many wonderful flavors and cooking techniques to Louisiana. This vegetable chili, with its green chiles and various beans, is a great example of Spanish-influenced cooking.

This recipe is from Chef John Folse's *The Encyclopedia of Cajun & Creole Cuisine*.

INGREDIENTS

- ½ pound dry (uncooked) white navy beans
- ½ pound dry (uncooked) red kidney beans
- ¼ cup vegetable oil
- 1 cup onions, diced
- ½ cup celery, diced
- ¼ cup green bell peppers, diced
- ¼ cup garlic, minced
- 2 teaspoons chili powder
- One 4-ounce can diced green chiles
- One 14-ounce can peeled tomatoes, with juice
- 5 cups cold water
- 1 cup zucchini, diced
- 1 cup summer squash, diced
- ½ cup broccoli, chopped
- Salt and black pepper, to taste
- Louisiana hot sauce, to taste
- Sprig of fresh cilantro
- ¼ cup parsley, chopped
- Serve with: hot garlic bread or cornbread sticks

Directions

1. Combine the navy and kidney beans in a colander and rinse under cold water. Place the beans in a ceramic bowl, cover with cold water, and keep in the refrigerator overnight. This process will reduce the cooking time by a third. When ready to cook, rinse the beans in cold water.

2. In a cast iron pot, heat the oil over medium-high heat. Add the onions, celery, bell peppers, and garlic. Sauté for 3–5 minutes or until the vegetables are wilted.

3. Stir in the beans, chili powder, chiles, and tomatoes with juice. Pour in the water and bring to a rolling boil. Reduce the heat to a simmer and cook for approximately 1 hour 30 minutes or until the beans are tender.

4. Add the zucchini, squash, and broccoli. Season to taste using salt, pepper, and hot sauce. Flavor with the cilantro and parsley, then allow the chili to cook until the squash is tender but not mushy.

5. Serve with hot garlic bread or cornbread sticks.

CHEF JOHN FOLSE,
New Orleans, Louisiana

Chef John Folse, Louisiana's Culinary Ambassador to the World, is proud to share his passion for Louisiana's swamp floor pantry around the world. As an entrepreneur, his interests range from restaurateur to manufacturer, author to educator. Some of his national and international accolades include being named Louisiana Restaurateur of the Year, National Chef of the Year, and several others. Author of 10 cookbooks, his *Can You Dig It* vegetable cookbook won the Benny Award for Best Cookbook. Folse hosts a national PBS television cooking show, *A Taste of Louisiana*. He was recently inducted into the American Academy of Chefs Culinary Hall of Fame and the Chef John Folse Culinary Institute at Nicholls State University is named in his honor.

Good-to-Know Info

Some surprising and unexpected ingredients dubbed as "flavor bombs" that some people use in their chili include: balsamic vinegar, beer, coffee, chocolate, sriracha, olives, cola, mango, dried cranberries, coconut milk, honey, whiskey, cauliflower, bacon, soy sauce, and so much more. The possibilities are endless!

Righteous Three-Bean Vegetarian Chili

This chili features three types of beans: red kidney, black, and navy. It includes some standout ingredients, like maple syrup from New York state and sriracha, and it is finished with a special touch: The Most Righteous New York Straight Bourbon from the Catskill Distilling Company. Paired with homemade New York state cheddar biscuits and homemade maple syrup butter, it celebrates the New York autumn harvest and is perfect for tailgating parties.

COOK TIME
2 hrs.

Makes 7+ servings

INGREDIENTS

- One 15-ounce can light red kidney beans
- One 15-ounce can black beans
- One 15-ounce can navy beans
- 2 tablespoons olive oil
- 5 cloves garlic, minced
- 1 cup onions, diced small
- 1 cup carrots, diced small
- 1 cup green bell pepper, diced small
- 1 jalapeño, minced, to taste
- 1 cup corn on the cob, removed from cob
- 1 cup zucchini, diced small
- Two 28-ounce cans diced tomatoes, with juice
- 1 cup ketchup
- ¼ cup maple syrup (I use syrup from New York state)
- 1 tablespoon sriracha, to taste
- Salt and black pepper, to taste
- 4 ounces bourbon (I use The Most Righteous New York Straight Bourbon)
- Cheddar cheese, grated, to taste

Directions

1. Drain, rinse, and soak the beans in cold water.

2. While the beans soak, heat a large saucepot. Add the oil, garlic, onions, and carrots. Cover and sweat until the onions are translucent.

3. Add the green bell peppers and jalapeño and sauté for 2 minutes. Add the corn and sauté for 3 minutes. Add the zucchini and sauté for 2 minutes. Add the diced tomatoes.

4. Drain the beans. Add the beans to the tomatoes and vegetables. Then add the ketchup, maple syrup, sriracha, and salt and pepper to taste. Stir to combine. Bring to a boil. Reduce the heat and simmer for 1 hour.

5. Finish with the bourbon and grated cheddar.

DEBRA ARGEN,
Greenwich, Connecticut

Debra C. Argen is the cofounder and editor in chief of Luxury Experience (www.Luxury Experience.com), where she brings her passion and creativity to creating culinary and cocktail recipes for clients for the Liquor Cabinet and Wine Cellar sections. She honed her culinary experience by attending top culinary schools in the United States, Italy, and Mexico. An award-winning cook and photographer, she travels the world working with clients to tell their unique stories to a global audience.
Facebook: @LuxuryExperience
Twitter, Instagram: @LuxuryPair
YouTube: @edwardnesta

COOK TIME

45 mins.

Makes 6 servings

Santa Fe "Christmas" Red and Green Chili

I grew up in Santa Fe and love to celebrate local culinary traditions. My chili recipe combines several New Mexican favorites into one delicious pot. Corn is a staple in the Southwest, and hominy is the main ingredient in a local stew called posole. Pinto beans with red chile sauce is also a traditional dish in New Mexico. Finally, "Frito pies" (red meat and pinto bean chili poured over Fritos® corn chips) are a common meal. These all come together for a yummy, hearty vegetarian chili.

INGREDIENTS

- 2 tablespoons vegetable oil
- 1 medium yellow onion, diced
- 2 tablespoons garlic, minced
- 3 tablespoons ground Chimayó red chile powder
- 1 tablespoon cumin
- 1 tablespoon brown sugar
- 1 cup fresh tomatoes, diced
- One 14.5-ounce can stewed tomatoes
- 2 cups cooked white hominy (homemade or 15.5-ounce can, drained)
- 2 cups cooked pinto beans (homemade or 15.5-ounce can, drained)
- 1 cup Hatch green chiles, roasted and diced (homemade, canned, or frozen)
- 1½ cups vegetable broth
- Salt and pepper, to taste
- Garnishes: sour cream, grated cheese (any kind), diced red onion, crushed Fritos® corn chips

Directions

1. Heat the oil on medium to high heat, then add the onion. Cook for about 3 minutes, then add the garlic. Cook another 2 minutes, stirring often.

2. Add the red chile powder, cumin, brown sugar, and diced fresh tomatoes. Mix all the ingredients together well.

3. Add the stewed tomatoes, hominy, pinto beans, and green chiles. Gently stir to mix.

4. Add the vegetable broth, salt, and pepper. Lower the heat and let simmer for 20–25 minutes, stirring occasionally.

5. Remove from the heat and let sit for 5 minutes.

6. When it's ready to serve, ladle the chili into bowls and add garnishes to taste.

NATALIE BOVIS,
Santa Fe, New Mexico

Natalie Bovis is the award-winning founder of The Liquid Muse, New Mexico Cocktails & Culture Festival, TACO WARS, and OM Chocolate Liqueur. She produces culinary events, such as the James Beard Foundation's "Taste America" dinner in Santa Fe, and teaches cooking and cocktail classes. Her fourth book, *Drinking with My Dog*, hits shelves in January 2023.
Website: www.The LiquidMuse.com
Instagram, Twitter, Facebook: @TheLiquidMuse

Easy Mango Chili

This vegetarian chili is packed full of tasty, hearty goodness. Both vegetarians and non-vegetarians are sure to be satisfied. Plus, its unexpected mango flavors will surprise even chili experts.

COOK TIME

45 mins.

Makes 4 servings

INGREDIENTS

- 3 tablespoons olive oil
- 1 onion, chopped
- 2 cloves garlic, chopped
- 2 carrots, chopped
- 2 celery stalks, chopped
- 1 red bell pepper, chopped
- 1 ripe mango, chopped
- One 14.5-ounce can fire-roasted tomatoes
- 2 teaspoons cumin (I use Simply Organic®)

- 2 teaspoons coriander (I use Simply Organic®)
- 2 teaspoons smoked paprika (I use Simply Organic®)
- 3 cups vegetable stock
- 3 tablespoons tomato paste
- 2 teaspoons apple cider vinegar
- One 15.5-ounce can kidney beans
- One 15.5-ounce can black beans
- 2 tablespoons cilantro

Directions

1. Add the olive oil to a pan over a low-medium flame and let it warm up. Add in the chopped onions and sauté, constantly stirring, for about 20–25 minutes, until the onions are caramelized.

2. Add in all the remaining ingredients except for the cilantro. Let the chili simmer for about 10–15 minutes.

3. When ready to serve, top with cilantro and enjoy.

Good-to-Know Info

Avoid gritty sauces by making sure all your spices are finely ground by using a spice grinder or a coffee grinder.

SHASHI CHARLES,
Covington, Georgia

Shashi is the blogger behind Savory Spin, a collection of super easy, economical, mostly fusion recipes made with ingredients from the local grocery store. She is a huge proponent of "a little spice is always nice" and passionately incorporates it into eats and treats that tickle the tastebuds and not mess with waistlines—too much. Facebook, Instagram: @savoryspin

VEGAN

Chickpea and Lentil Chili

I love this chili because it's a healthier alternative to chili and spaghetti (aka Cincinnati chili), which is a favorite in a lot of places in Ohio, where I am originally from.

COOK TIME
30 mins.
Makes 4 servings

INGREDIENTS

- 1 tablespoon avocado oil
- 1 medium yellow onion, diced
- 3–4 cloves garlic, minced
- 1 pound cooked chickpeas
- 1 cup cooked lentils
- 1½ cups vegetable broth
- 2 tablespoons tomato paste
- 1 cup tomato sauce
- 2 cups tomatoes, diced
- 2 tablespoons and 1½ teaspoons chili powder

- 1 tablespoon and 2 teaspoons ground cumin
- 1 tablespoon cocoa powder
- 2 teaspoons organic cane sugar (optional)
- 1½ teaspoons Himalayan pink salt
- ½ teaspoon ground black pepper
- Serve with: cornbread, spaghetti, or your choice of sides

Directions

1. In a pot on medium heat, add the oil and onions. Sauté for 5 minutes or until the onions are translucent. Add the garlic and cook until fragrant.

2. Add the remaining ingredients and stir until well combined. Bring to a boil and reduce the heat to low. Simmer, uncovered, for 20–25 minutes, stirring occasionally.

3. Remove the chili from the heat and serve warm with cornbread, spaghetti, or your choice of sides.

RYAN SHEPARD,
Boca Raton, Florida

Ryan, a self-made plant-based chef, can often be found experimenting in the kitchen with colorful whole-food ingredients. He enjoys promoting a healthy lifestyle and sharing accessible, vegan-friendly recipes (inspired by popular dishes from around the world) with the masses. When the apron's off, he's likely at the beach or kickin' it with close friends. Visit www.theveganrhino.com or follow him on Instagram @theveganrhino for tasty finds, eco-friendly tips, and updates on his upcoming cookbook, *From Roots to the Kitchen.*
Website: www.thevegan rhino.com
Instagram: @theveganrhino

COOK TIME

45 mins.

Makes 8 servings

Electric Pressure Cooker Vegetarian Three-Bean Chili

This chili is proof that a meatless chili satisfies big cravings and a hungry crowd. It debuted years ago at our neighborhood Halloween party. Guests were floored by the deep chili flavor of this meatless wonder and kept requesting more. The kiddos did too! I just love how a pressure cooker can turn three beans, everyday veggies, tomatoes, and classic seasonings into big chili flavor in under an hour. It's a long-standing vegetarian favorite to this day!

INGREDIENTS

- 2 tablespoons olive oil
- Half of 1 onion, diced
- 2 large carrots, diced
- 2 ribs celery, diced
- 3 cloves garlic, minced
- One 15-ounce can black beans, rinsed and drained
- One 15-ounce can great northern beans, rinsed and drained
- One 15-ounce can red kidney beans, rinsed and drained
- 1 cup corn
- 1½ cups vegetable broth
- One 14.5-ounce can diced tomatoes; do not drain
- 3 ounces tomato paste
- 3 tablespoons chili powder
- ½ teaspoon ground cumin
- ½ teaspoon kosher salt
- ¼ teaspoon black pepper

Directions

1. Select "sauté" on your electric pressure cooker and heat the olive oil.
2. Add the onions, carrots, celery, and garlic. Sauté until tender.
3. Add the beans, corn, vegetable broth, diced tomatoes (with juice), tomato paste, chili powder, cumin, salt, and pepper. Press "cancel." Secure the lid and turn the pressure release valve to the sealing position. Select "manual" or "pressure cook" high for 2 minutes.
4. Allow the cooker to sit undisturbed for a 15-minute natural pressure release and carefully release any remaining steam.
5. Serve warm.

TRACI ANTONOVICH,
Sonoma County, California

Traci owns and operates www.thekitchen girl.com, featuring hundreds of easy, delicious recipes for every occasion. As The Kitchen Girl, she prides herself in testing and developing every recipe to be approachable and successful for any cooking level. Her followers love her content for the use of wholesome, everyday ingredients and straightforward instructions. Traci invites you to find yourself among her countless readers saying, "This was so easy, and everyone loved it!" Facebook, Instagram, Pinterest: @thekitchengirl

WATCH HOW TO MAKE THIS RECIPE

Black Bean Chili

Black bean chili can be made either with or without meat, so long as there are lots (and lots) of black beans! Veggies and spices can also be included, which makes for some great vegetarian and vegan options.

The Recipes

Buffalo Chicken Chili

Chipotle Chorizo Chili

Kevin's Famous Chili
Recreated

Christmas Eve Chili

Checkerboard Chili

In 2000, one of my neighbors made too much chili and shared some with my wife and me. We thought it was the best chili we had ever had, so we asked for the recipe. We have been making that recipe now for more than 20 years—we still have the original recipe written on notebook paper. This particular chili is based on that recipe, but with a few custom tweaks. The name refers to the mixture of black beans and dark red kidney beans.

COOK TIME

1 hr.

Makes 7+ servings

INGREDIENTS

- ½ pound bacon, cut into small pieces
- 1 medium onion, chopped
- 2 stalks celery, chopped
- Half of 1 yellow bell pepper, chopped
- Half of 1 red bell pepper, chopped
- 2 pounds ground beef
- 3 teaspoons garlic, minced
- One 15-ounce can black beans, drained and rinsed
- One 15-ounce can dark red kidney beans, drained and rinsed
- One 6-ounce can vegetable juice (I use V8®)

- One 10-ounce can diced tomatoes and green chiles (I use Rotel®)
- Two 15-ounce cans tomato sauce
- One 15-ounce can petite diced tomatoes
- 1½ teaspoons chili powder
- 1 teaspoon New Mexico chile powder
- 1 teaspoon ancho chile powder
- ½ teaspoon chipotle powder
- 1 teaspoon paprika
- 1 teaspoon cumin
- 1 teaspoon oregano
- 1 tablespoon sugar
- 1 tablespoon salt
- 1 tablespoon black pepper

Directions

1. Add the bacon to a pot and cook until crisp. Remove the cooked bacon and set aside.
2. Add the onion, celery, and bell peppers to the pot. Cook until tender.
3. Add the ground beef and garlic. Cook until the meat is browned.
4. Add the beans, juice, diced tomatoes and green chiles, tomato sauce, diced tomatoes, and all seasonings.
5. Add any reserved bacon pieces that have not yet been eaten back into the pot. Simmer for 30 minutes, stirring often.
6. Serve!

BRAD HUYSER,
Ankeny, Iowa

Brad Huyser is an Iowa native. He is an IT professional by day and experimental cook by night. He enjoys cooking for his family and trying out new recipes. He especially likes to improve upon favorite recipes such as chili, pizza, and anything barbecued.

COOK TIME

1 hr. 45 mins.

Makes 4 servings

2Chefs Black Bean and Chorizo Chili

After living in Los Angeles for 12 years and now living in Austin, we've become obsessed with chorizo. We love the spiciness and the texture, and we're suckers for all things pork. We're fans of the combination of black beans and chorizo, so we came up with a chili recipe that combines both. The best part of this recipe is the incredibly bold flavors, despite having few ingredients, and that it's super simple to make, which is perfect for the beginner cook.

INGREDIENTS

- 2 teaspoons olive oil
- 1 pound spicy chorizo
- 1 red onion, finely diced
- 2 red bell peppers, medium diced
- 2 cloves garlic, minced
- 1 teaspoon cumin
- 1 teaspoon smoked paprika
- 1 teaspoon dried oregano
- 2 teaspoons salt
- 2 cups chicken stock
- 1 lime, zest and juice
- Three 15.5-ounce cans black beans
- 1 teaspoon fresh oregano, chopped
- Garnish: Mexican crema

Directions

1. Place a pot over medium-high heat and add the olive oil and chorizo. Brown for about 5 minutes.
2. Lower the heat to medium and add the onions. Sauté for 3 minutes.
3. Add in the bell pepper, garlic, cumin, smoked paprika, dried oregano, and salt. Sauté for 3 minutes.
4. Deglaze with the chicken stock. Add the black beans, lime juice, and lime zest, bring the mixture back to a boil, and then lower it to a simmer. Simmer for 90 minutes.
5. When the chili is done, stir in the fresh oregano. Garnish with Mexican crema.

CHEFS MARA AND RYAN WOLLEN,

Austin, Texas

2Chefs are a husband-and-wife private chef team who prepare healthy weekly meals for their clients using quality seasonal ingredients. Additionally, they teach online cooking classes, for all levels of skill, from beginners seeking some cooking basics to seasoned home cooks who are looking for pro tips to up their game. Instagram, Facebook: 2chefs.food YouTube: Cooking with 2chefs

WATCH HOW TO MAKE THIS RECIPE

Buffalo Chicken Chili

This chili recipe was inspired by my love of spicy food and a warm, comforting bowl of chili. It has all the flavor of hot wings, but without the messy fingers.

COOK TIME
1 hr. 30 mins.

Makes 10 servings
(2 quarts)

INGREDIENTS

- 2 tablespoons olive oil
- 2 tablespoons butter
- 5 cloves garlic, minced
- 6 celery stalks with leaves, diced
- 2 cups onions, diced
- 2 cups carrots, chopped
- Two 15-ounce cans pinto beans, drained
- Two 15-ounce cans black beans, drained
- One 28-ounce can crushed tomatoes
- One 28-ounce can tomatoes with green chiles

- 2 bottles full-bodied (not light) beer
- 3 cups chicken stock
- 1½ cups hot sauce
- 3 teaspoons cumin
- 3 teaspoons smoked paprika; use hot smoked for more heat
- 1 whole chicken, baked and shredded, or substitute a store-bought rotisserie chicken
- Salt and pepper, to taste
- ¼ cup sweet and hot jalapeño juice (optional)
- Garnishes: blue cheese crumbles, cheese crisps (see recipe at right)

Directions

1. In a large 6-quart stock pot, heat the oil and butter on high heat. Add the onion, celery, and carrots. Sauté for 5 minutes.
2. Add the chicken, garlic, salt, pepper, cumin, and paprika. Mix well and let the mixture cook on medium heat for 10 minutes.
3. Add the beer and simmer for 10 minutes.
4. Add all the tomatoes, hot sauce, stock, beans, and jalapeño juice. Simmer over low heat for 1 hour.
5. Serve with blue cheese crumbles and a cheese crisp.

KIM WILCOX,
Knoxville, Tennessee

From her first Easy Bake oven to her owning restaurants, Kim Wilcox finds joy in making others smile through food. Kim is a regular on local TV stations, has been featured in print media as having one of the most unique ice cream flavors in Knoxville, and has been featured on both The Cooking Channel and Food Network. She wrote *The Great Book of Grilled Cheese* and has published recipes in *The Ultimate Spam® Cookbook*. Kim has also been a two-time winner at the March of Dimes Celebrity Chefs auction with her unique and savory ice cream desserts. Kim grew up in a family who gathered in the kitchen, and she sees food as the universal language that we all speak.
Instagram: @itsallso yummycafeowner
Twitter: @ItsAll SoYummy
Facebook: Its All So Yummy Cafe/Hilton Head Ice Cream

Cheese Crisps

INGREDIENTS

- Shredded cheese of your choice
- Seasoning of choice (optional)

Directions

1. Shred or crumble your own cheese if possible. Pre-shredded cheese won't melt as well due to the nonstick agents that are added.
2. While shredding the cheese, preheat a griddle to 375 degrees Fahrenheit.
3. Place handfuls of the cheese on the griddle, with a little space in between each one.
4. Let each crisp melt until the edges are brown, then turn each one over. They will be easy to turn when they are brown enough. If you try to turn them too soon, they will stick to the griddle.
5. After you turn each crisp, let the side that is down get brown, them remove the crisps from the heat and drain them on paper towels.
6. For added flavor, sprinkle them while they're still warm with your favorite seasoning. These are the perfect accompaniment for soups or salads—and, of course, chili!

Spicy Bison Chili

My husband has always wanted to go on a big game hunt. So when a friend asked him to go on a bison hunt, he jumped at the chance! After the successful hunt, the meat was split equally, yielding 860 pounds in total. As a result, I was left with the task of creating various bison recipes to free up room in our overloaded freezer. This chili is one of our favorite recipes that I created.

COOK TIME

1 hr. 15 mins.

Makes 6 servings

INGREDIENTS

- 2 tablespoons vegetable oil
- 1 pound ground bison
- 1 medium onion, diced
- 5 medium Anaheim chiles, diced
- 3 cloves garlic, minced
- 1 teaspoon salt
- 1 teaspoon garlic powder
- 1 teaspoon cumin powder
- 1 tablespoon chili powder
- 1 tablespoon smoked paprika
- ½ teaspoon black pepper
- ¼ teaspoon ground cloves
- One 14-ounce can diced tomatoes
- 2 tablespoons tomato paste
- Two 14-ounce cans chicken broth
- One 7-ounce can chipotles in sauce
- Two 15-ounce cans black beans
- Garnishes: sour cream, tortilla chips

Directions

1. Heat the oil in a 6-quart Dutch oven. Add the ground bison, diced onion, chiles, and garlic. Cook until the meat is browned, then add the salt and all spices.

2. Stir in the diced tomatoes, tomato paste, and chicken broth. Add the chipotles, one at a time, until you achieve the right level of spiciness.

3. Simmer over low heat for 30 minutes, then add the black beans. Cover and simmer for an additional 30 minutes over low heat. Serve with a dollop of sour cream and tortilla chips.

HILDA STERNER,
Trego, Montana

Hilda Sterner is a cookbook author and a food blogger at www.HildasKitchenBlog.com. She is involved in church ministry, is a Navy Veteran, and is a retired Deputy Sheriff. In 2008, Hilda published *Mom's Authentic Assyrian Recipes Cookbook*. Hilda is married to her best friend, Scott, and has two adult children, Nena and Scott.
Website: www.hildaskitchenblog.com
Facebook: @HildasKitchenBlog
Instagram: @hildaskitchenblog
TikTok: @hildaskitchenblog
Social media handles

Chipotle Chorizo Chili

COOK TIME

1 hr. 30 mins.

Makes 6 servings

My business partner introduced me to a lot of different ethnic foods and made a chorizo chili for meal prep that I loved. He is the most cryptic person you will ever meet, and he never gave me his recipe, just some broad ingredients, so I spent the next six months making a pot or two a week to really get it perfected.

INGREDIENTS

For Chili:
- Six 5-ounce chorizo links
- 1 medium onion, diced
- 1 tablespoon extra virgin olive oil
- Two 28-ounce cans crushed tomatoes
- Two 15-ounce cans black beans

For Spice Dump:
- 1 teaspoon ancho chile powder
- 1 teaspoon annatto powder
- 1 teaspoon coriander
- ½ teaspoon cumin
- ½ teaspoon salt
- ½ teaspoon black pepper

For Chipotle Paste:
- ½ tablespoon apple cider vinegar
- One 8-ounce can chipotles
- ¼ teaspoon ancho chile powder
- ¼ teaspoon annatto chile powder
- ¼ teaspoon coriander
- 3 tablespoons crushed tomatoes
- ½ tablespoon fresh cilantro
- Small squirt of lime juice

Directions

1. Remove the chorizo links from their casing; discard the casing. Chop the meat and cook it three-quarters of the way through.

2. Cook the onion with the olive oil until the onions are translucent.

3. Mix the spice dump. Add the spice dump to the onions and coat well.

4. Add 1 can of crushed tomatoes to the onions. Turn the heat to medium-low and stir often.

5. Make the chipotle paste, taking the 3 tablespoons of crushed tomatoes for the paste from the unused can.

6. Add 2 tablespoons of the chipotle paste to the onions as well as the rest of the crushed tomatoes. Add the chorizo and cook on low heat for 45 minutes, stirring often.

7. Add the beans 30 minutes before serving. Add more chipotle paste to taste; I stay under 3 tablespoons during this last step.

BRIAN D. SANTAY,
Toms River, New Jersey

Brian Santay is a mechanic turned restaurant owner. When he is not experimenting in the kitchen, he is spending time with his son.

Christmas Eve Chili

Ever since I can remember, my mom made chili for us on Christmas Eve. It was our traditional meal before the much-anticipated opening of gifts. I've carried that tradition on, and, for 38 years, I've made chili for my kids and grandkids every Christmas Eve. Now, I am a beans-in-my-chili kind of gal, and I use at least three types of beans. You can use whatever you like best in yours. You will also see that I use Chili-O® seasoning. It's what my mom used and it's what my family loves. I won't forget the one Christmas when I used my own mix instead, and the next morning my stocking was full of coal!

COOK TIME

1 hr. 30 mins.

Makes 20 servings
(6 quarts)

INGREDIENTS

- 2½ pounds ground beef
- 2 cups onions, diced
- ¾ cup chili seasoning (I use French's® Chili-O® Seasoning Mix)
- 2½ tablespoons brown sugar
- 46 ounces tomato juice
- 28 ounces crushed tomatoes
- 28 ounces diced tomatoes
- 28 ounces tomatoes and green chiles

- Two 15-ounce cans dark red kidney beans, drained
- Two 15-ounce cans black beans, drained
- Three 15-ounce cans chili beans, undrained
- Salt and pepper, to taste
- Garnish and serve with: corn chips, shredded cheese, diced onions, olives, jalapeños, sour cream

Directions

1. In a large stock pot on medium-high heat, brown the ground beef and onions. When the beef is brown, drain the fat.

2. Add the chili seasoning and stir well to incorporate.

3. Add the remaining ingredients and mix well. Bring to a boil, then turn the heat to low and simmer all day if you can, stirring about every hour.

4. Serve piping hot with whatever fixings you enjoy! Our family loves to make chili pies. We set up a buffet of corn chips, shredded cheese, diced onions, olives, jalapeños, and sour cream and let everyone make their own.

5. If you have extra chili, you can freeze it in smaller containers and use it for chili dogs, nachos, or a quick meal when you don't feel like cooking.

KIM WILCOX,
Knoxville, Tennessee

From her first Easy Bake oven to her owning restaurants, Kim Wilcox finds joy in making others smile through food. Kim is a regular on local TV stations, has been featured in print media as having one of the most unique ice cream flavors in Knoxville, and has been featured on both The Cooking Channel and Food Network. She wrote *The Great Book of Grilled Cheese* and has published recipes in *The Ultimate Spam® Cookbook*. Kim has also been a two-time winner at the March of Dimes Celebrity Chefs auction with her unique and savory ice cream desserts. Kim grew up in a family who gathered in the kitchen, and she sees food as the universal language that we all speak.
Instagram: @itsallso yummycafeowner
Twitter: @ItsAll SoYummy
Facebook: Its All So Yummy Cafe/Hilton Head Ice Cream

Kevin's Famous Chili Recreated

I'm a massive fan of *The Office*! Last summer, I posted a video recreating "Kevin's Famous Chili" to my accounts, and it went viral overnight, gaining over two million views. This recipe was the closest I could come up with to what Kevin described in the show, down to the ancho chiles, diced whole tomatoes, and undercooked onions.

COOK TIME
1 hr. 30 mins.

Makes 7+ servings

WATCH HOW TO MAKE THIS RECIPE

INGREDIENTS

- Olive oil
- 2 onions, diced
- 5 cloves garlic, minced
- 2 jalapeños, finely chopped
- 3 dried ancho chiles, rehydrated in hot water for 10 minutes and finely chopped
- 3 pounds ground beef
- 10–12 fresh plum tomatoes, peeled and diced
- 2 tablespoons tomato paste

- One 15-ounce can dark kidney beans
- One 15-ounce can light kidney beans
- One 15-ounce can pinto beans
- One 15-ounce can black beans
- One 15-ounce can navy beans
- 4 cups beef broth
- 3 tablespoons cumin
- 3 tablespoons coriander
- 3 tablespoons oregano
- Salt and pepper, to taste

Directions

1. Heat the olive oil in a large pot and gently sauté the onions, leaving them slightly undercooked (as Kevin instructs!).
2. Add the garlic, jalapeños, and ancho chiles, toasting them lightly.
3. Pour in the ground beef. Allow the beef to brown before adding the diced tomatoes, tomato paste, beans, beef broth, and spices.
4. Simmer for about 1 hour on medium-low heat, stirring frequently.
5. Enjoy with your favorite chili toppings!

ARIANA FEYGIN,
Excelsior, Minnesota

Ariana Feygin is a 17-year-old chef, philanthropist, food content creator, and former contestant on *MasterChef Junior* with Gordon Ramsay. From sharing creative recipes with her two million followers on social media to raising over $500,000 in support of a variety of charitable causes, touching people's lives is what brings Ariana the most joy.
Facebook, YouTube, Instagram, TikTok: @ArianaFeygin

Timmy Chili

Developed on active duty (Navy) and perfected throughout local and state cook-offs, this *rojo* (also known as red chili) has continuously received first place and people's choice awards! It has received accolades in Hawaii, Colorado, Iowa, and Kansas. One of my highest accomplishments is bringing this US-style chili to Australia during my assignment there. It's easy to make, goes with anything or tastes great on its own, and no matter how full you get, you always want more!

COOK TIME
1 hr. 30 mins.
Makes 7+ servings

BLACK BEAN CHILI

INGREDIENTS

- Two 16-ounce cans tomato sauce
- Two 16-ounce cans diced tomatoes
- Two 16-ounce cans black beans
- Two 16-ounce cans dark red kidney beans
- Two 16-ounce cans pinto beans
- Two 4-ounce cans diced green chiles
- 8 ounces jalapeños, sliced
- 1 large onion, diced
- 3 tablespoons garlic, minced
- 3 tablespoons chili powder
- 1 tablespoon parsley
- 1 tablespoon basil
- 1 tablespoon oregano
- 2 teaspoons cumin
- 2 teaspoons smoked paprika
- 2 teaspoons chipotle powder
- 2 teaspoons ancho chile powder
- 1 teaspoon black pepper
- 1 teaspoon red pepper flakes
- 1 pound ground beef
- 1 pound hot ground sausage
- 1 pound hot Italian sausage

Directions

1. Combine the tomato sauce, diced tomatoes, and beans in a large pot. Turn on medium heat, cover, and bring to a bubble.

2. Stir in the green chiles, jalapeños, and onion. Continue to cook, covered, on medium heat.

3. Add the garlic and each spice. Cover again and turn heat to low.

4. Brown all the meat. Drain the cooked beef, but keep the sausage juices. Add all the meat (and sausage juice) to the pot.

5. Simmer for at least an hour, stirring occasionally. The longer the chili sits, the better blended the spices will be. This chili is best after overnight refrigeration.

Chili Recipe Awards

- 1998 – Iroquois Lagoon Yacht Club 1st Place
- 2003 – Iroquois Lagoon Yacht Club 1st and 3rd Place
- 2009 – Member, International Chili Society
- 2010 – State of Hawaii Chili Cook-Off Honorable Mention
- 2011 – State of Hawaii Chili Cook-Off Entrant
- 2012 – Joint Intelligence Operations Center 1st Place
- 2013 – Hawaii Sail and Power Squadron 1st Place and People's Choice
- 2014 – Joint Intelligence Operations Center 1st Place and Certificate of Awesomeness
- 2016 – US Army Command and General Staff Officer Course 1st Place and Spiciest

TIMOTHY J. BANES,
Aiea, Hawaii

Originally from Palo, Iowa, Timmy has lived in Hawaii for the last 25 years. He spent 20 years in the U.S. Navy before retiring and has been married for over 27 years. He and his wife, Karen, have two cats, Linus and Lucy. He loves chili for its dynamic and versatile nature, as well as being able to take it to the limits of the imagination. Timmy joined the International Chili Society in 2009, and his highest honor was winning First and Spiciest for the U.S. Army Command and General Staff Officer Course in 2016. Facebook: @Timothy J. Banes

www.crepesnokool.com

WATCH HOW I ADD TOMATOES, SAUCE, AND SPICES HERE.

SERIOUS ABOUT CHILI

Pumpkin and Black Bean Chili

When fall arrives, we all start craving two things—pumpkin and chili. So why not put them together? I tried this recipe on my family, truly not knowing if it would pass muster—but it did, with flying colors! The pumpkin creates a smooth, velvety texture and the black beans amp up the fiber and heartiness.

COOK TIME
30 mins.

Makes 7+ servings

INGREDIENTS

- 1 small onion, diced
- 1 pound ground beef
- 4 cloves garlic, minced
- 2 tablespoons chili powder
- 1 teaspoon cumin
- 1 teaspoon salt
- ½ teaspoon red pepper flakes
- 1 cup pumpkin purée
- One 15.5-ounce can diced tomatoes
- One 15.5-ounce can black beans, drained and rinsed
- One 15.5-ounce can chili beans
- Two 15.5-ounce cans tomato sauce
- 1 cup water

Directions

1. Heat a large soup pot or Dutch oven to medium-high heat.
2. Add the onion and sauté until slightly translucent.
3. Add the ground beef. Crumble and cook it until it is no longer pink. Add the garlic and sauté for a few minutes. Drain off any excess grease.
4. Add all the seasonings—chili powder, cumin, salt, and red pepper flakes. Stir to combine.
5. Dump in the pumpkin, tomatoes, beans, and tomato sauce. Stir and let simmer, keeping the chili warm until it's ready to serve.

Good-to-Know Info

Every great chili recipe needs a secret ingredient! Some people swear by a shot of bourbon, but any sweet or acidic ingredient will add something extra and unique.

ALLY BILLHORN,
Wilton, Iowa

A popular Midwest food blogger since 2009, Ally Billhorn highlights simple, family-friendly meals; ones that are homemade and easy, even for the non-cook! She takes pride in showing others fun ways to put meals on the table without much fuss. Ally has been featured in multiple Midwest newspapers, including *The Des Moines Register* and *dsm* magazine, as well various podcasts and local television shows. Her recipes have been featured by many national food brands and companies, including Blue Bunny®, Cuisinart®, ALDI®, Hy-Vee®, Iowa Beef Industry Council®, Cookies BBQ & Seasonings®, and more.
Facebook,
Instagram, Twitter:
@sweetsavoryeats
Pinterest: @allybillhorn

COOK TIME

3 hrs.

Makes 10 servings

Game Day Chili

Hickory-smoked blade steak adds character and depth to this chili, while giving you the opportunity to defy winter by using a grill or smoker. I smoked about 4 pounds of blade steak for 30 minutes on my daily-use grill, a Kamado Joe® ceramic grill. The meat will have plenty of time to cook and tenderize in the pot—the focus here is on imparting the smoke flavor that will distinguish this chili. Make sure you don't use a leaner cut of beef, because it will lead to a dry and disappointing meat. Also, go with dried beans rather than canned beans—dried beans retain their integrity throughout the cooking process.

INGREDIENTS

- One 16-ounce bag dry (uncooked) mixed beans, or a combination of black, pinto, and kidney beans
- 4 pounds blade steak
- 6 dried ancho chiles
- 3 chile de árbol peppers
- 3 tablespoons cornmeal
- 2 tablespoons molasses
- 2 teaspoons oregano
- 1 tablespoon cumin seeds
- 3 teaspoons cocoa
- 3 cups chicken broth
- 3 large yellow onions, chopped
- Vegetable oil
- 5 cloves garlic
- One 28-ounce can diced tomatoes
- Garnishes: lime slices, avocado, sour cream, shredded cheddar cheese

Directions

1. Add the beans to salted water. Bring to a full boil, remove from the heat, cover, and set aside for 1 hour.

2. Meanwhile, start the grill with hardwood charcoal. Add 2–3 pieces of hickory hardwood. When the hickory is fully aflame, place the blade steak on the grate and close the lid. Flip the steak after 15 minutes; remove it after 30 minutes. Slice the steak into small cubes.

3. Stem and seed the dried ancho chiles and chile de árbol peppers. Shred the ancho chiles and toast them and the chile de árbol peppers in a skillet. Transfer the toasted chiles to a blender, add the remaining solid ingredients (cornmeal, oregano, cumin, and cocoa), and pulse. Add 1 cup chicken broth and blend until a paste forms.

4. Sauté the chopped onions in vegetable oil in a large Dutch oven. Sauté the garlic separately because it browns so quickly.

5. Add the chile paste, the molasses, the tomatoes, 2 cups of chicken broth, the drained beans, the garlic, and the meat cubes to the pot. Mix thoroughly and place the covered pot in the oven at 300 degrees Fahrenheit.

6. After 2 hours, verify that the beans are softened. Top with lime slices, avocado, sour cream, and shredded cheddar cheese.

ROSS BOWEN,
Taylors, South Carolina

Ross Bowen's first BBQ experience came at age six in his home state of South Carolina. Years later, he formed the Two Little Pigs BBQ team and competed nationally and internationally, winning many awards, including the Minnesota State championship. He is a career actuary and applies an analytical rigor to his craft, saying it is better to be very good with a few dishes than mediocre at many.

Content submitted by Cynthia Sutter. She is the founder and editor of Spirited Table®, which provides seasonal and holiday lifestyle tips, epicurean news, and recipes.

Zesty Black Bean Chili

This is one of my favorite bowls of chili—a comforting, easy black bean chili with plenty of piquant spices and just the right amount of heat. Chop, pour, simmer, done.

COOK TIME

45 mins.

Makes 6 servings

INGREDIENTS

- 1 tablespoon olive oil
- 2 jalapeños, diced
- 1 medium onion, diced
- 4 cloves garlic, chopped
- 1½ pounds ground turkey, or use ground beef, ground chicken, or ground pork
- 3 ounces tomato paste
- Two 16-ounce cans black beans, drained
- 2 cups chicken stock or a good-flavored amber beer (I use a white ale)
- 1 tablespoon chili powder
- 1 tablespoon ancho chile powder
- 1 teaspoon cayenne pepper
- 1 teaspoon oregano
- 1 teaspoon cumin
- Salt and pepper, to taste
- Hot sauce, to taste
- Garnishes: crumbly white cheese (like cotija), spicy chili flakes, chopped red onion, chopped fresh parsley, sliced jalapeños, lemon or lime wedges

Directions

1. Heat the oil in a large pot and add the jalapeños and onions. Cook them down for about 5 minutes, or until they become tender.

2. Add the garlic and cook for another minute, until the garlic becomes fragrant.

3. Add the ground turkey and break it apart with a wooden spoon. Cook until the turkey is mostly cooked through, about 5 minutes.

4. Stir in the tomato paste and cook another minute.

5. Add in the beans, chicken stock (or beer), and all the seasonings, plus the hot sauce to taste. Bring to a boil, then reduce the heat and simmer for at least 30 minutes. You can easily let it simmer for 1 hour to let the flavors develop even further.

6. Serve with your desired garnishes!

WATCH HOW TO MAKE THIS RECIPE

MICHAEL J. HULTQUIST,
Huntersville, North Carolina

Mike Hultquist is the author of *The Spicy Dehydrator Cookbook* and *The Spicy Food Lovers' Cookbook*. You can find more of his culinary work at the popular food blog, Chili Pepper Madness (www.chili peppermadness.com). Facebook, Instagram, YouTube: @chilipeppermadness

COOK TIME
1 hr. 30 mins.
Makes 8 servings

Sirloin Black Bean Chili

This recipe was created one evening long ago when I wanted to make chili but had no ground meat and no kidney beans. I used choice sirloin and black beans and improvised the spice blend. What a treat for a cool evening or when watching football in the fall. Add a frosty mug of cold beer and life is good!

INGREDIENTS

- ⅓ cup olive oil
- 2 pounds boneless sirloin, cut into ½-inch cubes
- 2 cups yellow onion, chopped
- 2 tablespoons garlic, minced
- 5 fresh jalapeños, seeded and finely chopped (wear rubber gloves)
- ⅓ cup masa harina (corn flour mix for tortillas)
- ⅓ cup plus 1 teaspoon chili powder
- ½ teaspoon cayenne pepper
- ½ teaspoon ground cumin
- ½ teaspoon white pepper
- 2 teaspoons salt
- 1 cup dry red wine
- 4 cups beef broth
- 2 cups cooked black beans, rinsed and drained if canned
- One 14-ounce can petite diced tomatoes
- Garnishes: grated mild cheddar cheese, minced red onion, cilantro

Directions

1. In a heavy kettle, heat the oil over moderately high heat until it is hot but not smoking. Brown the sirloin in batches, transferring it as it is browned with a slotted spoon to a bowl.
2. In the fat remaining in the kettle, cook the yellow onion, garlic, and jalapeños over moderate heat, stirring until the onion is softened.
3. Add the masa harina, chili powder, cayenne pepper, cumin, white pepper, salt, and wine. Cook the mixture, stirring for 5 minutes.
4. Add the broth and the sirloin and simmer the mixture uncovered, stirring occasionally, for 45 minutes or until the meat is tender.
5. Stir in the beans and diced tomatoes. Simmer the mixture for 20–30 more minutes.
6. Serve the chili garnished with cheddar cheese, red onion, and cilantro.

GUY BOWER,
Wichita, Kansas

Guy Bower is a retired Air Force fighter pilot and retired FedEx Airbus A300 captain. Both careers involved many years of living, traveling, cooking, and eating in Europe. He has been a dedicated food and wine enthusiast and home chef since growing up and working in his parents' Miami restaurant. He is the host/producer of *The Good Life* radio show on KNSS since 1991, the WSU Wine Educator, an International Wine Judge, and a level-1 sommelier with the Court of Master Sommeliers. Guy lives The Good Life and promotes food, wine, and fun every Saturday on his radio show.
Radio Show Website: www.goodlifeguy.com
Facebook, Twitter: @goodlifeguy

Homestyle Chili

For homestyle chili, beans are required, but anything else goes!
Any kind of meat in any kind of cut, any combination of veggies, any color—
homestyle is whatever you like. You can even throw in seafood!

The Recipes

Slow Cooker Chili with Tomatoes

Kids' Favorite Chili

George Lulos Chili

Hannah Dasher's Bad-Mamma-Jamma Chili

George Lulos Chili

George S. Lulos owned and operated a small-town restaurant called the Liberty Lunch in Buckhannon, West Virginia, after taking over from his Greek father in 1948. Customers traveled for miles to enjoy his menu, especially his secret Greek chili recipe and homemade pies. George was quite a character with his jokes and his enthusiasm. His children and grandchildren (including me!) carry on this exact recipe to this day.

COOK TIME
5 hrs.

Makes 7+ servings

INGREDIENTS

- 2 white onions
- 3 tablespoons butter, or substitute 2 tablespoons oil
- 2 pounds 73% lean ground beef
- Two 6-ounce or 15-ounce cans tomato paste
- 12–15 ounces water
- 6–8 cloves garlic, diced (or as much as your heart desires)
- Two 15-ounce cans tomato sauce
- ½–1 cup tomato juice or water
- 2–3 tablespoons chili powder
- 2 tablespoons oregano
- 2 tablespoons parsley
- 1 tablespoon paprika
- ½ teaspoon allspice
- 1 teaspoon seasoned salt (I use Morton® Season-All®)
- Salt and pepper, to taste

Directions

1. Cook the chopped onions in the butter (or oil) in a large pot or Dutch oven until soft.
2. Add in the ground beef and cook together until the beef is browned. Do not drain the fat—it will bring flavor to the chili as it cooks.
3. Add in the tomato paste, water, and garlic. Cook on medium to medium-low heat for 1 hour.
4. Add in the tomato sauce and juice (or water). Add all the remaining spices. Cook on low for 4–5 hours.
5. Once the chili is done, skim off the excess fat.

WATCH HOW TO MAKE THIS RECIPE

NATALIE WHELCHEL,
Coralville, Iowa

Natalie Whelchel is a home cook and food content creator, who also works full-time as a special education teacher for Kindergarten through 3rd grade. She has been cooking since she was a child, but really started exploring the kitchen in 2009. Her grandfather's recipe she holds dear to her heart because she never got to know him. She was five years old when he passed away, so she hopes that others get to enjoy his recipe that so many loved.
Website: www.living inmidwest.com
Instagram, TikTok, YouTube: @Livinginmidwest

COOK TIME

4 hrs.

Makes 7+ servings

Slow Cooker Chili with Tomatoes

I have been making this chili recipe for my family for as long as I can remember. It is a staple of our gatherings and big events like game day. I love to make it during the fall and winter, as it is super easy—you basically just throw everything in the slow cooker and go. And who doesn't love simple?

INGREDIENTS

- 3 pounds lean ground beef
- One 28-ounce can stewed tomatoes
- Two 16-ounce cans dark red kidney beans
- Two 16-ounce cans light red kidney beans
- 1 purple onion, chopped
- One 12-ounce jar hot banana pepper rings (add more if you want to spice it up)
- Two packs hot chili seasoning (or mild, if you're scared!)
- Garnish: cheddar cheese cubes

Directions

1. Brown the ground beef in a large skillet and drain the grease.
2. Combine all the ingredients in a large slow cooker. Do not drain the liquid from any of the ingredients. Stir the chili to get an even mixture.
3. Cook on low for about 3–4 hours, depending upon your slow cooker.
4. After the chili is fully cooked, add some cubes of cheddar cheese and enjoy!

DAWN MCALEXANDER,
Mount Airy, North Carolina

Dawn's free time is spent traveling and working on her blogs, www.CheapIsTheNewClassy.com and www.EatPlayRock.com. She and her daughter, Amber, have binge-watched *The Office* too many times to count and love to use random quotes from the show in public to see who gets it. It is a great conversation starter. After all, if you dig long enough and hard enough in a conversation, you get to a friend. Dawn lives in NC with her boyfriend, Kenny, her dogs, Daisy and Marley, and his cat, TJ, where she patiently awaits her Dundee for "Best Chili."
Facebook: @cheapis thenewclassy
Instagram, Twitter, Pinterest: @thenewclassy

Fairy Dust Chili

I started cooking competition chili back in 1982 with my dad, Dan Edmonson, and sister, Lisa Edmonson Stone. After years of test kitchens working to perfect the recipe, I claimed the 2021 ICS World Chili Championship Homestyle Division against more than 100 competitors. Some folks say that true Texas chili never includes beans in the chili—that it's against the law. However, this Texas girl did use beans in her World Championship Homestyle chili. You could say this is a truly bold and flavorful Texas-style chili that has broken the law.

COOK TIME

2 hrs. 15 mins.

Makes 6 servings

INGREDIENTS

For Chili:
- 2 pounds 80% lean ground chuck (I use HEB®)
- 2 tablespoons canola oil
- One 14.5-ounce can beef broth (I use Swanson®)
- One 14.5-ounce can chicken broth (I use Swanson®)
- One 8-ounce can tomato sauce
- Two 16-ounce cans chili beans, drained (I use Bush's®)
- Hot sauce, to taste (I use Cholula®)
- Salt, to taste

For First Spice Mixture:
- 2 teaspoons onion granules (I use Mild Bill's®)
- 1½ teaspoons garlic granules (I use Mild Bill's®)
- 1 tablespoon beef granules (I use Knorr®)
- 1 tablespoon chicken granules (I use Knorr®)
- 2 tablespoons chili powder (I use Mild Bill's San Antonio Original®)
- 2 teaspoons chili powder (I use Mild Bill's Dixon®)
- ⅛ teaspoon cayenne pepper (I use Mild Bill's®)
- ⅛ teaspoon Tellicherry black pepper (I use Mild Bill's®)

For Second Spice Mixture:
- 1 tablespoon chili powder (I use Mild Bill's San Antonio Original®)
- 2 tablespoons chili powder (I use Mild Bill's Cowtown®)
- 1½ tablespoons cumin (I use Mild Bill's®)
- ½ teaspoon granulated garlic (I use Mild Bill's®)
- ⅛ teaspoon brown sugar
- 1 packet Sazón Goya® or similar seasoning

Directions

1. In a 3- or 4-quart pot, lightly brown the ground chuck in the canola oil. As you are browning, leave the meat in big chunks in your pot. Drain off the grease and set the meat aside.

2. Clean out your pot and add the meat chunks back into the pot. Add the beef and chicken broths. Cook on a low boil for 45 minutes.

3. Remove the meat and strain off the grease from the broth. Add the strained broth and meat chunks back into the pot. Add the tomato sauce and the first spice mixture. Cook on medium-low heat for about 30 minutes, being careful not to mash the meat.

4. After 30 minutes, turn off the heat. Cut the meat chunks down or use a potato masher to break the meat up to about fingertip size.

5. Turn on the heat to low and add the second spice mixture and the chili beans. Simmer on low heat for about 20 minutes.

6. Before serving, add 3 dashes of hot sauce, salt to taste, and, if needed, more cayenne pepper for heat.

Chili Recipe Awards

- 2021 WCCC ICS Homestyle Chili Championship
- 2018 ICS Louisiana Regional Homestyle Chili Championship
- 2016 CASI Oklahoma State Chili Championship

DIANNE LEWIS,
Boerne, Texas

You might say that Dianne was "born to cook chili." She and her sisters began competitively cooking in 2007 to honor their father, Richard "Dan" Edmonson. Dan had won the honor to cook at the CASI Terlingua International Chili Championship in Terlingua in 1983, but was tragically unable to attend. Dianne and her sisters, Lisa, Terry, and Elaine, have won multiple cook-offs, including the Terlingua International Chili Championship at Terlingua, Texas, Ladies State, and others. Dianne's win in September 2021 netted her the prestigious title WCCC ICS Homestyle World Chili Champion in Myrtle Beach, SC.

Dianne and her family and friends continue to cook competitively. Living outside of Boerne, she and her husband, Patrick, enjoy the outdoors, fishing at the coast, their three children, and six grandchildren.

Facebook, Instagram: @dianneedmonsonlewis

Kids' Favorite Chili

We love to make this chili right before we head out for a weekend of camping. Having a hearty and balanced meal ready to go when we arrive at camp is always so comforting. We enjoy this with chips or on top of hot dogs. This chili recipe is great for families since it doesn't pack too much heat, only flavor.

COOK TIME

40 mins.

Makes 6 servings

INGREDIENTS

- Half of 1 onion, chopped
- 2 tablespoons olive oil
- 1 pound ground sausage
- 2 tablespoons chili powder
- 1 tablespoon cumin
- ½ teaspoon salt
- ½ teaspoon pepper
- One 15-ounce can kidney beans, drained
- One 15-ounce can white beans, drained
- One 32-ounce can crushed tomatoes

Directions

1. Sauté the onions in olive oil until translucent, about 3 minutes.
2. Add the sausage and seasonings and cook through for 12 minutes.
3. Add the remaining ingredients (beans and tomatoes) and simmer for 20 minutes.

BRI GRAJKOWSKI,
San Diego, California

Brianne Grajkowski is the founder of BriGeeski, Inc., a food-focused lifestyle blog and online media agency. Bri features everyday recipes, adventures, travel, and design on the San Diego–based blog. Bri won Puesto's Next Top Taco contest and had her taco recipe as a special on their menu. Bri is a home cook who learned from watching her family and tasting food from local restaurants. She wrote her first book, *Cooking With Kids*, to teach her kids how to cook and help other families come together in the kitchen, too!
Website: www.Bri Geeski.com
Facebook, Instagram, Twitter, Pinterest: @BriGeeski

COOK TIME
2 hrs.
Makes 6 servings

Clean the Freezer Chili

There is so much debate about the origin of chili, but the use of game as the main ingredient, as seen in this recipe, originated in a convent of nuns in Texas back in the 1800s. With so many hunters here in the bayou state (Louisiana), there is no better dish than this one to clean the freezer of last year's hunt right before the upcoming season.

INGREDIENTS

- ½ cup vegetable oil
- 1 pound duck breast meat, diced
- 1 pound venison, diced
- 2 cups onions, diced
- 1 cup celery, diced
- ½ cup green bell peppers, diced
- ½ cup red bell peppers, diced
- ½ cup yellow bell peppers, diced
- 2 tablespoons garlic, minced
- 2 tablespoons jalapeños, diced
- One 16-ounce can pinto beans
- Three 8-ounce cans tomato sauce
- 2 cups chicken stock
- 1 tablespoon chili powder
- 1 teaspoon ground cumin
- Salt and black pepper, to taste
- Granulated garlic, to taste
- Serve with: cornbread

Directions

1. In a large Dutch oven, heat the vegetable oil over medium-high heat. Add the duck breast and venison and sauté for 20 minutes to render the juices, stirring often.

2. Add the onions, celery, bell peppers, minced garlic, and jalapeños. Sauté for 3–5 minutes or until the vegetables are wilted, stirring occasionally.

3. Add the pinto beans, tomato sauce, and chicken stock, stirring to incorporate. Bring to a low boil, then reduce to a simmer.

4. Stir in the chili powder and cumin. Cook for approximately 1 hour or until the duck and venison are tender, stirring occasionally.

5. Season to taste with salt, black pepper, and granulated garlic.

6. Ladle into soup bowls or mugs and serve hot with fresh cornbread.

CHEF JOHN FOLSE,
New Orleans, Louisiana

Chef John Folse, Louisiana's Culinary Ambassador to the World, is proud to share his passion for Louisiana's swamp floor pantry around the world. As an entrepreneur, his interests range from restaurateur to manufacturer, author to educator. Some of his national and international accolades include being named Louisiana Restaurateur of the Year, National Chef of the Year, and several others. Author of 10 cookbooks, his *Can You Dig It* vegetable cookbook won the Benny Award for Best Cookbook. Folse hosts a national PBS television cooking show, *A Taste of Louisiana*. He was recently inducted into the American Academy of Chefs Culinary Hall of Fame and the Chef John Folse Culinary Institute at Nicholls State University is named in his honor.

Good-to-Know Info

The dying words of frontier legend Kit Carson were, "Wish I had time for just one more bowl of chili."

Hannah Dasher's Bad-Mamma-Jamma Chili

My TikTok followers tell me they've been winning chili competitions with this recipe. I honestly just threw this together according to my personal tastes. . . . Anyhow, if you don't want any leftovers, make it this way.

COOK TIME
1 hr.

Makes 6–8 servings

INGREDIENTS

- 1 pound ground chuck
- 1 pound pork sausage (spicy is great)
- 1 medium onion, chopped
- 2 jalapeños, chopped and seeded
- One 28-ounce can petite diced tomatoes
- One 28-ounce can crushed tomatoes
- 4 ounces any domestic lager beer
- One 6-ounce can tomato paste

- One 28-ounce can black beans, drained
- Two 15-ounce cans hot chili beans
- 2 tablespoons yellow mustard
- 2–3 tablespoons chili powder
- 6 light dashes cumin
- ½ teaspoon garlic powder
- ¼ teaspoon cayenne pepper
- 2–3 tablespoons brown sugar
- 1 tablespoon salt
- ¼ cup instant potato flakes
- Garnishes: sour cream, cheese, hashbrown casserole

Directions

1. In a 7- to 8-quart pot, brown the meat. Set it aside on a paper towel.

2. On medium-low heat, sauté the onions and jalapeños in the meat drippings until tender.

3. Add the meat, tomatoes, and spices. Rinse out the crushed tomato can with beer and add the beer to the pot, along with the tomato paste, beans, and mustard. Stir well. Cover and simmer on medium-low for 20–30 minutes (simmer for longer if desired).

4. When just about ready to serve, thicken the chili with instant potato flakes. Top with sour cream and cheese. (Although it doesn't need a thing!) I also garnish mine with hashbrown casserole. Sinful.

HANNAH DASHER,
Nashville, Tennesee

Hannah Dasher is quickly becoming a household name with her viral TikTok series, "Stand By Your Pan," which is a country music–infused cooking show. Dasher, a Nashville recording artist and songwriter, says the series "accidentally blew up on her" during quarantine. She has rocked audiences across the country opening for her heroes like Hank Williams Jr., Lynyrd Skynyrd, and Reba McEntire.
Instagram:
@hannahdasher
TikTok:
@hannahdamndasher
Apple Music, Spotify:
Hannah Dasher

Blade Steak Chili

Here's the chili I whip up while watching the playoffs. It's not particularly hot. I usually use a chuck roast, but you can use a brisket if you have more time. Two spices are at the heart of this chili's flavor: cumin and coriander. Use fresh whole spices rather than pre-ground spices. Do not cut this corner—it will be worth it.

COOK TIME

3 hrs.

Makes 10 servings

INGREDIENTS

- 1 pound blade steak
- Cooking oil of choice
- 1 large yellow onion, chopped
- 2 cloves garlic, pushed through a garlic press
- One 14-ounce can crushed tomatoes
- Two 14-ounce cans pinto beans
- 3–5 cups beef or chicken stock
- 1 large dried ancho chile
- 1 large dried Hatch chile
- 1 tablespoon fresh, whole cumin seeds
- 1 teaspoon fresh, whole coriander seeds
- 1 tablespoon oregano
- ¼ teaspoon cayenne pepper
- 1 tablespoon cornmeal
- Garnishes: sour cream, cheddar cheese, cilantro, crackers

Directions

1. Throw the steak in a snowbank for about 30 minutes while it is 0 degrees Fahrenheit outside. If you don't live in Minnesota like I do, put the streak in your freezer instead. This will make it easy to cut into small cubes. Cut the meat into ¾-inch cubes.

2. In a large heavy pot, like a Dutch oven, sauté the meat in oil until brown. I use a high smoke point oil by Eniva®, which is comprised of avocado and safflower oils. Vegetable oil or canola oil work fine too.

3. Set the meat aside. Add more oil to the pot if necessary, then add and cook the chopped onion. Scrape the bottom to release any browning from the meat. After a few minutes, add the garlic. Garlic cooks faster than onion, and burned garlic never did anybody any good.

4. Add the beef, tomatoes, and beans to the pot, along with 3 cups of beef stock (chicken stock will also work). Keep the mixture on a low-medium heat while you work on the chiles and spices next.

5. Choose your chiles; I use chiles about 4 inches long and 1 inch wide each. Remove the seeds and tops of the chiles, then shred them into smaller pieces. Place them on a hot skillet and punch them around continuously, until they start to smoke, which will only take a few minutes. Then process the chiles in a food processor until they become as atomized as possible.

6. Add the pulverized chiles to the chili pot. If you want to make the chili hotter, add the chile seeds you removed earlier.

7. Next, it's time to process the spices. For the cumin and coriander, use the freshest whole spices you have, rather than starting from pre-ground spices. Toast them on the hot skillet until they start to smoke, then grind them with a mortar and pestle or place them in a food processor and pulse until they are broken down.

8. Add the cumin and coriander to the chili. Also add the oregano and the carefully measured cayenne pepper. Never free-pour cayenne pepper—too much heat is a hard problem to correct.

9. Simmer the chili for a few hours, stirring occasionally, and adding more beef stock if more liquid is needed. Add the cornmeal to help the chili thicken.

10. For garnishes, add sour cream, cheddar cheese, and cilantro. Serve with crackers.

ROSS BOWEN,
Taylors, South Carolina

Ross Bowen's first BBQ experience came at age six in his home state of South Carolina. Years later, he formed the Two Little Pigs BBQ team and competed nationally and internationally, winning many awards, including the Minnesota State championship. He is a career actuary and applies an analytical rigor to his craft, saying it is better to be very good with a few dishes than mediocre at many.

Content submitted by Cynthia Sutter. She is the founder and editor of Spirited Table®, which provides seasonal and holiday lifestyle tips, epicurean news, and recipes.

Italian Chili

This Italian Chili has so many unique ingredients that make it exceptionally hearty and delicious. During the winter months of the pandemic, I would host walks with friends on the frozen creek behind my home. Following vigorous exercise in chilly fresh air, we would gather around our fire pit and enjoy a steaming bowl of Italian Chili. (It was kept warm in a Slow Cooker with a long extension cord so everything was outdoors.)

COOK TIME
1 hr. 15 mins.
Makes 8–10 servings

INGREDIENTS

- ½ pound mild Italian sausage
- ½ pound hot Italian sausage
- 1 pound ground beef
- 2 cups onion, sliced
- 2 cups red bell peppers, sliced
- 2 cups green bell peppers, sliced
- 5 cloves garlic, finely chopped
- 2 tablespoons tomato paste
- 2 cups green cabbage, shredded
- One 15-ounce can red kidney beans, drained and rinsed
- Two 15-ounce cans diced tomatoes
- One 10-ounce can diced tomatoes and green chiles
- One 15-ounce can cannellini beans, drained, rinsed, and slightly mashed
- 1 tablespoon chili powder, or more if desired
- 3 tablespoons fresh parsley, chopped, divided, 1 tablespoon reserved for garnish
- 2 tablespoons dried oregano
- 1 teaspoon salt, or to taste
- 1 tablespoon basil pesto
- 1 bay leaf
- Garnish: shredded Pecorino cheese

Directions

1. In a large Dutch oven, brown the sausages and ground beef. Drain the meat on paper towels.
2. Cook and stir in the onion and bell peppers in the same pot, cooking for 8 minutes.
3. Add the garlic and cook for 2 minutes, stirring constantly.
4. Add the tomato paste and continue cooking and stirring another 1–2 minutes.
5. Add the browned meats, cabbage, kidney beans, and all three cans of tomatoes.
6. Add the cannellini beans and all remaining seasonings, stirring everything into the chili. Bring the mixture to a boil, reduce the heat, and simmer, uncovered, for about 45 minutes, stirring occasionally.
7. Before serving, remove the bay leaf. Top each serving with cheese.

VICKI BRUNSVOLD,
Edina, Minnesota

Vicki is a self-proclaimed foodie, a tastemaker for the lifestyle website Spirited Table, and the reception coordinator for her church. She has catered for concert receptions, formal dinners, and hors d'oeuvres buffets. Vicki also loves serving on several boards of directors, golfing, biking, meeting for book club, and playing weekly games of bridge and mah-jongg. Content submitted by Cynthia Sutter. She is the founder and editor of Spirited Table®, which provides seasonal and holiday lifestyle tips, epicurean news, and recipes.

COOK TIME
2 hrs.

Makes 7+ servings

Timer Farms Chili

This is great for tailgates or large parties! It's made from easy pantry ingredients you can throw together for a quick yummy meal that will satisfy everyone's hunger.

INGREDIENTS

- 2 pounds beef
- 2 pounds pork
- 1 pound cooked bacon, diced
- Eight 30.5-ounce cans chili beans, medium and hot (I use Brooks®)
- Four 10-ounce cans diced tomato with green chiles
- One 28-ounce can can diced tomatoes
- One 6-ounce can tomato paste
- 2 tablespoons Worcestershire sauce
- 2 tablespoons hot sauce (I use Frank's®)
- 2 stalks scallions, chopped
- 4 red and green bell peppers, chopped
- 6 jalapeños, chopped
- 2 tablespoons cumin
- ¼ cup chili powder
- 1 tablespoon salt
- 1 tablespoon pepper
- 1 tablespoon cayenne pepper
- 1 tablespoon paprika
- 1 tablespoon garlic powder
- 1 tablespoon dried oregano
- 1 tablespoon basil
- 1 pint maple syrup

Directions

1. Cook the ground beef and ground pork in a turkey roaster.
2. Add the bacon, all the beans, diced tomato with green chiles, tomatoes, tomato paste, Worcestershire sauce, and hot sauce. Also add the chopped vegetables. Finally, add all the spices.
3. Stir to mix well, then cook for 1 hour.
4. After 1 hour, add the maple syrup and cook for 1 more hour.

KATIE TIMER,
Fowlerville, Michigan

Katie is a native Michigander and inherited her love of cooking and competition from her mom. Born and raised in Lansing, Katie attended Michigan State University where she received her bachelor's degree in English. A long-time employee of the State of Michigan, Katie currently works as an analyst for the WIC program and enjoys testing out new chili recipes on her unsuspecting coworkers. This chili recipe, which took years to perfect, has consistently won first prize at local chili cook-offs. Katie lives on a working farm in Fowlerville with her husband and two daughters. Check out their website at www .TimerFarms.com.

Chili Recipe Awards

- **Rosemary Motz Chili Cook-Off 2016**
- **St. Agnes K of C 2017, 2018, 2019, 2020**
- **Village of Fowlerville: 2017 Judges' Choice and 2018 Best Business/ Organization**

Chili Takes
Chili Dogs, Nachos, Cornbread, and More

Not just to be enjoyed in a bowl, chili can take your nachos,
hot dogs, and other dishes to a whole new level!

The Recipes

Good-to-Know Info

Tomato paste offers a more intense,
concentrated flavor, so mix in a
few tablespoons along with the
spices. This is also a huge help
when you're low on time but still
want a slow-cooked flavor.

Cornbread Waffle with Chili

Slow Cooker Mexican Goulash

Chili Pasta Casserole

Chili for Chili Dogs

Soy Chorizo Chili and Fries

I used to own a popular Southern California food truck. One of our most popular items was this dish. Soy chorizo, despite its name, has a wonderful chorizo flavor and barely takes any time to prepare. This is a crowd-pleaser that just happens to be vegetarian. Customers sometimes felt betrayed when they discovered it was meatless!

COOK TIME
30 mins.

Makes 7+ servings

INGREDIENTS

- 1 pound soy chorizo (I use Melissa's®)
- 1 onion, finely diced
- 1 teaspoon ground cumin
- 1 teaspoon salt
- ¼ teaspoon ground black pepper
- ¼ teaspoon chili powder
- 1 cup broth or water
- One 14-ounce can black beans
- One 14-ounce can pinto beans
- 1 pound potato fries or fresh potatoes julienne cut
- 1 tablespoon cilantro
- 1 cup finely shredded Jack or cheddar cheese

Directions

1. Heat a heavy-bottomed pan to medium-high. Add the soy chorizo and diced onion. Cook and stir for 1 minute.
2. Add all of the dry spices and turn the heat down a bit. Cook for 1 minute, stirring a little.
3. Add the broth or water, black beans, and pinto beans. Bring to a simmer for 10 minutes.
4. Check the seasoning and add more salt or heat as desired.
5. Toast, air-fry, or deep fry the potato fries.
6. Serve a generous dollop of chili on top of the fries. Garnish with cilantro and shredded cheese.

Chili Recipe Awards

- "Best" Award at the Annual Harvest Festival Chili Cook-Off 2008 (San Diego, CA)

KARI RICH,
Vacaville, California

Chef Kari Rich began her career following in her brother's footsteps in professional kitchens. After culinary school, Chef Rich honed her skills in fine dining premier restaurants in San Diego, California. She continued in her career as a professional chef running kitchens for more than 20 years. After selling her successful food truck venture, Food Farm, Chef Kari has continued working as a restaurant consultant as well as food writing and research. Instagram: @Chef_K_Rich_

COOK TIME

45 mins.

Makes 6 servings

Best Chili Dog Sauce

This homemade chili dog sauce will be the best chili dog sauce you have ever made—and it has a secret ingredient (ground-up hot dogs) that puts it completely over the top!

INGREDIENTS

- 2 tablespoons butter
- 1 onion, chopped
- 1 clove garlic, minced
- 1½ pounds ground beef
- 3 tablespoons chili powder
- 1 tablespoon yellow mustard
- One 6-ounce can tomato paste
- One 6-ounce can water
- Salt and pepper, to taste
- Two 12-ounce packs skinless beef hot dogs (I use Nathan's Famous®)
- Hot dog buns

Directions

1. Add the butter and onions to a skillet and sauté until tender.
2. Add in the garlic and sauté for a minute longer.
3. Add in the ground beef, chili powder, mustard, tomato paste, water, salt, and pepper. Mix together. Cook over medium heat for about 20–25 minutes.
4. Turn down to a simmer and let the mixture continue cooking.
5. While the mixture is cooking, grind up the hot dogs or mince them finely.
6. Add one package of hot dogs to the ground beef mixture and let it cook for another 15 minutes to let everything come together.
7. Serve over hot dogs.

JENNIFER SIKORA,
Calvert City, Kentucky

Jennifer Sikora is a food and travel blogger living her best life in Western Kentucky. She spends her days making delicious recipes to share with her friends and family. Her recipes are inspired by her Southern background, where she learned that a sprinkle of this and a pinch of that can make any dish sing. When Jennifer is not in the kitchen cooking, you can find her exploring and traveling with her family and her two Australian Shepherds. Website: www.jen aroundtheworld.com Instagram: @JenniferSikora Facebook: @JenAroundTheWorld

Cornbread Waffle with Chili

Who says we can't eat chili for breakfast? This recipe is perfect for all you breakfast and brunch connoisseurs! It has become a staple brunch dish in my home since it offers such a unique and fun way to eat chili. Enjoy!

COOK TIME

1 hr.

Makes 4 servings
plus extra chili

INGREDIENTS

For Chili:
- 1 onion, medium diced
- 3–5 cloves garlic, smashed and minced
- 1 pound ground beef
- 1 tablespoon garlic powder, or to taste
- 1 tablespoon onion powder, or to taste
- 1 tablespoon chili powder, or to taste
- Salt and pepper
- One 15-ounce can diced tomatoes, or 1 large tomato, diced
- One 6-ounce can tomato paste
- One 15-ounce can tomato sauce
- Three 15-ounce cans beans of choice (such as kidney beans, black beans, and chili beans)
- ½–1 cup water
- Garnish: chives, sour cream, and shredded cheddar (optional)

For Cornbread Waffle:
- 1 teaspoon butter
- 1 cup cornbread mix (I use Trader Joe's® Corn Cookie Mix)
- 1 cup flour
- 1 egg
- 1 tablespoon baking powder
- ¼ cup melted butter
- 1 teaspoon salt
- ½ cup sugar (or other sweetener of choice, such as maple syrup or honey)
- 1 cup milk
- 1–2 cups corn

Directions

For Chili:
1. Sauté the onions and garlic together in a large pot.
2. Add the ground beef and season with all the spices. Sauté until brown.
3. Once the meat is brown, add the diced tomatoes, tomato paste, and tomato sauce. Add all the cans of beans. Add ½–1 cup of water if the mixture is too thick.
4. Let simmer for 1 hour, or transfer to a slow cooker and simmer on low overnight or on high for 4 hours.
5. Serve on top of cornbread waffles.

For Cornbread Waffle:
1. Pre-heat a waffle maker. Once the waffle maker is heated, butter it.
2. While the waffle maker is heating up, mix all the waffle ingredients in a large bowl.
3. Place the batter in the waffle maker and close. Flip it when the light indicates to flip it.
4. Remove the waffle when it is done cooking. Let cool for 5 minutes.
5. Top with chili and garnishes, and enjoy!

JULIA SILVA,
Charlotte, North Carolina

Julia Silva was born and raised in the Philippines where she was exposed to various cuisines and cooking methods at a young age. In the middle of the pandemic, she found cooking to be her form of therapy. It not only brought her comfort, but it ignited this strong passion of hers. Julia then decided to start her food blog to share the roots of her culture and her love of all things food with the world. She hopes to inspire people to pursue their true passions, and to truly find happiness within themselves. Instagram, TikTok: @julia.not.child

15-Minute Sweet and Salty Chili Sheet Pan Nachos

I've been making these sheet pan baked bean nachos for nearly 10 years now. My sister Tera originally shared her recipe with us years ago, and I have since adapted it slightly to my own flavor preferences. They are just as delicious as hers! I love this bean and meat mixture on nachos. It is slightly sweet thanks to the baked beans but salty with the ground beef. Sometimes on busy nights I don't even get plates out—we just eat together at the table right out of the pan.

COOK TIME
15 mins.

Makes 7+ servings

INGREDIENTS

- 1 pound ground beef
- One 28-ounce can baked beans (I use Bush's®)
- One 15-ounce can corn, drained
- Gluten-free corn tortilla chips
- 3 cups shredded cheddar cheese
- 1 teaspoon smoked paprika
- Garnishes: gluten-free sour cream, salsa, cilantro, chopped tomatoes, smoked paprika

Directions

1. In a frying pan, brown the beef. Add paprika.
2. While the beef is cooking, spread the tortilla chips onto a baking sheet. Sprinkle them with lots of shredded cheese.
3. Once the beef is browned, add the corn and beans and stir until heated.
4. Spoon the bean and beef mixture onto the chips and cheese and broil everything for 2 minutes.
5. Top with gluten-free sour cream, salsa, cilantro, and fresh tomatoes. A sprinkle of smoked paprika is optional.

CHANDICE PROBST,
Washington, Utah

Chandice Probst is the bubbly personality behind the food and entertainment blog, This Vivacious Life. She co-authored the book *Gluten-Free on a Budget* with her mom who also has celiac disease. Chandice has led the charge in hosting celiac awareness nights with MLB and NBA teams around the nation, raising money for research. While she loves to cook and entertain, Chandice loves being a wife and mother most. Instagram, Pinterest, Twitter: @chandiceprobst Facebook: @thisvivaciouslife

COOK TIME

2 hrs.

Makes 6 servings

Slow Cooker Mexican Goulash

I love making Mexican goulash because it is so simple. It reminds me of the meals my mom made when I was a little girl. Mexican goulash was always a go-to for her, but she used canned chili con carne. This was before we were diagnosed with celiac disease. Now that I can't eat gluten or most canned chili con carne, I have had to get creative on how to recreate this dish with just a slow cooker. This meal is a great way to use your leftover ground beef after taco night, and it only takes 2 hours!

INGREDIENTS

- ½ pound ground beef, cooked
- Two 15.5-ounce cans kidney beans, drained
- One 15-ounce can tomato sauce
- 15 ounces salsa
- Gluten-free tortilla chips
- Lettuce, shredded
- Garnishes: sour cream, additional salsa, shredded cheddar cheese, ranch, lime juice

Directions

1. Place the beef, beans, tomato sauce, and salsa in a slow cooker. Cook on high for 2–3 hours.
2. Crush the tortilla chips onto plates, then add some shredded lettuce. Top this with the chili.
3. Garnish with sour cream, salsa, cheese and fresh lime juice and ranch if desired.

CHANDICE PROBST,
Washington, Utah

Chandice Probst is the bubbly personality behind the food and entertainment blog, This Vivacious Life. She co-authored the book *Gluten-Free on a Budget* with her mom who also has celiac disease. Chandice has led the charge in hosting celiac awareness nights with MLB and NBA teams around the nation raising money for research. While she loves to cook and entertain, Chandice loves being a wife and mother most. Instagram, Pinterest, Twitter: @chandiceprobst Facebook: @thisvivaciouslife

Dr Pepper®-Inspired Chili

I created this recipe to fuse my family's two favorite things together: chili and Dr Pepper®. This is perfect for a busy family to make.

COOK TIME

30 mins.

Makes 6 servings

INGREDIENTS

- 1 pound lean ground beef
- 1 cup onions, diced
- ½ cup red bell pepper, diced
- 1 tablespoon chili powder
- 2 teaspoons cumin
- ¾ teaspoon salt
- ½ teaspoon oregano
- ¼ teaspoon garlic powder
- 1 cup chicken broth
- One 12-ounce can Dr Pepper®
- One 14-ounce can fire-roasted tomatoes
- 2 tablespoons tomato paste
- 1 teaspoon Worcestershire sauce
- One 15-ounce can kidney beans
- Garnishes: sour cream, red onion, cilantro

Directions

1. Heat a nonstick skillet over medium-high heat and add the ground beef. Break the beef down with a wooden spoon as it browns until half cooked.

2. Add the onion and bell pepper and continue to stir until the vegetables are softened. Strain out any excess grease.

3. Stir in the chili powder, cumin, salt, oregano, and garlic powder, cooking for an additional 30 seconds.

4. Add the chicken broth, Dr Pepper®, tomatoes, tomato paste, and Worcestershire sauce. Mix well and simmer for 20–30 minutes, or until chili has the desired thickness.

5. At the end, add the kidney beans.

6. Serve with sour cream, red onion, and cilantro.

SARA LUNDBERG,
Portland, Oregon

Sara Lundberg is a cookbook author and founder of the lifestyle blog BudgetSavvyDiva.com. She is a wife and a mother to five children, and she loves cooking and getting messy in the kitchen with her two oldest. Facebook: @thebudgetsavvydiva Instagram, TikTok: @budgetsavvydiva

Chili Pasta Casserole

If you are craving a casserole but you also always want chili, this is the perfect choice. Adding in that sour cream at the end is a must! This is a huge family favorite.

COOK TIME

30 mins.

Makes 6 servings

INGREDIENTS

- ½ tablespoon canola or vegetable oil
- 1 whole onion, chopped
- 1 pound ground beef
- 1 dash salt
- 1 dash black pepper
- ½ pound pasta (I use small shells or elbows)
- 15 ounces tomato sauce
- One 14.5-ounce can diced tomatoes and green chiles
- One 15-ounce can kidney or black beans, rinsed
- 1½ tablespoons chili powder
- 2 teaspoons cumin
- 3 dashes cayenne pepper
- ¼ cup water
- 2 cups shredded cheddar cheese
- ½ cup sour cream
- 4 tablespoons green onions, chopped

Directions

1. Preheat the oven to 350 degrees Fahrenheit. Lightly grease a 9-inch by 13-inch pan.
2. In a large skillet, add the oil and onions and cook for 5 minutes.
3. Add the beef to the skillet and cook until brown.
4. While cooking the beef, cook the pasta in a separate pan. Once the pasta is cooked, drain and set aside.
5. Add the tomato sauce, diced tomatoes and green chiles, beans, salt, pepper, chili powder, cumin, cayenne, and water to the skillet. Mix and cook for 5 minutes.
6. Add the pasta to the mixture. Pour the entire mixture into the greased pan. Sprinkle with cheese. Bake for 20 minutes.
7. Serve topped with sour cream and green onions.

SARA LUNDBERG,
Portland, Oregon

Sara Lundberg is a cookbook author and founder of the lifestyle blog BudgetSavvyDiva.com. She is a wife and a mother to five children, and she loves cooking and getting messy in the kitchen with her two oldest.
Facebook: @thebudgetsavvydiva
Instagram, TikTok: @budgetsavvydiva

Chili for Chili Dogs

My husband wooed me with his famous Chili Cheese Dilly Dogs—but his chili came from a can. I knew if our union was to last, we'd have to do better. This tangy, sweet, spicy chili is the perfect consistency for hot dogs, chili cheeseburgers, and "tot-chos"—whatever else you can dream up! And it's ready to use in just over 30 minutes.

COOK TIME

30 mins.

Makes 4 servings

INGREDIENTS

- 1⅓ pounds ground round
- ½ cup ice water
- 1 tablespoon olive oil
- 1 medium onion, chopped
- 2 cloves garlic, minced
- 1 teaspoon kosher salt
- 2 teaspoons cumin
- 1 tablespoon chili powder
- 1 teaspoon onion powder
- ½ teaspoon cayenne pepper, or more to taste
- 1 cup ketchup
- 2 tablespoons mustard
- 1 teaspoon Worcestershire sauce
- 1 teaspoon cider vinegar

Directions

1. Add the ground beef to a large bowl and pour the ice water over it. Mix to combine.

2. Heat the oil in a skillet over medium heat. Add the onions and sweat them for 2–3 minutes until they are softened and slightly translucent.

3. Add the garlic, salt, cumin, chili powder, onion powder, and cayenne to the onions and stir until well combined and very fragrant.

4. Add the ground beef to the onions and cook until browned.

5. Stir in the ketchup, mustard, Worcestershire sauce, and vinegar. Simmer for 15 minutes with a covering lid slightly askew.

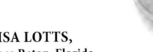

LISA LOTTS,
Boca Raton, Florida

Lisa is a South Florida–based food blogger. She started her website, Garlic and Zest, in 2013, which focuses on fresh, well-prepared, family-style dishes. Soups, stews, and chilis are just some of her everyday go-to's, but she also creates innovative salads, comfort food classics, and fresh seafood, along with grilling and barbecue favorites. In each post, she takes her readers step-by-step through the recipe to build kitchen confidence and help them master the dish.
Website: www.garlic andzest.com
Facebook, Instagram, Pinterest, and TikTok: @garlicandzest

COOK TIME

3 hrs.

Makes 7 servings

Smoked Beer Brat Chili Cheese Hot Dog

I belong to the International Chili Society (ICS) and have been competing since 2018. My dad got me into cooking chili because he won local chili competitions, so I wanted to get more serious and compete at the professional level with the ICS. The recipe is a labor of love, but it's well worth the effort!

INGREDIENTS

- 10 smoked bratwursts
- ½ cup (1 stick) butter
- 3 onions, sliced
- 3 red bell peppers, sliced
- 2 cans beer
- 16 ounces chicken stock
- 32 ounces beef broth with 50% less sodium
- Two 7.75-ounce cans hot tomato sauce (I use El Pato®)
- 1 can light beer
- ½ cup black coffee
- 1 tablespoon chili paste (I use Santa Cruz®)
- 3 ounces ground cumin
- 1 ounce granulated garlic
- 2 packets Sazón Goya® or similar seasoning
- 1½ ounces Hatch red chile powder (I use Santa Cruz®)
- ½ ounce onion powder
- 1 teaspoon brown sugar
- Package of hot dogs (I use Nathan's Famous®)
- Large hot dog buns, toasted
- Garnishes: queso cheese, jalapeños, pickled red onions

Directions

1. If you can't purchase smoked bratwurst, smoke them yourself with charcoal/hickory wood. They should be done in 15 minutes.

2. After smoking, put the brats in an aluminum pan with the butter, onions, red bell peppers, 2 cans of beer, and chicken stock. Keep the aluminum pan on the grill for 45 minutes until the red bell peppers are tender.

3. While the vegetables and brats are cooking, add the beef broth, tomato sauce, light beer, black coffee, and chili paste to a large pot. Mix up a batch of homemade chili powder using the cumin, granulated garlic, seasoning, chile powder, onion powder, and brown sugar. Add 1 cup of this mixture to the liquids and bring to a simmer.

4. Take the aluminum pan off of the heat. Cut the brats into cubes. Add the brats and vegetables to the chili liquid. Cook until the chili is very thick.

5. Top hot dogs with chili. Garnish as desired.

SEAN GALLOWAY,
El Mirage, Arizona

Sean is a U.S. Marine Corps Iraq War veteran who currently lives in Arizona and has been cooking his entire life. Some of his passions include competing in the International Chili Society, barbecuing, and spending time with family. A member of the ICS since 2018, he has placed second numerous times and recently placed first in a regional chili competition. Sean was fortunate to compete in the 2021 World Chili Championship, a competition he hopes to one day win!

ICS World Championship

After appearing at the World Championship Chili Cook-Off in 2021, I knew I needed some of their recipes in this cookbook. They are the best of the best, after all. But how much of their success was due to the recipe and how much was due to the chef? You have to try them to find out. For over 50 years, the International Chili Society (ICS) has been inviting chili competitors to participate in their cook-offs. This collection of 50 Award-Winning recipes represents a sampling of the winners. The year(s) that each recipe won is included.

215

216

218

220

221

229

232

233

234

236

239

242

History of the International Chili Society

By Carol Hancock, CEO and Owner of the ICS, 2003–2017

What began as a publicity stunt in 1967 has evolved into the International Chili Society (ICS), an organization that has contributed over one million dollars to charity. The first eight championship cook-offs were held in Terlingua, Texas, and winners ranged from foodies like Wick Fowler and Joe DeFrates to celebrities like C.V. Wood Jr. and Carroll Shelby, champion racecar driver, automotive icon, and founder of the ICS and the World Championship Chili Cook-Off.

In 1975, Shelby moved from Texas to California and formally organized the International Chili Society in Newport Beach, California. Entertainers and celebrities quickly became a feature of the World Championship Chili Cook-Off (WCCC). 1978 was the first year that the winner was awarded a cash prize in addition to a trophy and the title of World's Champion. At the beginning, the WCCC held its competition for Texas "red" chili only. As the years went by, salsa, chili verde, homestyle, and the youth division were introduced into ICS competitions and the WCCC. The ICS is run exclusively by volunteers.

It seemed that by 1985, public awareness had been raised for competitive chili cooking and the WCCC. Carol Hancock, that year's champion, appeared on numerous TV shows, became a spokesperson for Frito-Lay Company, and had her recipe printed in magazines, cookbooks, and the food pages of nationwide newspapers and websites. In 2003, due to his advancing age and failing health, from the World Championship stage in Reno, Nevada, Shelby announced that Hancock would become the CEO and owner of the ICS. Carroll and wife, Cleo, continued to be on hand at WCCCs until Carroll Shelby's death in 2012.

In 2017, Hancock retired as CEO and Owner of the ICS. Today, Mike McCloud, owner of MMA Creative, Inc. and the World Food Championships, has taken over as President. He has re-established the ICS as a viable organization after the COVID-19 pandemic and is currently making strides toward making the ICS bigger and better for its members and all chiliheads.

WORLD CHAMPION CHILI COOK-OFFS
ICS
EST. 1967

C.V. Wood's
World Championship Chili
by C.V. Wood

Ingredients

- One 3-lb. stewing chicken, cut into pieces
- 1½ quarts water or 10 oz. can chicken broth
- ½ lb. beef suet or oil (I used Wesson®)
- 4 lb. flank steak
- 5 lb. thin, center-cut pork shops

- 6 long green chiles, peeled
- 2 tsp. sugar
- 3 tsp. ground oregano
- 3 tsp. ground cumin
- ½ tsp. MSG (optional)
- 3 tsp. pepper
- 4 tsp. salt

- 5 tbsp. chili powder (I used Gebhardt®)
- 1 tsp. cilantro
- 1 tsp. thyme
- 8 oz. Budweiser® beer
- Four 15-oz. cans tomatoes (I used Hunt's®)
- ½ cup celery, finely chopped

- 2 cloves garlic, finely chopped
- 3 medium onions, cut into ½-inch pieces
- 2 green peppers, cut into ⅜-inch pieces
- 1 lb. jack cheese, grated
- 1 lime
- Tabasco®

Directions

1. Combine chicken with water in a large pot and simmer 2 hours.
2. Strain off broth and reserve chicken for other use (or use canned chicken broth).
3. Render suet to make 6 to 8 tbsp. oil (or use cooking oil).
4. Trim all fat and bones from pork and cut it into ¼-inch cubes. Trim all fat from flank steak and cut it into ⅜-inch cubes.
5. Boil chiles 15 minutes or until tender. Remove seeds and cut the chiles into ½-inch squares.
6. Mix sugar, oregano, cumin, MSG, pepper, salt, chili powder, cilantro, and thyme with beer until all lumps are dissolved.
7. Add the tomatoes, celery, chiles, beer mixture, and garlic to the chicken broth.
8. Pour about ⅓ of the reserved suet or oil into a skillet. Add pork and brown. (Do only ½ of total amount at a time.)
9. Add the pork to the broth mixture and cook slowly for 30 minutes.
10. Brown beef in the remaining oil, about ⅓ of the total amount at a time.
11. Add the beef to the pork mixture and cook slowly about 1 hour. Then, add onions and peppers.
12. Simmer 2 to 3 hours until meat is broken down, stirring with a wooden spoon every 15 to 20 minutes.
13. Cool 1 hour and refrigerate 24 hours. Reheat chili before serving it.
14. About 5 minutes before serving time, add grated cheese.
15. Just before serving, add the juice of the lime and stir the mixture with a wooden spoon.

1971, 1969

Donovan's Code 3 Salsa
by Gail Donovan

Ingredients

- 8 to 10 Roma tomatoes, seeded and chopped
- ¼ cup fresh cilantro, chopped
- 1 medium onion, diced
- 4 jalapeños, seeded and finely diced
- 1 medium green bell pepper, seeded and chopped
- 1 medium yellow bell pepper, seeded and chopped
- 1 medium red bell pepper, seeded and chopped
- 2 cloves fresh garlic, minced
- Two 6-oz. cans tomato juice
- 2 tbsp. lime juice, freshly squeezed
- 1 tsp. white balsamic vinegar
- ½ tbsp. olive oil (light)
- 1 tbsp. honey
- 1 tbsp. salt
- 1 tbsp. Tabasco® sauce

Directions

1. Mix all ingredients together. Cook.
2. Just before serving, adjust Tabasco® and salt to taste.

2013, 2016, 2021

Rosie's Chili Verde
by Rosie Taylor

Ingredients

- 2½ lb. cubed pork loin (½-inch squares)
- 2 tbs. oil
- One 15-oz. can green enchilada sauce
- ½ onion, finely chopped
- One 14-oz. can chicken broth (I used College Inn Chicken Broth®)
- 4 cloves minced garlic
- 4 serranos, seeded and finely diced
- 2 jalapeños, seeded and finely diced
- One 27-oz. can whole green chiles (I used Hatch® Whole Green Chiles), seeded and diced in ½-inch squares
- One 7-oz. jar salsa verde
- ½ cup finely chopped cilantro leaves
- 1 tsp. green pepper hot sauce (I used Cholula® Green Pepper Hot Sauce)

Spice Mix
- 1 tsp. oregano (I prefer All Things Chili® brand)
- 1 tsp. salt
- 3 tsp. cumin (All Things Chili®)
- 4 tsp. green chile powder (I used Verde Bravo Green from All Things Chili®)
- 4 tsp. chile verde mix (I used Homestyle Chili Verde mix from All Things Chili®)
- ¼ tsp. MSG, salt substitute, or salt (I used Accent® seasoning)

Directions

1. Brown meat in oil, drain, and place in 5-quart chili pot.
2. Add chicken broth, enchilada sauce, onion, peppers, and garlic to chili pot. Bring to a boil. Reduce to a simmer and continue simmering for approximately 2 hours.
3. At 2 hours, add green chiles (diced), cilantro, green pepper hot sauce, jar of salsa verde, and spice mix. Simmer for another hour. Adjust salt to taste.

2021

Trailer Trash "Impossible" Veggie Chili
by Nathan Gramm

Ingredients

Spice Mix (I used all spices from Mild Bills)

- 2 tsp. paprika
- 5 tbsp. chili powder
- ½ tbsp. onion powder
- ½ tbsp. garlic powder

Cumin Mix

- 1 tbsp. cumin
- 1 tsp. salt
- ½ packet Sazón Goya®
- ⅛ tsp. red jalapeño powder

Sauce

- 1 tsp. chicken-flavored base (I used Better Than Bouillon®)
- 2 tsp. beef-flavored base (I used Better Than Bouillon®)
- 20 oz. water
- 10 oz. tomato sauce

Meat Substitute (I used Impossible brand products)

- 1 lb. plant-based burger
- ¾ lb. plant-based sausage

Vegetables (chop all)

- 1 oz. green bell pepper
- 1 oz. red bell pepper
- 2 oz. sweet onion
- 2 oz. orange bell pepper
- 2 oz. yellow bell pepper
- 2 oz. pickled jalapeño
- 2 oz. roma tomato
- 2 oz. dill pickle

Beans and Spices

- One 14-oz. can of chili beans (I used Bush's® chili beans), rinsed and drained
- Salt
- Brown sugar
- Cumin
- Hot sauce (I used Crystal® hot sauce)

Directions

1. Combine the spice mix ingredients and separate into 4 "dumps." Combine all the cumin mix ingredients and set aside. The sauce should be combined and set aside, as well.

2. Add 2 cups of the sauce to a large pot. Then add the first "dump" and cook for 45 minutes. Add the second "dump" with ⅔ cup of sauce and simmer for 45 minutes.

3. While sauce is simmering, sauté the meat substitutes, being sure to separate into bite-size pieces. Add to the pot and mix well.

4. Add "dump" three and ⅔ cup of sauce. Simmer for 30 minutes. Add all the chopped veggies and simmer another 15 minutes before adding "dump" four and the remaining sauce. Continue to simmer for 30 minutes, then add the cumin mix. Wait 15 minutes, then add the can of chili beans.

5. Adjust to taste using salt, brown sugar, cumin and hot sauce.

2021

Trailer Trash Chili Jr.
World Championship Traditional Red Chili
(12-year-old and over)
by Connor Gramm

Ingredients

- 2½ lb. of tri-tip beef cut into small pieces
- Cumin, salt, and hot sauce (I used Crystal®), to taste

Spice Mix

- 7 tbsp. chili powder
- 1 tbsp. paprika
- 1 tbsp. onion powder
- 1 tbsp. garlic powder
- ¼ tsp. jalapeño
- 2 tbsp. cumin
- 2 tsp. salt

Sauce

- 8 oz. tomato sauce
- 12 oz. beef broth
- 12 oz. chicken broth
- 1 tbsp. dill pickle juice

Directions

1. Prepare the spice mix by combining the chili powder with the paprika, onion, and garlic. Separate mixture into 4 equal parts or "dumps." Then, combine the sauce ingredients in a bowl and set aside.

2. Brown the tri-tip (in small batches) in oil and drain. Add the meat to a large pot with 1 cup of the sauce and the first "dump." Simmer for 45 minutes. Add 1 cup of sauce and a "dump" every 45 minutes thereafter and continue to simmer pot. Fifteen minutes after your last "dump," add the cumin and salt mixture.

3. Make necessary adjustments to taste with cumin, salt, and hot sauce.

4. Stir chili pot three times to the left before serving.

2021

WolfHaven Homestyle Chili
"It's Howlin' Good!"
by Lloyd Weir

Ingredients

- 1¼ lb. chili grind beef
- 1¼ lb. tri-tip beef, cubed
- One 14-oz. tomato sauce (I used Hunt's®)
- One 15-oz. can beef broth (I used Swanson's®)
- One 15-oz. can chicken broth (I used Swanson's®)
- Two 15-oz. cans black beans, drained and rinsed (I used Bush's®)
- ½ sweet onion, diced

First Spice Mix

- 1 tbsp. cumin (I used Ray's®)
- 1 tbsp. onion powder (I used Ray's®)
- ½ tbsp. garlic powder (I used Ray's®)
- 1 tbsp. Hungarian paprika (I used Mild Bill's®)
- ½ tsp. white pepper (I used Mild Bill's®)
- ½ tbsp. chicken granules (I used Wyler's®)

Second Spice Mix

- 1 tbsp. chicken base (I used Better Than Bouillon®)
- 2 tbsp. chili seasoning (I used Ray's® Original Chili Seasoning)
- 2 tbsp. chili powder (I used Chilli Man®)

Third Spice Mix

- 2 tbsp. red chili powder (I used Ray's®)
- 1 tbsp. cumin (I used Ray's®)

Fourth Spice Mix

- 1 tbsp. New Mexico hot chile powder (I used Mild Bill's®)
- 1 packet Sazón Goya®

Fifth Spice Mix

- 1 tbsp. chili powder (I used Mild Bill's San Antonio Red®)
- ½ tbsp. cumin (I used Ray's®)
- ½ tbsp. brown sugar
- Hot sauce (I used Cholula®)
- Cayenne pepper (I used McCormick's®)

Directions

1. Lightly brown the tri-tip and drain the excess fat. Add to pot with beef broth and first spice mix. Simmer for 30 minutes.

2. Brown the chili grind, then drain and add to the pot along with the second spice mix. Simmer for an hour.

3. Sauté onion until tender, then add to the pot along with the third spice mix. Continue to simmer for 30 minutes.

4. Add fourth spice mix, tomato sauce, beans, and enough chicken broth to fully cover the meat. Simmer for another 30 minutes.

5. Add the fifth spice mix along with two shakes of hot sauce. Add salt to taste. If needed, add cayenne pepper for heat.

Bobble Head White Veggie Chili
by Henry Stephens

Ingredients

- Olive oil
- 1 white onion, diced
- 2 jalapeños, diced
- 2½ tbsp. white chili powder (I used Mild Bill's K-H®)
- 1½ tsp. garlic granules (I used Mild Bill's®)
- 1 tsp. Mexican oregano (I used Mild Bill's®)
- 1 tsp. Cayenne Pepper (I used Mild Bill's 40K®)
- 1 tsp. white pepper (I used McCormick's®)
- 1 tbsp. granulated vegetable bouillon (I used Knorr Selects®)
- 1 cup vegetable broth
- ¼ cup water
- 1 lime, juiced
- 1 cup sour cream (I used Daisy®)
- 1 cup table cream (I used Mexicana®)
- 16 oz. white cheese dip (I used Gustoso®)
- 1 head cauliflower, chopped (about 2 cups)
- One 8-oz. can yellow corn, drained (I used Del Monte®)
- 1½ cups fresh Roma tomatoes, diced
- One 15-oz. can black beans, drained (I used Bush's®)
- One 4-oz. can diced green chiles (I used Hatch® Select Hot Diced Green Chiles)
- 1 bunch green onions, thinly sliced
- Celery salt

Directions

1. In a stock pot, add enough olive oil to coat the bottom, then add diced onion and jalapeños. Sauté until clear.
2. Add the first six dry ingredients. Sauté those ingredients for a few minutes. Stir often until all oil is absorbed.
3. Whisk in the water, vegetable broth, and lime juice, and then add chopped cauliflower. Heat to a slight boil—about 10 to 15 minutes. Let pot rest for 30 minutes.
4. Add sour cream, table cream, and white cheese dip. Simmer on low for 20 minutes, stirring constantly.
5. Add canned corn, diced tomatoes, black beans, and green chiles. Simmer very low for another 15 to 20 minutes.
6. Add sliced green onions and two pinches celery salt. Stir pot counterclockwise.

2019

Knockout Chili
by Brayden Herrera

Ingredients

- 3 lb. meat cut into ¼-inch cubes
- Cooking oil or spray
- 4 tbsp. chili powder
- 2 tbsp. cumin
- ½ tsp. black pepper
- Seven ¾-oz. cans tomato sauce (I used El Pato®)
- 2 tsp. salt, plus more to taste
- 2 tsp. onion powder
- 2 garlic cloves, finely chopped

Directions

1. Lightly coat pan with cooking oil or spray. Once pan is warm, add meat and cook until browned.
2. Add chili powder, cumin, pepper, and salt.
3. Allow to cook for 1 hour, stirring occasionally.
4. Add tomato sauce, onion powder, and garlic. Simmer until done.
5. Add salt and heat, if necessary.

2016

Rudy Valdez
World Champion Chili
by Rudy Valdez

Ingredients

- 1 lb. pork shoulder, chopped into ⅜-inch pieces
- 1 lb. beef flank steak, chopped finely
- 1 tsp. cumin, divided into two portions
- 1 tomato, chopped
- 1 clove garlic, minced
- 1 medium white onion
- Six 6-inch-long celery stalks, chopped
- One 8-oz. can green chile salsa (I used Ortega®)
- One 8-oz. can green chile peppers, diced (I used Ortega®)
- 1 tsp. oregano
- 1 tsp. Tabasco®
- 1 tbsp. New Mexico hot chile powder
- 1 tbsp. New Mexico medium chile powder
- 1 tbsp. New Mexico mild chile powder
- Water
- Salt, to taste

Directions

1. Cook pork and beef in separate pans for 20 minutes.
2. Add ½ tsp. cumin to each skillet.
3. In a 6-quart sauce pan, combine tomato, garlic, onion, cilantro, chile salsa, green chiles, oregano, and Tabasco®.
4. Make a paste, adding a small amount of water, with the three grades of chile powder and add it to the vegetable mixture in the saucepan.
5. Cook this mixture 20 minutes.
6. Drain the juice from the meat, except 4 tbsp., and add the meat to the vegetable mixture.
7. Cook about 1½ hours or until the meat is tender.
8. Just prior to serving, add salt to taste.

1976

Chili Daddy Salsa
by Tom Calvert

Ingredients

- 4 to 5 cups diced tomatoes
- 1 cup diced red onion
- ¼ cup diced white onion
- 2 tbsp. minced garlic
- 1 green bell pepper, diced
- ½ of each of the following bell peppers: red, yellow, gold, and orange (diced)
- 4 to 5 jalapeños, diced
- 2 tbsp. cilantro, chopped
- Juice from ½ lime
- Juice from ½ lemon
- ½ tsp. black pepper
- ½ tsp. celery salt
- One or two 8-oz. cans tomato sauce (optional)

Directions

1. Combine all ingredients. Add salt to taste. Adding the tomato sauce tightens the consistency.

2004

Grand Slam Chili
by Sean Griffith

Ingredients

- 2 lb. 80/20 ground chuck (original recipe uses meat from H-E-B Texas Grocery)

First Batch

- 24 oz. beef broth (I used Swanson®)
- One 8-oz. can tomato sauce
- ⅛ tsp. hot sauce (I used Louisiana®)
- 1 jalapeño, pierced so that it will float

Second Batch

- 2 tsp. onion granules (I used Mild Bill's®)
- 1 tbsp. beef granules (I used Knorr®)
- 1 tbsp. chicken granules (I used Knorr®)
- 1½ tsp. garlic granules (I used Mild Bill's®)
- 4 tbsp. chili powder (I used 2 tbsp. Mild Bill's San Antonio Original®, 1 tbsp. Mild Bill's Dixon Medium Hot®, and 1 tbsp. Mild Bill's Cowtown Light®)
- ⅛ tsp. cayenne (I used Mild Bill's®)
- ⅛ tsp. white ground pepper (I used Mild Bill's®)
- ⅛ tsp. fine black pepper (I used Mild Bill's®)

Third Batch

- 1 tbsp. cumin (I used Mild Bill's®)
- ½ tsp. garlic granules (I used Mild Bill's®)
- 2 tbsp. chili powder (I used 1 tbsp. Mild Bill's San Antonio® original and 1 tbsp. Mild Bill's Cowtown Light®)
- 1 packet Sazón Goya® seasoning
- ⅛ tsp. brown sugar

Directions

1. In a 3- or 4-quart pot, brown meat and leave it in big chunks or balls. Drain and set aside.
2. Remove all grease and clean out your pot. Then add meat chunks back to pot.
3. Add first batch ingredients and bring to a boil. Once boiling, reduce heat to low simmer and keep lid on the pot.
4. Cook for about 45 minutes to tenderize the meat.
5. About 1 hour before serving, add the second batch. Bring to a boil, being careful not to mash the meat. Instead, push the meat around with a spoon.
6. Once boiling, reduce heat to low. Keep lid on the pot.
7. Thirty minutes before serving, remove jalapeño (save pepper juice, should you want to add spiciness later).
8. With scissors, cut meat chunks down to about fingertip size.
9. About 25 minutes before serving, add the third batch.
10. Before serving, taste for salt and heat. Adjust heat as necessary by using pepper juice or hot sauce. Check gravy consistency. If it is too thick, add a little water.

2018

Chuck's Outlaw Verde
by Chuck McCrory

Ingredients

- 2 lb. pork, cubed
- 2 cans (14 oz. each) chicken broth (I used Swanson®)
- 1 can (28 oz.) whole green chiles, seeded and chopped (I used Hatch®)
- 2 cloves garlic, minced
- 5 jalapeños, seeded and chopped
- 1 medium onion, chopped
- 8 oz. green enchilada sauce (I used Hatch®)

Spice Mix

- 3 tbsp. cumin (I used Mild Bill's®)
- 3 tbsp. Hatch green chili powder (I used Mild Bill's®)
- 1 tbsp. salt (I used Morton®)
- ¼ tsp. oregano (I used Mild Bill's®)

Directions

1. Gray cubed pork in 1 can of chicken broth. Set aside
2. Combine cumin, green chili powder, salt and oregano. This is the spice mix. Set aside.
3. Chop or blend jalapeños and green enchilada sauce and divide in three equal parts. Set aside.
4. Combine 1 can chicken broth, onion, and garlic in cooking pot and heat until onion is translucent.
5. Add ⅓ of the blended jalapeños, pork, and 1½ tbsp. spice mix. Cook on medium heat for an hour.
6. Add another ⅓ blended jalapeños, 1½ tbsp. spice mix. Continue cooking for an hour, then add the last ⅓ of blended jalapeños and remaining spice mix. Cook for 30 min.

2018

Red Rat Chili
by Clif Dugan

Ingredients

- 2½ lb. cut tri-tip beef
- 1 can beef broth (I used Swanson®)
- ½ can chicken broth (I used Swanson®)
- One 8-oz. can tomato sauce

First Spice Mix

- 3⅓ tbsp. chili powder (I used 3 tbsp. Pendery's Colleen Wallace® and ⅓ tbsp. All Things Chili Deadly Dudley® chili powder)
- 1 tbsp. New Mexico light chile powder (I used Pendery's®)
- 1 tbsp. garlic granules (I used Mild Bill's®)
- 2 tsp. beef granules (I used Wyler's®)
- 2 tsp. chicken granules (I used Wyler's®)

Second Spice Mix

- 4 tbsp. chili powder (I used 2 tbsp. Pendery's Bo Prewitt®, 1 tbsp. All Things Chili Champion, and 1 tbsp. Pendery's Texas Road Dawg® chili powder)
- 1 tbsp. cumin (I used Mild Bill's®)
- 2 tsp. onion granules (I used Mild Bill's®)
- ¼ tsp. black pepper (I used Pendery's Tellcherry®)

Directions

1. Add meat to greased pot and cook 15 minutes then drain into colander.
2. Place back into chili pot along with beef broth, chicken broth, and tomato sauce.
3. When boiling, add first spice mix.
4. Cook for one hour, then turn off fire to rest.
5. Turn on fire after one hour. Once boiling, add second spice mix.
6. Turn off fire at five minutes before you are ready to serve.
7. Adjust thickness of gravy with water and add salt if needed. Serve.

2017

Duffy's Irish Chili Verde
by David Lorenz

Ingredients

- 3 lb. Boston butt, cubed
- ½ lb. sausage, sautéed and drained
- 4 jalapeños, stemmed, seeded, and diced
- 4 serranos, stemmed, seeded, and diced
- 1 poblano, stemmed, seeded, and diced
- Three 7-oz. cans salsa verde
- One 10-oz. can enchilada sauce
- Two 10-oz. cans green chiles, finely diced
- 3½ tbsp. cumin
- 2 tsp. New Mexico hot chile powder
- 2 tsp. jalapeño powder
- 1 tbsp. chicken soup base
- 1 tbsp. finely minced garlic
- 1 cup of diced white onion

Directions

1. Sauté pork and drain, then add to your favorite pot.
2. Add fresh peppers, chicken broth, half the canned peppers, chicken soup base, 2 cans salsa verde, 2 tbsp. cumin, diced onion.
3. Cook for 1 hour.
4. Add enchilada sauce, 1 can salsa verde, 1 tbsp. cumin, sausage.
5. Cook for 15 minutes, turn off, and let sit for 15 minutes.
6. Add powders: garlic, ½ tbsp. of cumin, remainder of canned chilies.
7. Simmer lightly for an additional hour. Salt to taste and enjoy!

2017

Joe's Jet Lag Homestyle Chili
by Joe Harter

Ingredients

- 3 lb. beef, chili grind

Broth

- One 14-oz. can beef broth
- One 14-oz. can chicken broth
- 4 oz. tomato sauce
- Salt

First Spice Dump

- 2 tbsp. ground red chili pepper
- 1 tbsp. onion powder
- 1 tsp. garlic powder
- ½ tsp. ground pepper

Second Spice Dump

- 3 tbsp. ground red chili pepper
- 2 tsp. garlic powder
- ½ tsp. oregano

Third Spice Dump

- 3 tbsp. chili powder
- 3 tbsp. cumin
- 1 mini brick Velveeta Cheese Original®
- Hot sauce
- Salt

Directions

1. Start heating the broth mixture.
2. Brown the chili grind and add to the broth along with the first spice dump, bring to a boil and simmer for about an hour.
3. One hour before serving, add second spice dump.
4. 45 minutes before serving, add third spice dump.
5. About 15 minutes before serving, add the Velveeta cheese.
6. Use the hot sauce and salt to your liking.

2016

Giants Tailgate Chili Too
by Joseph Callahan

Ingredients

- 3 lb. boneless chicken thighs
- 1 lb. boneless pork spare ribs
- 10 to 12 tomatillos
- 2 poblanos
- 2 long hot peppers
- One 8-oz. can diced green peppers
- 1 large (2 small) diced onions

Spice Mix

- 5 tsp. cumin
- 2 tbsp. jalapeño powder
- 2 tbsp. garlic powder
- 2 tbsp. onion powder
- 2 tbsp. white pepper
- 2 quarts chicken stock
- 12 oz. Goya® Sofrito
- Two 16-oz. cans pinto beans

Directions

1. Take all the spices and mix in a small container for use later in recipe.
2. Wash chicken thighs and pork spare ribs under cold water.
3. Remove any extra fat (some fat is good, too much is not).
4. Cut meat into small cubes, keeping chicken and pork separate.
5. In a small frying pan, add vegetable oil and sauté chicken for about five minutes, or until the meat is white in color.
6. Drain meat and wash in cold water.
7. Repeat the same process for the pork.
8. Dice all the peppers and onions into small cubes.
9. In a large pot, add some vegetable oil and sweat down your peppers and onions until about half the size.
10. Mix in about half of your spice mix and cook for five minutes.
11. Add the can of diced green peppers, the meat, Goya® Sofrito, chicken stock, and half of the remaining spices.
12. This should cook for about 1½ hours on low to medium heat.
13. Add remaining spice mix and pinto beans.
14. Turn heat to low setting and cook another 30 minutes.
15. Let it sit for about an hour and check spice level.
16. At this point, you can add more if needed. Always remember you can add heat, but you cannot take it out.
17. You can serve as is or top it off with cheddar and onions, if you like.
18. Corn bread would go nicely with this dish.

2017

Happy Trails Chili
by Thomas H. Hoover, Jr.

Ingredients

- 2¾ lb. tri-tip sirloin beef, cut in ⅜ cubes
- One 15-oz. can beef broth
- One 8-oz. can chicken broth
- One 8-oz. can tomato sauce
- 1 tbsp. granulated onion
- 1 tbsp. granulated garlic
- 1 tbsp. pasilla chile powder
- 4 tbsp. Gebhardt® chili powder
- 3 tbsp. California chile powder
- 1 tbsp. New Mexico chile powder
- 1 tbsp. cumin
- 1 fresh minced serrano
- 2 tsp. salt.
- 2 tbsp. Happy Trails Chili Seasoning® (if available)

Directions

1. In large skillet, brown the meat.
2. Once cooked, drain fat and juice. Then, add to stock pot.
3. Add beef broth, chicken broth, and tomato sauce. Simmer for 30 minutes.
4. Add remaining ingredients. Cover and simmer until meat is tender.
5. Right before serving, add 2 tbsp. Happy Trails Chili Seasoning Mix and simmer five minutes longer.
6. Check salt and adjust to taste.

2010

California Road Chili
by Chuck Harber

Ingredients

- 1 cup chopped white onion
- 14 oz. beef broth
- 1 can (8 oz.) tomato paste
- 1 can (8 oz.) tomato sauce
- 4 to 6 cloves of garlic, minced
- 2½ tbsp. chili powder, divided (I used Gebhardt®)
- 3 tbsp. New Mexico mild powder, divided
- 1½ tsp. garlic granules
- 1 tbsp. onion granules
- 4 tbsp. California mild powder, divided
- 2 tbsp. New Mexico hot powder, divided
- 1½ tsp. salt
- 1 tbsp. Chimayó powder
- 3 tbsp. cumin (divided)
- 3 lb. tri-tip beef, cubed
- ½ tsp. light oil
- ½ tsp. cayenne powder
- 1 tsp. Mexican oregano
- 1 (7¾ oz.) tomato sauce hot
- 14 oz. chicken broth
- 1½ tbsp. pasilla powder
- ½ tsp. arbol powder

Directions

1. Add to pot: onions, beef broth, tomato paste and tomato sauce, fresh garlic, chili powder (I used Gebhardt), ¾ tbsp. New Mexico mild powder, onion and garlic granules, 2¾ tsp. California mild powder, 1½ tsp. New Mexico hot powder, salt, Chimayó powder and 2 tbsp. cumin.
2. Simmer pot for 30 to 40 minutes.
3. In another pot, brown meat in oil.
4. Put in ¼ tbsp. of New Mexico mild powder, salt, sprinkle of garlic granules and ¼ tsp. of California powder.
5. Drain and add to pot the contents of the first pot, combining well.
6. Add 3 tbsp. of California mild powder, pasilla powder, New Mexico oregano, and hot tomato sauce.
7. Simmer for 1½ to 2 hours.
8. Add 1 tbsp. of cumin to pot and salt to taste.
9. Continue to simmer.
10. If needed, add chicken broth, arbol powder, and 1½ tsp. of Mexico hot powder.
11. Prepare to serve.

2016

Moose Tracks Chili
by Eileen Beaty

Ingredients

- 2½ lb. pork sirloin, cut into small cubes
- 2 tbsp. lard
- ¾ cup onions, chopped
- 14 oz. chicken broth
- 1 tbsp. chicken base
- 1 tbsp. fresh garlic, minced
- 1 tsp. celery salt
- ½ tsp. oregano leaves, crushed
- 2 tbsp. cumin
- 4 serranos, seeded and chopped
- 1 tsp. hot green chili powder
- 14 oz. green enchilada sauce
- 27 oz. green chiles, chopped into ⅜-inch cubes
- 4 oz. hot green chiles, chopped
- 1 tsp. salt
- 1 packet Sazón Goya®
- 1 oz. fresh cilantro leaves, finely chopped
- Green Tabasco® sauce

Directions

1. Brown pork in the lard and drain.
2. Add onion, serranos, chicken broth and green enchilada sauce.
3. Simmer for 1½ hours, stirring often.
4. Add cumin, celery salt, fresh garlic, ½ tsp. oregano leaves, chicken base, Sazón Goya®, and 1 tsp. salt.
5. Continue to cook for 1 hour (thin as needed with water), stirring often to avoid sticking.
6. Add the chopped green chiles, hot green chiles, and hot green chili powder and cook for another 15 minutes.
7. Add 1 oz. finely chopped cilantro leaves.
8. Adjust flavor with 1 tsp. hot green chili powder, green Tabasco® sauce, and salt to taste.

2015

Dago Reds Too
by Dave Hipskind

Ingredients

- 4 lb. tri-tip top sirloin, cubed
- 1 to 2 lb. pork chop (bone in)

First Spice Mix

- Two 14-oz. cans chicken broth (I used Swanson®)
- One 7¾-oz. can tomato sauce (I used regular El Pato Mexican®)
- One 6-oz. can spicy V-8® juice
- 4 tsp. onion powder (or 1 to 2 medium finely diced onions)
- 2 tsp. garlic powder (or 6 to 8 cloves finely diced garlic)
- 2 tbsp. chili powder (I used McCormick®)

Second Spice Mix

- 2 tbsp. chili powder (I used McCormick®)
- 3 tsp. California chile powder
- 5 tsp. ground cumin (I used McCormick®)
- ½ tsp. accent of MSG (optional)
- 1 tbsp. Tabasco®
- Salt to taste

Third Spice Mix

- 1 tsp. New Mexico chile powder
- 1½ tsp. Tabasco® red pepper sauce
- 1 tbsp. chili powder (I used McCormick®)
- 1 tsp. ground cumin (I used McCormick®)
- Salt to taste

Fourth Spice Mix

- 5 tsp. arrowroot or corn starch
- ½ tsp. garlic powder (I used McCormick®)
- ½ tsp. brown sugar
- 1 tsp. ground cumin (I used McCormick®)
- 1 tbsp. chili powder (I used McCormick®)
- ¼ tsp. New Mexico chile powder
- Salt, pepper, and Tabasco® to taste

Directions

1. Brown 4 lb. tri-tip (top sirloin), cubed, in three batches. Each batch should have 1 tsp. salt and ½ tsp. white pepper. Use a non-stick skillet (or spray non-stick cooking spray in a regular heavy-duty frying pan).
2. Rinse each batch with clear water and place in stock pot.
3. Brown 1 to 2 lb. pork chops (bone in), lightly seasoned with seasoning salt.
4. Place in stock pot with chili meat.
5. Add the first spice mix to your stock pot. Cook for 1 to 1½ hours.
6. Add second spice mix to your stock pot. Mix with broth from your chili pot until rich paste is formed.
7. At 2 hours, add third spice mix to stock pot. Mix with broth from your chili pot until rich paste is formed.
8. At 2 hours and 40 minutes, add fourth spice mix to stock pot. Mix with broth from your chili pot until rich paste is formed.

2015

Hillbilly Bob's Homestyle Verde
by Bob White

Ingredients

- 2½ lb. cubed pork
- 1 cup chicken broth (I used Swanson®)
- Two 15-oz. cans green enchilada sauce (I used Hatch®)
- ½ medium white onion, finely chopped
- 4 jalapeños, finely chopped
- 2 serranos, finely chopped
- Two 4-oz. cans diced chiles (I used Ortega®)
- 1 bundle cilantro, finely chopped
- 3 tbsp. garlic powder
- 3 tbsp. cumin
- 3 tbsp. onion powder

Directions

1. Brown pork and add to pot along with the chicken broth, enchilada sauce, and 3 tbsp. garlic powder.
2. Simmer for 1½ hours.
3. Add onion, jalapeño, serranos, and 3 tbsp. cumin. Continue to simmer for another 30 minutes.
4. Add diced chiles, finely chopped cilantro, and 3 tbsp. onion powder. Simmer for 1 hour.
5. Adjust the thickness with chicken broth as needed.
6. Salt to taste.

2015

Chili Verde from Heaven
by Christian Parker

Ingredients

- 2 lb. pork tenderloin, cut into small cubes
- 1 sweet onion finely chopped
- One 28-oz. can green chiles, seeded and chopped
- Two 14½-oz. cans chicken broth
- ½ cup tomatillo sauce (I used Herdez®)

Spice Mix
- 2 tsp. garlic powder
- 2 tbsp. cumin
- 1½ tbsp. green chili powder
- 1 tsp. jalapeño powder
- 1 tsp. salt (adjust to taste)

One Hour Before Serving
- 4 oz. can whole green chiles, seeded and peeled
- 2 tsp. cumin
- 1 tsp. jalapeño powder
- 2 tbsp. Tabasco® green pepper sauce

Directions

1. In five-quart pot, brown the pork. Then, add onion and chicken broth.
2. Add ½ cup tomatillo sauce and simmer for 1 hour, occasionally testing meat for tenderness.
3. Additional water or chicken broth may be needed to keep ingredients covered.
4. Add spice mix and simmer for an hour.
5. Add the remaining four ingredients and cook for an hour, adjusting the thickness with chicken broth or water.
6. During the last 10 minutes, add additional heat, if desired, using Tabasco green pepper sauce.
7. Salt to taste.

2013

Alf's Colorado Red
by Al Henry

Ingredients

- 3 lb. chili grind beef (chuck tender), coarse grind
- One and a half 14½-oz. cans beef broth
- One and a half 14½-oz. cans chicken broth
- Two 8-oz. cans tomato sauce
- Water

First Spice Mix

- 4 tbsp. onion powder
- 1 tbsp. garlic powder
- 1 tbsp. New Mexico chile powder
- 2 tbsp. California chile powder
- 1 tbsp. chili powder (I used Gebhardt®)

Second Spice Mix

- 1 tbsp. New Mexico hot chile powder
- 1 tbsp. California chile powder
- 2 tbsp. New Mexico mild chile powder
- ½ tbsp. garlic powder
- 1 tbsp. cumin
- Dash of seasoned salt

Third Spice Mix

- 2 tbsp. California chile powder
- 2 tbsp. New Mexico chile powder
- 1 tbsp. cumin
- 1 tsp. garlic powder
- Fourth Spice Mix
- 1 tbsp. chili powder (I used Gebhardt®)
- 1 tbsp. cumin
- ½ tbsp. garlic powder

Directions

1. In chili pot, brown the beef, then drain the fat.
2. Add both broths and tomato sauce to the pot along with the first spice mix.
3. Simmer for an hour.
4. Add the second spice mix.
5. Continue to simmer for another hour, being sure to check on the tenderness of the meat.
6. Add the spice mix 30 minutes before serving.
7. Add water as needed for consistency.
8. Add the spice mix 15 minutes before serving.
9. Five minutes before serving, adjust the cumin and salt, and add tabasco for heat.

2013

Old No. 7 Chili Verde
by Gary Ray

Ingredients

- 1 tbsp. minced garlic
- 2½ tbsp. chicken base or bouillon
- 1 tsp. celery salt
- 1 tbsp. flour
- 2 tsp. dried oregano
- 1 tbsp. cumin
- 1 tbsp. dried cilantro or cup finely chopped fresh cilantro
- 3 tbsp. green chile powder

Meat

- 2 tsp. canola oil
- 2 lb. pork tenderloin, cut into small cubes
- 1 cup chopped onion
- 1¾ cups chicken broth
- 1¼ cups canned green chili salsa
- 20 oz. canned chopped green chiles
- Dash of Tabasco® green pepper sauce
- Salt

Directions

1. In a small bowl, combine spice mix ingredients.
2. In a large pot over medium heat, gently brown pork in oil.
3. Drain.
4. Add onion and chicken broth to pot and simmer over medium heat for 1 hour, stirring often.
5. Add spice mix and salsa. Simmer for 1 hour.
6. Add green chiles, Tabasco®, and salt to taste.
7. Continue simmering for 1 more hour.
8. Garnish with pepper jack cheese!

2011

Tom's Famous Green Chili Stew
by Tom Pardikes

Ingredients

- 3 lb. cubed pork roast
- 4 slices semi-cooked bacon, finely chopped
- 14 oz. chicken broth
- 1 cup diced onion
- One 10-oz. can green enchilada sauce
- One 16-oz. jar verde salsa
- 1 diced green pepper
- 1 diced red sweet pepper
- 1 diced yellow sweet pepper
- 2 tbsp. chicken base
- 24 oz. diced green chile peppers, divided in half

- 4 cloves diced garlic
- ¼ cup cilantro, finely chopped
- 2 diced serranos
- 8 oz. cooked navy beans
- 8 oz. cooked northern white beans

Spices

- 2½ tbsp. cumin
- 2½ tbsp. green chili powder
- 1 tsp. celery salt
- ¼ cup ground corn chips
- Tabasco green sauce for heat

Directions

1. Cook pork until gray. Drain meat well.
2. In large pot, combine all ingredients except the spices and corn chips, adding only 12 oz. diced green chile peppers.
3. Simmer for 1 hour, then add spices and remaining diced green chile peppers.
4. Cook for 30 to 60 minutes more, or until the pork is tender.
5. Salt to taste.
6. Add Tabasco green hot sauce for heat!
7. Stir in ground corn chips before serving.

2012

Chili Verde by Jerry
by Jerry Simmons

Ingredients

- 2 lb. pork, cut into small cubes
- 1 cup chopped onion
- 14 oz. chicken broth
- 1½ tsp. granulated garlic
- 2½ tbsp. chicken base
- 1 tsp. celery salt
- 1 tbsp. cornstarch
- ½ tsp. oregano

- 1 tbsp. cumin
- ½ tbsp. jalapeño
- 1 tbsp. dried cilantro
- ½ tbsp. green chili powder
- 10 oz. green enchilada sauce
- 27 oz. green chili, chopped
- 8 oz. green chili, puréed
- 1 tsp. salt

Directions

1. Brown pork and drain. Then, add onion and chicken broth (will not cover meat).
2. Simmer for 1 hour, stirring often. After an hour, add spice mix and a little water.
3. Simmer another hour, stirring often to avoid sticking.
4. Add green enchilada sauce. Simmer for 30 minutes.
5. Add chopped green chili. Cook for 15 minutes.
6. Add 8 oz. green chili, puréed. After 10 minutes, adjust with ½ tsp. jalapeño, 1 tsp. salt, and a liberal dose of hot sauce.

2006

Chef Boy-R-Bob Chili Verde
by Bob Hall

Ingredients

- 2½ lb. pork tenderloin cut into ⅜- to ½-inch cubes
- 1 cup diced onion
- 4 cloves garlic, pressed
- 4 jalapeños, seeded and chopped
- 2 green chiles, seeded and chopped
- 4 serranos, thinly sliced
- ½ lb. canned green chiles combined with ½ lb. frozen green chiles
- One 14-oz. can chicken broth
- 1 cube chicken bouillon (I used Knorr®)
- One 14-oz. can green enchilada sauce
- One 7-oz. can green salsa verde
- 2 tbs. cumin
- 1 tbs. powdered green jalapeño
- 2 tsp. powdered green chili
- 2 tsp. corn starch for thickening
- Salt to taste
- Tabasco® green pepper sauce (as needed for heat)

Directions

1. Allow three hours for cook time.
2. In a five-quart pot, brown the pork.
3. Add the remaining ingredients (except the powders), adding half of the combined green-chiles* to the pot.
4. Simmer for 2 hours.
5. You may need to add some water during the cooking time to keep the mixture covered.
6. With 30 to 40 minutes of cooking time left, add the remaining green chiles, the green jalapeño powder, and the green chili powder.
7. Adjust thickness and salt 10 minutes before serving.
8. Add Tabasco® green pepper sauce as needed for heat.
9. *The salt level drops each time you add the green chiles. Be sure to add salt each time to taste.

2012, 2009

Southern Chili Georgia Style
by Georgia Weller

Ingredients

- 3 lb. tri-tip roast or chuck tender, cut in small chunks
- One 15-oz. can beef broth (I used Swanson®)
- One 15-oz. can chicken broth (I used Swanson®)
- One 10-oz. can tomato purée (I used Hunt's®)
- 2 green chiles from a 4 oz. can of whole ones, blended

Spice Mix

Reserve 4 tbsp. of mix and set aside. Divide the remaining amount into two equal parts.

- 4 tbsp. California chile powder
- 3 tbsp. chili powder (I used Gebhardt®)
- 1 tbsp. pasilla chile powder
- 1 tbsp. Chimayó® chili powder
- 2½ tbsp. cumin
- 1 tbsp. granulated garlic
- 1 tbsp. onion powder
- ½ tsp. cayenne powder
- 2 tsp. salt

Directions

1. In chili pot, combine beef broth, chicken broth, tomato purée, and half of remaining spice mix.
2. In skillet, brown the meat, drain and add to chili pot.
3. Cook for about 1½ hours.
4. Add other half of spice mix and blended green chiles. Simmer for an additional hour.
5. Add reserved 4 tbsp. of spice mix and cook a 30 minutes more or until meat is tender.
6. Adjust salt if necessary.
7. Add Tabasco to taste.

2008, 1996

John's Chili
by John Jepson

Ingredients

- 3 lb. lean tri-tip beef, ¼-inch cubes
- 10 oz. chicken broth (I used Swanson®)
- 8 oz. beef broth (I used Swanson®)
- 2 tbsp. New Mexico hot chile powder (I used Rancho De Chimayó®)
- 2 chicken bouillon cubes
- 4 oz. tomato sauce (I used Hunt's®)
- 3 tbsp. New Mexico medium hot chile powder
- 4 tbsp. chili powder
- 1 tbsp. garlic powder
- 1½ tbsp. onion powder
- 1 tsp. sea salt
- 2 oz. tomato sauce (I used Hunt's®)
- 3 tbsp. California mild chile powder
- ½ tbsp. New Mexico hot chile powder
- 1 tbsp. cumin
- 2 tsp. corn starch
- 1 tsp. sea salt

Directions

1. Rinse off the meat.
2. Lightly brown tri-tip in small batches until gray in color. Add to pot.
3. Add next five ingredients, bring to a boil, cover, and reduce to a light boil for 2 hours or until meat is very tender.
4. Add the next six ingredients and turn to a very low simmer for 30 minutes.
5. Add the next five ingredients and leave at a very low simmer for 30 minutes.
6. You may adjust to taste by adding small amounts of cayenne or red Tabasco, cumin, salt or brown sugar.
7. Add chicken broth as necessary to cover meat.
8. Simmer until tender.
9. For a smoother sauce, run powders through a spice grinder and soak them in a very small amount of chicken broth.

2011

Jim Weller's Macktown Chili
by Jim Weller

Ingredients

- 3 lb. tri-tip beef, cubed
- One 14-oz. can beef broth
- One 14-oz. can chicken broth
- One 8-oz. can tomato sauce (Hunt's®)
- 1 tsp. Tabasco® sauce
- Water

Spice Mix

- 8 tbsp. California chile powder (mild)
- 2 tbsp. New Mexico hot chile powder
- 3 tbsp. cumin
- 1 tbsp. garlic granules
- 1 tbsp. onion granules
- ½ tbsp. arrowroot

Directions

1. Brown meat, drain, and add to chili pot with broths and tomato sauce.
2. Add ¾ of spice mix, bring to boil, and simmer for 2 hours.
3. Add Tabasco® and remaining spices.
4. Thin gravy with water, if necessary.
5. Cook additional half hour or until meat is tender. Add salt to taste.

2000

Maureen's Almost Famous Red Chili
by Maureen Barrett

Ingredients

- 3 lb. tri-tip beef, cubed
- One 8-oz. can tomato sauce
- One 15-oz. can chicken broth
- ⅛ tsp. red pepper powder
- 1 tsp. chicken base
- 4 tbsp. chili powder (I used 2 tbsp. Gebhardt® and 2 tbsp. Ray's®)
- One 15-oz. can beef broth
- 1 tbsp. onion powder (I used Ray's®)
- 1 whole jalapeño, seeded and halved
- ½ tsp. white pepper

- 1 packet Sazón Goya® seasoning
- ½ tsp. salt
- 3 tbsp. Gebhart® chili powder
- 1 tbsp. garlic powder (I used Ray's®)
- 2 tbsp. cumin (I used Ray's®)
- 2 tbsp. New Mexico light chile powder
- ¼ tsp. brown sugar
- 1 tbsp. New Mexico light chile powder
- 1 tsp. cumin (I used Ray's®)
- 1 tbsp. Gebhardt® chili powder

Directions

1. Brown cut up tri-tip in pot until gray in color.
2. Add the next 9 ingredients and bring to a boil. Cover and simmer for 1 hour.
3. Add the next 7 ingredients. Cook for another 30 minutes before adding the brown sugar, New Mexico light chile powder, and cumin.
4. Continue to simmer pot for another 30 minutes.
5. Add remaining ingredients 20 minutes before serving. Adjust to taste with salt, brown sugar, or tomato sauce. Thicken with arrow root, if needed.

2009

Doc's Secret Remedy
by Ed Pierczynski

Ingredients

- 3 lb. cubed sirloin, London broil, or tri-tip
- 4 tbsp. oil (I used Wesson®)
- 6 oz. sausage
- One 14½-oz. can beef broth
- 8 oz. can tomato sauce (I used Hunt's®)

- 6 oz. can Snap-E-Tom®
- 12 oz. can beer (I used Budweiser®)
- 11 tbsp. chili powder (I used Gebhardt®)
- 1 tsp. garlic powder
- 1 tbsp. onion powder
- 1 tbsp. cumin
- 2 tsp. Tabasco®

Directions

1. Sauté beef in oil.
2. Fry sausage till done and drain well.
3. Put beef, sausage, and ½ can beef broth in your favorite chili pot and bring to slow simmer.
4. Add 8 oz. can of tomato sauce, Snap-E-Tom®, 6 oz. beer (drink the other 6 ounces), 6 tbsp. chili powder, 1 tsp. of garlic powder, 1 tbsp. onion powder, 1 tsp. Tabasco.
5. Simmer slowly for about 1½ hours or until meat is tender.
6. Add the remaining 5 tbsp. chili powder, 1 tbsp. cumin, and 1 tsp. Tabasco®.
7. Simmer for 30 minutes. Salt to taste.

1992

Gambler's Chili
by Lauren Ray

Ingredients

- 2 lb. pork tenderloin, cut in small cubes
- 1 cup onion, medium chopped
- 14 oz. chicken broth (I used Swanson®)
- 10 oz. green salsa (canned or bottled)
- 20 oz. canned whole green chiles, seeded and chopped

Spice Mix

- 3 tsp. garlic (minced or mashed)
- 2½ tbsp. chicken base
- 1 tsp. celery salt
- 1 tbsp. flour
- 2 tsp. oregano
- 1 tbsp. cumin
- 3 tbsp. jalapeños, diced
- 1 tbsp. dried cilantro (Pendrey's® powder or 3 tbsp. fresh, finely chopped)
- 1 tbsp. green chili powder
- Tabasco® (green)
- Salt

Directions

1. Brown pork and drain
2. Add onion and broth. Simmer for 1 hour. Stir often to avoid sticking.
3. Add spice mix ingredients and 10 oz. green chili salsa. Simmer for 1 hour.
4. Add 20 oz. chopped green chiles. Salt to taste.
5. Add dash of green Tabasco®. Continue to simmer for another hour.

2008

J.R.'s Rough and Ready Chili
by J.R. Knudson

Ingredients

- 3 lb. tri-tip beef, chopped
- 2 oz. sausage
- 1 oz. rendered beef fat
- 1 medium onion, diced
- 1 tbsp. garlic powder
- 1 green pepper, remove seeds and dice fine (I used Ortega®)
- ½ oz. salt
- ¼ tsp. fine black pepper
- 2 oz. chili powder (I used Gebhardt®)
- ½ oz. California chile powder
- ½ oz. New Mexico powder
- ½ oz. cumin
- ½ tsp. pequin powder
- One or two 14-oz. cans chicken broth
- One 6-oz. can tomato sauce (I used Hunt's®)
- ¼ tsp. cayenne
- Tabasco® sauce to taste

Directions

1. Sauté onion and green pepper in rendered beef fat in a three-quart pot.
2. Add garlic powder and half of chili powder.
3. Add half a can of chicken broth. Mix well and set aside.
4. Brown sausage and beef in a skillet (about 1 lb. at a time).
5. Drain and add meat to onion mix.
6. Add remaining chili powder and remaining can of chicken broth.
7. Cook for 30 minutes on low heat.
8. Add tomato sauce, cumin, cayenne pepper, and pequin powder.
9. Add more broth as needed and cook until meat is tender (about 2 to 3 hours).
10. Add a dash of Tabasco® sauce, if needed, for heat.

2006

Black Coyote Green Chili
by Wes Carlson

Ingredients

- 2 lb. pork loin, cubed
- One 28-oz. can whole green chiles, seeded and cut into small cubes
- 1 tbsp. salt
- 2 cloves garlic
- 2 cups water
- 5 jalapeños, seeded
- 1 medium sweet onion, chopped
- 5 tbsp. ground cumin
- ¼ tsp. oregano
- 2 cans chicken broth (I used Campbell's®)
- 2 tbsp. green Tabasco® sauce
- 8 oz. green sauce

Directions

1. Combine salt, cumin, and oregano. Set aside.
2. Blend together jalapeños and green sauce. Set aside.
3. Gray pork in frying pan. Set aside.
4. Combine chicken broth, half the water, onion, and garlic in cooking pot. Heat until onion is translucent.
5. Add blended jalapeños, pork, and 1½ tbsp. of cumin mixture to pot. Continue cooking over medium heat.
6. After 1 hour, add ⅓ can green chiles (blended), 1 tbsp. green Tabasco® sauce, and another 1½ tbsp. of cumin mixture.
7. After 2½ hours, add remaining green chiles, green Tabasco sauce and remaining cumin mixture.
8. Salt, thicken, or thin sauce to taste.

2004

Chillie Willie's Chili Salsa
by Judith Omerza

Ingredients

- 1 medium Vidalia onion
- 1 medium white onion
- 2 large Anaheim peppers
- 2 jalapeños
- 2 habaneros
- Juice of 1 lime
- Juice of 1 lemon
- 1 large bunch cilantro
- 1 pint cherry tomatoes
- 1 pint grape tomatoes
- 2 vine tomatoes
- 1 small turnip
- Salt and cumin to taste

Directions

1. Chop all ingredients except the lime and lemon juices.
2. Combine all ingredients and season with salt and cumin.

2003

Warning Shot Chili
by Ron Burt

Ingredients

- 1 tsp. ground cayenne pepper (I used Tradewinds®)
- 1 tbsp. MSG (I used Tradewinds®)
- 5 tbsp. ground cumin (I used Tradewinds®)
- 2 tbsp. ground Chimayó® chile powder
- 2 tbsp. ground pasilla chile powder
- 2 tbsp. New Mexico hot chile powder
- 6 tbsp. California chile powder (I used Tradewinds®)

- 5 tsp. granulated garlic (I used Tradewinds®)
- 5 tsp. granulated onion (I used Tradewinds®)
- 3 tsp. non-iodized salt (I used Smart and Final®)
- ¼ tsp. ground chile pequin powder
- 4 cans chicken broth
- 2 tbsp. apple cider vinegar
- 2 sweet onions, minced
- 8 tbsp. garlic, puréed

- 5 lb. tri-tip beef, cubed (I used Smart and Final®)
- Two 8-oz. cans Mexican tomato sauce (I used El Pato®)
- 2 oz. pork tenderloin (I used Smart and Final®)
- 4 oz. hot sausage (I used Jimmy Dean®)
- 2 small cans fire-roasted green chiles, seeded and minced (I used Ortega®)
- 2 tsp. Tabasco® sauce (traditional flavor)

Directions

Preparation Prior to Cooking

1. Place onion, garlic, and two minced green chiles in a blender with a small amount of chicken broth. Purée and pour into chili pot.
2. Pour Mexican tomato sauce in pot with pork tenderloin.
3. Add one can of chicken broth to blender and the entire setup, reserving 2 tbsp. of setup mixture.
4. Blend broth and setup. Pour ⅓ of broth/setup mixture into chili pot.

First Hour

1. Boil ingredients in chili pot, keeping temperature between 180 and 200 degrees. Meanwhile, in a frying pan, sauté the cubed tri-tip until no longer pink. Strain, reserving juices, then set aside.
2. Sauté the hot sausage. Then, place sausage in a bouquet garnI bag, place bag in the chili pot, and allow sausage bag to float in chili pot. Watch pot and add broth as needed.

Second Hour

1. Add half of remaining broth/setup mixture into chili pot. Then, add two minced green chiles.
2. Take reserved meat juices and run through a coffee filter. Then, add strained meat juices to chili pot.
3. After 30 minutes, add sauteed meat to chili pot.
4. Add broth as necessary.

Third Hour

1. Remove pork tenderloin and bouquet garnI bag and discard.
2. Add half of remaining broth/setup mixture into chili pot. Continue to boil, watching consistency.
3. Add all remaining ingredients, including Tabasco®, 30 minutes before conclusion of cooking. Blend well.
4. Adjust salt to taste. WEAR A TABASCO® T-SHIRT WHEN YOU COOK FOR BEST RESULTS.

Karen's Chili Verde
by Karen Ray

Ingredients

- 1 tsp. dried oregano, crumbled
- 1 tbsp. ground cumin
- 3 tbsp. green chile powder
- 19-oz. can green enchilada sauce
- 32 oz. canned tomatillos with their liquid
- 7-oz. can hot salsa verde
- 3½ lb. pork sirloin, cubed
- Lard or oil as needed to brown
- 2 cups onions, finely minced
- 1½ tbsp. fresh garlic, pressed
- 2 lb. diced green chiles, fresh or frozen
- 2 cups mixed fresh green peppers, very finely minced
- 1 tsp. lime juice
- ½ cup finely chopped cilantro leaves

Directions

1. Combine powders.
2. Combine enchilada sauce, tomatillos, and salsa verde in a chili pot.
3. Press tomatillos against the side of the pot to crush.
4. Add powders to the liquids. Heat to boiling.
5. Reduce heat and simmer, stirring frequently.
6. Brown meat in lard or oil in batches with onions and pressed garlic.
7. Drain meat and add to chili pot.
8. Add diced green chiles. Return pot to simmer.
9. After 2 hours, add half of finely minced green peppers.
10. Add salt as desired. Taste and adjust, adding additional minced peppers as desired.
11. After 2½ hours, thicken or thin as needed. After 2¾ hours, adjust salt and other seasonings as needed.
12. Just before serving, add lime juice and cilantro.

2001

Backdoor Chili
by David Valega

Ingredients

Part 1

- 3 lb. beef chuck tender
- 1 to 2 tbsp. vegetable oil
- Two 14½-oz. cans beef broth
- One 8-oz. can tomato sauce (I used Hunt's®)
- 4 dashes of Tabasco®

- 1½ tbsp. onion powder
- ¾ tsp. cayenne
- 2 tsp. beef bouillon granules
- 1 tsp. chicken bouillon granules

Part 2

- ¾ tsp. garlic powder
- 1½ tbsp. cumin
- ¾ tsp. white pepper
- 6 tbsp. chili powder (I used Gebhardt®)
- Salt to taste

Directions

1. Brown meat in vegetable oil. Cover with two 14½-oz. cans of beef broth. Mix in all part 1 ingredients.
2. Boil on medium until the meat is tender; add water as needed.
3. 30 minutes before you're going to serve, add the ingredients of part 2 and simmer.

1990

Mark Ward's
World Championship Salsa
by Mark Ward

Ingredients

- Two 8-oz. cans tomato sauce (I used Hunt's®)
- 8 ripe tomatoes, chopped
- 6 green onions, chopped
- 1 medium red onion, chopped
- 1 tsp. garlic
- 1 bunch fresh cilantro, chopped
- 2 or 3 fresh jalapeños
- 5 to 8 fresh serranos
- 1 medium avocado
- 1 tsp. ground cumin
- Cayenne pepper
- 1 tbsp. lime juice

Directions

1. Chop peppers, cilantro, onions, and tomatoes.
2. In a large bowl, combine all ingredients.
3. Add salt and cayenne pepper to taste.
4. Let sit 30 minutes.

2000

High Country Chili Verde
by Joseph Barrett

Ingredients

- 2 lb. diced green chiles (mild)
- 1 bunch chopped cilantro
- 1 lb. diced green chiles (hot)
- 1 pasilla pepper, seeded and diced
- 1¼ lb. diced green tomatillos, husked and quartered
- 4 minced jalapeños (2 seeded and deveined)
- 1 bell pepper, seeded and chopped
- 4 serranos, seeded and minced
- 2 bunches green onions, chopped
- 8 cloves garlic, pressed
- 19 oz. green enchilada cauce (I used Las Palmas®)
- 3 lb. pork sirloin tip, ½-inch cubed
- 2 tbsp. green chili powder
- ½ lb. sausage, fried and finely chopped
- 7 tbsp. cumin
- 5 oz. can white meat chicken, drained and chopped
- 2 tbsp. MSG
- 6 tbsp. lard salt
- Tabasco® habanero hot sauce as needed

Directions

1. Place all vegetables and powders in large pot and stir well.
2. Fry pork with garlic in lard until light crust forms on cubes. Drain and pat dry with paper towels to remove excess lard, then add to pot with vegetables. Bring to boil and reduce to simmer.
3. After 1 hour, add sausage.
4. With 1 hour cooking time remaining, add chicken.
5. Stir occasionally through the 3-hour cooking time.
6. Check for salt and add as needed.
7. In the last 10 minutes, check for heat and add Tabasco® habanero hot sauce as needed.

1999

24 Karat Chili
by Kathy LeGear

Ingredients

- 2½ lb. beef roast, cubed
- 2 cans beef broth
- 2 cups water
- 2 cans tomato sauce (I used Hunt's®)
- Oil (I used Wesson®)

First Spice Mix

- 1 tsp. MSG
- 2 tbsp. onion powder
- 2 tsp. beef granules
- 1 tsp. chicken granules
- 1 tsp. garlic powder
- ¼ tsp. season salt
- 1 tbsp. paprika
- 1 tbsp. Texas-style chili powder
- 1 tbsp. ground chili pepper

Second Spice Mix

- 1 tsp. MSG
- 2 tsp. cumin
- 1 tsp. garlic powder
- ¼ tsp. season salt
- 1 tbsp. Texas-style chili powder
- 1 tbsp. chili powder (I used Gebhardt®)

Third Spice Mix

- 1½ tsp. cumin
- 1 tsp. onion powder
- ½ tsp. garlic powder
- 1 tbsp. chili powder (I used Gebhardt®)
- 1 tbsp. Texas-style chili powder

Fourth Spice Mix

- 1½ tsp. cumin
- 1 tbsp. Texas-style chili powder
- ½ tsp. garlic powder

Directions

1. Brown beef in 2 tsp. oil.
2. Add 2 cans beef broth, 2 cups water, 1 can tomato sauce, and first spice mix.
3. Bring to boil, cover, and cook at medium boil until beef is almost tender (approximately 2½ hours).
4. Add second spice mix and second can of tomato sauce 30 minutes before serving.
5. Add third spice mix 20 minutes before serving.
6. Add fourth spice mix 10 minutes before serving.
7. Adjust to taste for salt. For heat, add Tabasco sauce.

1998

Nevada Annie's Champion Chili
by Laverne Harris

Ingredients

- 3 medium onions
- 2 medium green peppers
- 2 large stalks celery
- 2 small cloves garlic
- ½ (or more) small fresh jalapeño, diced
- 8 lb. lean chuck, coarsely ground
- One 7-oz. can diced green chilies
- Two 14½-oz. cans stewed tomatoes (I used Hunt's®)
- One 15-oz. can tomato sauce (I used Hunt's®)
- One 6-oz. can tomato paste (I used Hunt's®)
- Two 3-oz. bottles chili powder (I used Gebhardt®)
- 2 tbsp. cumin
- Tabasco sauce to taste
- One 12-oz. can beer, divided into two portions (I used Budweiser®)
- One 12-oz. bottle mineral water
- 2 or 3 bay leaves
- Garlic salt to taste
- Salt and pepper to taste

Directions

1. Dice and sauté the first five ingredients.
2. Add the meat and brown it.
3. Add the remaining ingredients, including ½ can beer (drink the remainder).
4. Add water just to cover the top of the mixture. Cook about three hours on low heat, stirring often.

1978

Stoney Road Tomato Salsa
by LeAnn Nienow

Ingredients

- 3 long, green Anaheim peppers (use pepper and seeds; take out seed pod)
- 2 fresh yellow peppers, deseeded and minced
- 6 or more medium tomatoes
- 1 or 2 medium red onions
- 2 green onions
- 1 clove garlic, minced
- 1 tbsp. rice vinegar
- 1 tbsp. fresh lime juice
- 1 tsp. sugar
- 1 tsp. olive oil
- ¼ to ½ cup minced fresh cilantro leaves

Directions

1. Chop and mix peppers, tomatoes, onions and garlic.
2. Add other ingredients. Salt to taste.

1997

Puppy's Breath Chili
by Catch R. Wilkey

Ingredients

- 3 lb. tri-tip beef or sirloin tip, cut in small pieces or coarse ground
- 2 tsp. o (I used Wesson®)
- 1 small yellow onion
- One 14½-oz. can beef broth
- 3½ tbsp. ground cumin
- ½ tsp. oregano
- 6 cloves garlic, finely chopped
- 3 tbsp. chili powder (I used Gebhardt®)
- 1 tbsp. New Mexico mild chile powder
- 5 to 6 tbsp. California chile powder
- One 8-oz. can tomato sauce (I used Hunt's®)
- 1 dried New Mexico chile, boiled and puréed
- 3 dried California chiles, boiled and puréed
- One 14½-oz. can chicken broth
- 1 tsp. Tabasco®
- 1 tsp. brown sugar
- 1 lime
- Dash of MSG

Directions

1. Brown meat in oil over medium heat for about 30 minutes.
2. Add onion and enough beef broth to cover meat. Bring to a boil and cook for 15 minutes.
3. Add 1 tbsp. cumin and ½ tsp. oregano. Reduce heat to light boil and add ½ of the garlic.
4. Add ½ half of the chili powder and cook for 10 minutes.
5. Add tomato sauce with the pulp from the dried peppers and remaining garlic.
6. Add any remaining beef broth and chicken broth for desired consistency.
7. Cook for 1 hour on medium heat, stirring occasionally.
8. Add remaining chili powders and cumin.
9. Simmer for 25 minutes on low to medium heat, stirring occasionally.
10. Turn up heat to light boil and add Tabasco®, salt to taste, brown sugar, and juice of lime.
11. Simmer on medium heat until you are ready to serve.
12. Keep your pot hot!

1993

7/8's Chili
by Kenton Stafford

Ingredients

- 3 lb. top sirloin, cut into ¼-inch squares
- 1 tsp. oil (I used Wesson®)
- ⅛ tsp. seasoned salt
- ¾ tsp. garlic salt
- ¼ tsp. garlic powder
- ¼ tsp. meat tenderizer
- Two 13½-oz. cans chicken broth

- 6 oz. beef broth
- 8 oz. tomato sauce (I used Hunt's®)
- ½ medium yellow onion, finely chopped
- ½ medium white onion, finely chopped
- 3 to 5 cloves garlic, finely chopped
- 5 tbsp. Gebhardt® chili powder
- 6 tbsp. California chile powder

- 4 tsp. New Mexico chile powder
- 1 tbsp. pasilla chile powder
- 2 tbsp. cumin (finely ground)
- 1 tsp. salt
- ¼ tsp. coriander (optional)
- 1 tsp. Tabasco® (optional)
- ½ tsp. oregano
- ¼ tsp. cayenne pepper

Directions

1. Brown meat about 1 lb. at a time with 1 tsp. oil, ⅛ tsp. seasoning salt, ¼ tsp. garlic salt, ¼ tsp. garlic powder, and ¼ tsp. meat tenderizer.

2. Drain all excess grease, put meat into cooking pot, and add the following ingredients: 1 can chicken broth, beef broth, tomato sauce, yellow and white onions, garlic, 5 tbsp. Gebhardt® chili powder, 5 tbsp. California chile powder, 1 tbsp. New Mexico chile powder, 1 tbsp. pasilla, 1 tbsp. cumin, ½ tsp. salt, ¼ tsp. coriander (optional), and 1 tsp. Tabasco® (optional).

3. Mix well, then simmer for 1½ hours. Add the other can of chicken broth if needed.

4. After it has simmered for an 1½ hours, add the following: ½ tsp. oregano, ¼ tsp. cayenne pepper, 1 tsp. New Mexico chile powder, 1 tbsp. California chile powder, ½ tsp. salt, 1 tbsp. cumin, and ½ tsp. garlic salt.

5. Cook 1 to 1½ hours more, checking on the pot from time to time. Salt to taste.

1988

Margo's Chili
by Margo Knudson

Ingredients

- 3 lb. tri-tip cut beef, cubed or coarsely ground
- 3 oz. sausage
- 2 tbsp. kidney suet or oil
- ½ oz. salt
- 2 oz. Gebhardt® chili powder
- ½ oz. chile powder
- ½ tsp. Hot New Mexico chile powder
- ½ oz. cumin
- Oregano tea (1 tbsp. oregano leaves in ½ cup hot water, let steep)
- White pepper to taste
- 5 to 7 cloves garlic
- 2 med onions, finely chopped
- ½ tsp. coriander (optional)
- 4 to 6 oz. tomato sauce (I used Hunt's®)
- ½ pint beef broth (add water if necessary)
- 1 med pepper, minced (I used Ortega®)
- ¼ tsp. cayenne pepper
- Dash of Tabasco®

Directions

1. Sauté onions and garlic in suet for about 3 minutes.
2. Add Gebhardt® chili powder and chile powder, mix well.
3. Brown beef in separate pan 1 lb. at a time. Pepper while browning. Add onions and spices. Use a little beef broth to keep from sticking.
4. Sauté sausage and pepper together for about 2 minutes.
5. Add to pot and cook for about 15 minutes.
6. Add remaining spices, tomato sauce, water or broth, and mix well.
7. Cook for about 30 minutes. Add oregano tea.
8. Cook for about 2 hours or until meat is tender, stirring occasionally.
9. In the last 20 to 30 minutes, add salt and cayenne pepper if needed.

1987

Los Venganza Del Almo
by Bill Pfeiffer

Ingredients

- 1 tbsp. oregano
- 2 tbsp. paprika
- 2 tbsp. MSG
- 11 tbsp. chili powder (I used Gebhardt®)
- 4 tbsp. cumin
- 4 tbsp. beef bouillon (instant crushed)
- 3 cans beer
- 2 lb. pork cubed (thick butterfly pork chops)
- 2 lb. chuck cubed
- 6 lb. ground rump
- 4 large onions, finely chopped
- 10 cloves garlic, finely chopped
- ½ cup oil or kidney suet
- 1 tsp. mole (powdered)
- 1 tbsp. sugar
- 2 tsp. coriander
- 1 tsp. Tabasco®
- One 8-oz. can tomato sauce (I used Hunt's®)
- 1 tbsp. flour (I used Masa Harina®)

Directions

1. In a large pot, add paprika, oregano, MSG, chili powder, cumin, beef bouillon, beer, and two cups of water. Let simmer.
2. In a separate skillet, brown 1½ lb. meat with 1 tbsp. oil or kidney suet until meat is light brown. Drain and add to simmering spices. Continue until all meat has been added.
3. Sauté finely chopped onions and garlic in 1 tbsp. oil or kidney suet.
4. Add spices and meat mixture. Add water as needed. Simmer two hours.
5. Add mole, sugar, coriander, and tomato sauce. Simmer 45 minutes.
6. Dissolve flour in warm water (pasty) and add to chili.
7. Add salt to taste and simmer 30 minutes. For hotter chili, add additional Tabasco® to taste.

1982

Howard Winsor
World Champion Chili
by Howard Winsor

Ingredients

- 1 medium sized onion, chopped in blender
- 5 or 6 large cloves garlic, chopped in blender
- ½ cup water
- 2 lb. lean beef, cut into ¼-inch cubes
- 1 lb. pork, cut into ¼-inch cubes
- 7 oz. can green chiles, including liquid (I used Ortega®)
- 5 or 6 jalapeños
- 1 can #2 tomatoes, whole, chopped in blender (14¼ oz.)
- 1 can #303 tomatoes, whole, chopped in blender (16 oz.)
- 4 large bay leaves
- 1 tbsp. oregano
- 1 tbsp. salt
- 1 tsp. cumin powder

Directions

1. Chop onion, garlic, and water in blender. Cook until soft.
2. Add meat and brown.
3. Add green chiles and jalapeños to the blender and purée to make a chile pulp.
4. Add 1 cup chile pulp and tomatoes to meat. Cook 20 minutes.
5. Add other seasonings.
6. Remove bay leaves about halfway through cooking time.
7. Use covered pot. You might have to remove lid in the last part of cooking time if too thin. If you want to use beans, put in bottom of bowl before adding chili.

1972

Smith and Fowler Chili
by H. Allen Smith and Wick Fowler

Ingredients

- 4 lb. course-ground chopped sirloin or tenderloin
- Olive oil or butter
- 1 or 2 small cans tomato paste with water or fresh tomatoes, finely chopped, or canned tomatoes pressed through colander
- 3 or 4 medium onions, chopped
- 1 bell pepper, chopped
- 2 to 10 cloves garlic, minced
- 1 tbsp. oregano
- ½ tsp. sweet basil
- 1 tbsp. cumin seed or ground cumin
- 3 tbsp. (or more) chili powder or some chili pods

Directions

1. In a four-quart pot, brown meat in oil or butter (or in a blend of the two).
2. Add the remaining ingredients.
3. Simmer 2 to 3 hours with the lid on. Salt and pepper to taste.

1967

Top Chili Cook-Off Locations

There are chili competitions across the United States—some hosted by the International Chili Society, some not. These are some of the biggest and most well-known events where you can get a good bowl of chili. Try finding more in your neck of the woods!

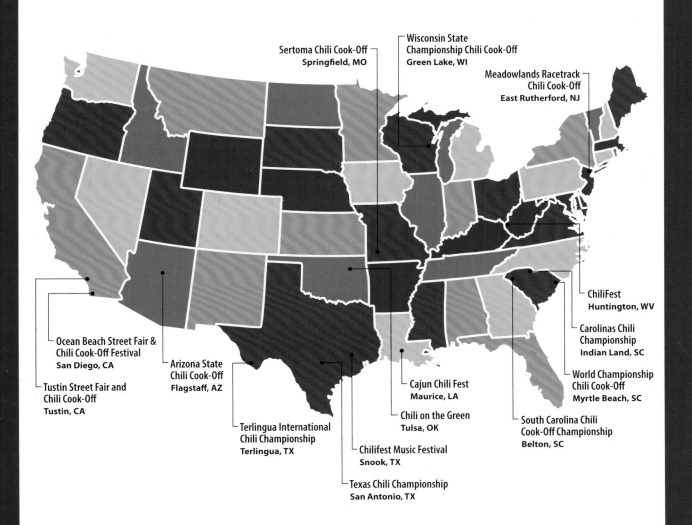

Sertoma Chili Cook-Off
Springfield, MO

Wisconsin State
Championship Chili Cook-Off
Green Lake, WI

Meadowlands Racetrack
Chili Cook-Off
East Rutherford, NJ

Ocean Beach Street Fair &
Chili Cook-Off Festival
San Diego, CA

Tustin Street Fair and
Chili Cook-Off
Tustin, CA

Arizona State
Chili Cook-Off
Flagstaff, AZ

Terlingua International
Chili Championship
Terlingua, TX

Chilifest Music Festival
Snook, TX

Texas Chili Championship
San Antonio, TX

Cajun Chili Fest
Maurice, LA

Chili on the Green
Tulsa, OK

South Carolina Chili
Cook-Off Championship
Belton, SC

ChiliFest
Huntington, WV

Carolinas Chili
Championship
Indian Land, SC

World Championship
Chili Cook-Off
Myrtle Beach, SC

Kevin's Famous Chili

From the moment the episode aired in 2009, the infamous chili scene from the beloved, Emmy-winning TV series *The Office* instantly went down in pop culture history. All it took was one fateful minute and Kevin Malone's sacred family recipe became his iconic claim to fame as it fumbled to the floor. The same heartbreaking but hilarious chili spill that's been viewed by millions is now your meal to make in this recipe below! (Just, please, don't drop it.)

INGREDIENTS

- 4 dried ancho chiles
- 2 tablespoons neutral oil (vegetable, canola, or grapeseed)
- 3 pounds ground beef (80/20 or 85/15 lean)
- 2 medium yellow onions, finely chopped
- 6 cloves garlic
- 1 large jalapeño, finely chopped
- 1 tablespoon dried oregano
- 2 teaspoons ground cumin
- ¼ teaspoon cayenne pepper
- 2 tablespoons tomato paste
- Two 12-ounce bottles of beer (lager or pale ale)
- 3 cans pinto beans, drained and rinsed
- 3 cups beef stock
- 2½ cups chopped ripe tomatoes
- 2 tablespoons kosher salt
- Serve with: chopped scallions, shredded Jack cheese, and sour cream

DIRECTIONS

1. Tear the ancho chiles into pieces, discarding the seeds and stems. In a large heavy pot or Dutch oven, toast the chiles over medium-high heat, stirring occasionally until very fragrant, 3 to 4 minutes. Transfer the toasted ancho chiles to a food processor or spice mill and process until very finely ground. Set aside.

2. Add oil to a pot and heat over medium-high heat. Add ground beef and cook, stirring occasionally to break the beef into small pieces, until well-browned (about 6 minutes). Using a slotted spoon, transfer the beef to a plate and set aside.

3. Add the onion to the pot and cook briefly over medium-high heat until barely softened, about 2 minutes. The secret is to undercook the onions.

4. Using a garlic press, press the garlic directly into the pot, one clove at a time. Then, stir in the jalapeños, oregano, cumin, cayenne pepper, and tomato paste. Stir and cook until fragrant, about 2 minutes. Add the beer and continue to cook, stirring and scraping the pan, for about 7 minutes.

5. Meanwhile, put the beans in a large bowl and mash briefly with a potato masher until broken up but not fully mashed.

6. Add the mashed beans, stock, tomatoes, salt, and cooked beef to the pot. Cover and bring to a simmer. Reduce heat to low to maintain simmer and cook for 2 hours so everything gets to know each other in the pot. Remove from heat, uncover, and let stand for at least 1 hour (can also be refrigerated for 8 hours or overnight).

7. Reheat gently, taste and add more salt if necessary, and serve with your favorite toppings. We recommend chopped scallions, shredded Jack cheese, and sour cream.

Kevin

Index

Photo Credits

Contributing chef recipes, photos, and headshots are courtesy of their associated chefs and used with permission.

ICS logo © International Chili Society, Inc., used with permission

Pages 2, 13: photographs © Bush's® Baked Beans, used with permission

Page 7: Oscar Nuñez headshot © Bruce Smith, used with permission

Page 16: *Breakfast on Military Plaza* from The New York Public Library. https://digitalcollections.nypl.org/items/510d47e1-b230-a3d9-e040-e00a18064a99

Page 17: Wolf® brand name and Can Car photograph © Wolf® Brand Chili, used with permission

Page 19: Carroll Shelby photograph by Dave Friedman, from the Collections of The Henry Ford, used with permission

Page 252: Brian Baumgartner headshot © Adam Hendershott, used with permission

Shutterstock photos: Used throughout: Abramov Valery (wooden cutting board); D_M (red peppers); govindamadhava108 (vegan symbol); Hortimages (green peppers); isaree (recipe paper); MaraZe (vegetables); neung_pongsak (red beans); Tanya_mtv (vegetables); Pages: nafanya241 (endpages); Everett Collection (middle 16); Jr images (bottom 16); Alexander Lukatskiy (bottom 17); AS Food studio (middle 18); Perry Correll (chili kit 19); Arkadiusz Fajer (30); mama_mia (27); Elena Eryomenko (33); Alexander Prokopenko (34); vm2002 (34); Pixel-Shot (46); Robert Briggs (63); Michelle Lee Photography (77); GROGL (75); Lynne Ann Mitchell (99); SWDiscovered (123); Liliya Kandrashevich (124); DronG (126, 157); TanyaCPhotography (134); AnastasiaKopa (138, 143); Elena Veselova (149); Brent Hofacker (153); Brian Maudsley (169); nelea33 (172); Lesya Dolyuk (195); SteAck (196); Foodio (200, 206); Vertes Edmond Mihai (US map 243); 32 Pixels (sticky note 244); Derya Cakirsoy (lined paper 244).

About the Author

Brian Baumgartner became a household name as Dunder Mifflin accountant "Kevin Malone" on NBC's Emmy-winning TV series, *The Office*. Just like his fictional character, Brian is passionate about chili. Brian was invited by the International Chili Society in 2021 to be one of their World Championship Chili Cook-Off judges. *Seriously Good Chili Cookbook* is Brian's first published cookbook and reflects his deep-rooted love for this classic comfort food. Brian is also a *New York Times* bestselling author of *Welcome to Dunder Mifflin*, as well as host of the award-winning iHeart Media podcast, *Off The Beat with Brian Baumgartner*.

Brian is a two-time SAG award winner, Daytime Emmy winner, and Webby award winner. He loves to golf.

Instagram and Twitter: @BBBaumgartner

Seriously Good
Chili Cookbook